The Russian Tea Room

A LOVE STORY

Faith Stewart-Gordon

A LISA DREW BOOK
SCRIBNER

A LISA DREW BOOK/SCRIBNER
1230 Avenue of the Americas
New York, NY 10020

SCRIBNER and design are trademarks of Macmillan Library
Reference USA, Inc., used under license by Simon & Schuster,
the publisher of this work.

A LISA DREW BOOK is a trademark of Simon & Schuster, Inc.

Designed by Colin Joh

Set in Sabon

Manufactured in the United States of America

1 3 5 7 9 10 8 6 4 2

Library of Congress Cataloging-in-Publication Data

Stewart-Gordon, Faith.
The Russian Tea Room: a love story/Faith Stewart-Gordon.
p.   cm.
Includes index.
(alk. paper)
1. Stewart-Gordon, Faith—Biography. 2. Russian Tea Room.
I. Title.
TX910.5.S48A3   1999
647.95'092—dc21
[B]   99-35600
CIP

ISBN 0-684-85981-5

To Sidney
And all the people who helped
make the Russian Tea Room what it was.
(The Past)

To Ellen and Ian
(The Future)

And
To Helen
Who believed in me and urged me to bring
these memories of the past into the present.
Without her this book would not have been written.

Acknowledgments

I owe thanks to many people who have helped me with this book.

For all those friends who have encouraged me, too numerous to mention here, my heartfelt thanks.

And my special thanks to the following:

Carolyn Blakemore, for her editing in the early stages;
Holly Bright, who saved me many times from computer madness;
Anne Tribbett, my invaluable assistant;
Patricia Vigueras, who always kept the home fires burning;
Elizabeth Henley and Charlotte Mears, who helped me get started;
and Dr. Bertram Schaffner, for his constant encouragement and understanding.

And to the following people who so generously gave me their time and support, in the present and in the past: Tom Ahrens, Hope Arthur, Roberta Ashley, Lyn Austin, Michael and Arianne Batterbury, James Beard, Bob Benton, Eleanor Bergstein, David Brown, Helen Gurley Brown, Gregory Camillucci, Michael Carlisle, Peggy Cass, Chris Chase, Craig Claiborne, Peter Duchin, David Dunlap, Andrew Freeman, Morton Gottlieb, Christopher Gray, Joan Hamburg, Al Hirschfeld, Ellen Kaye, Walter Kaye, Howard Kissel, Robert Lantz, Lionel Larner, Tom LoSquadro, Arthur Manson, Anne Meara, Sylvia Miles, Enid Nemy, Robert Osborne, Jacques Pépin, Flora Roberts, Don Smith, Anna Sosenko, Ona de Sousa, Richard Stein, Isabelle Stevenson, Jerry Stiller, Geraldine Stutz, Anita and Sol Summer, Lyn Tornabene, Nancy Vale, James Villas, Deborah Winer, Clark Wolf, Joanne Woodward.

My editor, Lisa Drew, whose wisdom, encouragement, and humor enabled me to create this book.

And to Teddy and Gorgeous, who slept patiently by my side.

Contents

	Acknowledgments	7
1	Beginnings	15
2	First Date	30
3	Newlyweds	40
4	New York Restaurants	46
5	Isaac	56
6	Hungry Artists	63
7	Location! Location! Location! Real Estate	67
8	RTR Divas and the Art of Having Lunch	88
9	Tall Tales	123
10	Into the Valley	157
11	Fires from Ashes	166
12	Jim	172
13	Caviar and Vodka and Other Epicurean Delights	186
14	Ellen—Heartbreak and After	189
15	The Art Collection	195
16	RTR Advertising	202
17	Making Movies and Making Trouble	209
18	Last Days	218
19	Cabaret	220
20	Endings	229
	Epilogue	235
	Index	237

The
Russian
Tea Room

In *The Madwoman of Chaillot,* the Countess is accused of wearing fake pearls and she says, "But don't you know? Pearls become real as you wear them!"

—*Jean Giraudoux*

I am growing old and frivolous. I miss the seriosity of my youth.

—*FS-G*

Beginnings

The last thing I expected to do was marry a man eighteen years older than I was who owned a restaurant. The fact that the restaurant was the Russian Tea Room on West 57th Street in New York, I expected even less. Here I was, at age twenty-three, after one year performing on the road with *New Faces of 1952* and one year in New York, determined to live my life on the stage, when I met Sidney Kaye, the owner of the Tea Room, which changed forever, without my realizing it, the pattern of my life.

Nor did my early years in Spartanburg, South Carolina, advertised locally as the "Hub City of the Southeast," designate me for a life involving the preparation and serving of food.

The town of Spartanburg is situated in the northwestern part of South Carolina, in the Piedmont area, at the foot of the mountains. Most people think of Charleston when they think of South Carolina, if they think of it at all, but we were far away from Charleston, not only in distance—it was two hundred miles southeast of us on the Atlantic coast—but in culture and history as well. Our heritage was a small community of Scotch-Irish farmers who settled in Spartanburg County after they fought there against the British at the Battle of Cowpens in the Revolutionary War. Charleston, by contrast, was settled more than a century earlier by wealthy members of the British and French aristocracy. The mystique of Charleston—its history, literary tradition, architecture, plantation culture, and Creole cuisine—had a great effect on my early life, as did the cult of Secession, still strong today in the rebellious spirit that often guides its politics. The only thing that tempers that bellicose insularity is economic prosperity, and it has made a big dent in the old ways. But the old spirit still prevails: a favorite joke we told about Charlestonians was that they believed the local Ashley and Cooper Rivers joined together to form the Atlantic Ocean.

Edgar Allan Poe, who spent time in the army at Fort Sumter, was one of the first writers I read, in books from my father's library. I was excited to visit Sullivan's Island, where he wrote "The Gold Bug," and the beach at Pawley's Island and the Isle of Palms seemed exotic and intoxicating. Our cabin on Lake Summit in North Carolina, where we spent the summers, seemed tame compared to the heaving waves, the sand dunes and palmetto trees, and, most of all, the history of the Low Country, as it is locally known. I used to get my family to stop at every country churchyard along the coast road so I could read the tombstones from the seventeenth, eighteenth, and nineteenth centuries. Charleston then was a sleepy, somewhat dilapidated town living in the past, but its pride was as strong as it ever had been. Its citizens were convinced Charleston was the center of the universe, and, for a while, I believed that, too.

At home we still lived with some traditions of the past. My mother didn't cook at all, unless you considered opening a can of mushroom soup for Sunday night supper cooking. Our beloved Bobbie Lee, who cooked for our family for forty years, had been my nurse and my brother's, Ernest, before me. She came to work for my mother when she was young and my mother was just married, neither of them knowing much of anything about keeping house, but they learned together, and Bobbie Lee moved on ahead of Mother and learned to cook. They were about the same age and Bobbie Lee established right away, after asking Mother when her birthday was, that her birthday was on the same day. This was the first little victory for Bobbie Lee. She may have had the disadvantage of being black and a servant, but she had the advantage of being quicker and smarter than my mother when it came to battle, and it would be hard to say who won more of the skirmishes that broke out periodically between them, and which lasted all the years they were together.

In Spartanburg there was only one restaurant, the Big Elite, not to be confused with the Petit Elite, which was not a restaurant but a soda fountain, drugstore, and newsstand conveniently across the street from the Presbyterian Church whose Sunday morning services I was forced to attend every week. My oldest friend, Bet Shepherd, and I, given ten cents each by our parents to put into the plate at church every Sunday, kept half of it and ran across the street to the Petit Elite for an ice cream cone—butter pecan for me—during the service. (Her parents thought she was sitting with my parents; mine thought I was sitting with hers.) My father bought the *Charlotte Observer* and the *Atlanta Constitution* there on Sundays, which meant lots of funny papers in color to read when we got home, and sometimes the *New York Times* with the Rotogravure section, printed in sepia. My favorite comic strips were "Dick Tracy," "Buck Rogers in the 21st Century," and "Terry and the Pirates"—that is, after "Batman," my most favorite of all, even before Robin the Boy Wonder existed.

The Big Elite was run by a Greek family, but the food was not Greek at all. I suppose they had to gear their menu to the spartan tastes of the local populace, which, as I remember, leaned mostly toward steak and potatoes with lots of gravy. But we went there very seldom because restaurants didn't play much of a part in our lives. The South was mostly rural then, and there was little money around during the Great Depression of the 1930s. The custom, anyway, was to eat at home. The state of South Carolina was dry, and that didn't encourage dining out, either. Men had to brown-bag it, and women were not expected to drink in public at all.

Men usually came home from work at midday to have dinner, the main meal of the day, though this custom changed during World War II, since most people, even middle-class women, helped with the war effort and worked at something during the day and started having their big meal at night. Sometimes my father would go to the "Dirty Spoon," the nickname for a diner where workingmen had lunch, so he could show his solidarity with "the boys" who worked for him at his Chevrolet agency. Only once did he invite me to join him there, and the experience fed my desire to be one of "the boys" so I could talk shop with Daddy about things like automobile parts and service and used car sales and new models. To my father the word *Chevrolet* meant quality and excellence: he fervently believed in his product. Just as he felt black cars were only good for funerals, he believed that Cadillacs, Oldsmobiles, and Pontiacs were unnecessary inventions that General Motors had created to make his life difficult, and Fords, Chryslers, and Studebakers were unmentionable. Foreign cars did not yet exist in the American market.

Supper was what we had in the evening in the breakfast room, unless we had company. Then we'd go into the dining room and my mother would ask Bobbie Lee to stay and serve. If there were more than six of us at the table, Mother would call up our neighbor Mrs. Blackford and ask her if L.C. was free to come over and help serve. L.C. worked for the Blackfords most of the time, but he tended our lawn one day a week, and helped out for dinners and parties. He always wore a starched white jacket, but his hands were outdoor hands, and they shook when he served. It may have been nervousness but it might have been alcohol, too. L.C. went on binges now and then on Saturday nights, and then Sunday morning he would call Mother from jail and ask her to come and bail him out, which she always did. (He never called Mrs. Blackford because she would not have understood.) L.C. and Bobbie Lee were great pals and were united in their secret struggle for equality. They laughed a lot in the kitchen after dinner while they were doing the dishes (they needed to laugh—we had no dishwasher in those days). I loved hearing Bobbie Lee laugh but she almost never did except when L.C. came around or when Brown Baby and Dan, two of her men friends, picked her up after work. I loved meeting Brown Baby and Dan. I loved their names and the way they laughed and the good time Bobbie Lee had flirting with them. I tried to imagine where they would go together— somewhere with music, I was sure, and good food and "some wine," as Bobbie Lee would say.

For company we would have things like roast lamb or fried chicken, mustard greens or turnip greens, both of which I hated, and avocado and grapefruit salad with French dressing. I hated that, too. Sometimes, when she cooked chicken, Bobbie Lee would hold back the drumsticks for a later snack, and when Mother asked where the legs were, she would say, "This chicken hasn't got no legs!" There was always a rich dessert, often a pie that Bobbie Lee made. And biscuits with the main course—no meal was complete without crumbly little buttered biscuits that Bobbie Lee served wrapped in a starched white linen napkin in a silver breadbasket.

We almost never had fish. There wasn't any fresh fish available except catfish, which was not considered edible for middle-class white Southerners in those days. There were trout in the rivers and lakes, but they never found their way to the seafood market. Two hundred miles from the Atlantic Ocean refrigeration for shipping was limited, so we just stayed away from fish as part of our regular diet. It was only during the war, when my father was in the navy and stationed in Charleston that we learned what fresh shrimp tasted like. He had them sent to us by train in barrels, packed in ice, and how poor Bobbie Lee would moan when she saw one of those barrels arriving—all those shrimp had to be peeled and cleaned and boiled right away. We would eat them and nothing else until they were all gone.

The foods I really loved as a child were things like peanuts boiled in salted water, seafoam candy we made from fresh sassafras root, molasses taffy we pulled ourselves, and homemade peach ice cream we made with fresh local peaches and churned in a cooler until we thought our arms would break. We liked hunting for wild fruits, too, which we gathered from the fields and woods when we went out exploring—wild cherries, persimmons, tiny wild tomatoes, and berries whose names I didn't even know. Most intriguing of all was rabbit tobacco, a weed with thin silver leaves, which grew on stalks in the fields and could be rolled in pieces of newspaper to make cigarettes or stuffed in a pipe for those who really wanted to show off. "You're just showin' out!" Bobbie would say to me on those occasions. The smoke was so strong it made our eyes burn and the taste was almost unbearable. In fact it was a relief later on to sneak real cigarettes—they were so much milder!

Spartanburg was a sleepy Southern college town before World War II. Memories of the Confederacy and the Lost Cause were still vivid in people's minds. I remember seeing Civil War veterans marching in the November 11 Armistice Day parade, and World War I was within the memory of everyone except the youngest children. But the "real" war, known as The War, though further back in time, was closer in the hearts of most Southerners. My grandfather, Marshall Marcus Courtney, though too young to fight in the Civil War, was left at home to mind the farm while his two older brothers went off to fight. One brother was killed, and the other, my mother's uncle Robert, had his leg shot off. Mother told us she used to hear her uncle late at night, thumping up the stairs, dragging his wooden leg behind him, and after he died she still heard those sounds at night. Was it his lost leg, she wondered, come back to find its owner? We enjoyed being frightened by this kind of gothic lore.

When World War II started, Camp Croft, an army infantry training camp, was built outside of town, and though it must have seemed to the soldiers stationed there that they had been sent to purgatory—a world of bigotry and rigid mores—they influenced that world by their very presence in its midst, and Spartanburg began to change. Some of the soldiers were attracted to its slow pace and old-fashioned ways and came back after the war, hoping to find a gentler life. But because of the new contacts with Northerners and the rapid dissemination of news through the national war effort, the South was beginning to join the Union, and by the end of the war we, too, were beginning to look forward to the American postwar boom, not backward to the poverty and shame of defeat eighty years before.

The soldiers had a hard time of it—nowhere to go, nothing to do—but the churches and synagogues began to have "socials" for the boys and soon love blossomed among the troops and the young women of Spartanburg, who must have been delighted to see some new faces, especially since the men their age were mostly at war somewhere else.

In those days we often had to seek out our entertainment, and so the impact of the experiences cut deep into our memory.

Zero Mostel was stationed at Camp Croft, and we used to go to see him entertain the troops, so I knew then how maniacally funny he was. Much later, at the Tea Room, I used to ask him to tell me about his experiences at Camp Croft, but he would only roll his eyes in horror.

The officers at Camp Croft had a better time of it than the enlisted men, as one might expect. They were invited into the best homes for meals and introduced to the finer young ladies of the town. Since both my father and brother were off in the navy—my father a lieutenant commander in naval Intelligence, my brother a navy medic—my mother decided to take in two young schoolteachers as boarders in our house, and she rented the apartment she had fixed up over the garage to a soldier and his wife from Morristown, New Jersey.

Julia and LaVerne, the two teachers, were both great girls, and they brought a lot of life to our otherwise dreary household of two. Their love stories point up what was taking place during the war. LaVerne, the prettier and quieter of the two, fell in love with Leslie, a handsome officer, married him, and left us. I fell in love with Leslie, too, and felt like Frankie in *Member of the Wedding,* watching from the sidelines at their ceremony.

Julia, the smarter and wittier of the schoolteachers, whom I had a great crush on, was called "Toot" by her friends. Almost everyone in the South had a nickname—mine was "Plum" for "Sugar Plum," which my father called me as a baby, and, since my mother was Faith, I continued to be called "Plum" by everyone I knew through school and even into college. Years later someone would come into the Tea Room and ask, "Is Plum here?" We all knew that person must go back a long way!

Julia fell in love with Bill, a soldier from Brooklyn, and had her heart broken because their backgrounds and cultures were so different that it was like rubbing two pieces of sandpaper together. I was the little girl in pigtails hanging over the balcony watching and listening to those emotional scenes between LaVerne and Leslie and Julia and Bill, and wishing I were old enough to fall in love and run away with a soldier or an officer myself. But I was still playing war games in the fields near our house after school, and wasn't ready for romance and that sort of thing until after the war, when the soldiers and officers had all gone home.

In some ways I have felt myself to be an outsider all my life, first as a member of the beleaguered female "minority," later as a Southerner in a Northern land. My struggle with my Southern accent was traumatic: to be cast to play parts I had to lose the accent, which meant not being me. And it also meant that every time I opened my mouth somebody, usually a man, would imitate my accent and make a stereotypical remark about pretty, dumb Southern girls. In addition, I was the child of divorced parents in a culture where divorce was taboo. My mother, who was very much against divorce on religious and personal grounds, fought my father's decision and felt socially ostracized when it was over, and passed those feelings on to me.

Because I felt like an outsider, and because of my natural curiosity, I became aware of the sharp contrasts between the prettified facade of Southern life and the ugly gothic darkness it often spawned underneath. It became second nature to me to search beneath the surface of things to try to find the truth.

For all these reasons and more, it was not surprising that my interest in the theater started when I was young. In 1939, when I was seven, my parents took my brother, Ernest, nicknamed "Buster," and me to the New York World's Fair, an experience that changed my life. It was then and there that I set my heart on living in New York when I grew up. It was that year, too, that I decided I wanted to be one of three A's—an actor, an author, or an artist. At the time I was taking painting lessons, and still drawing scenes of squirrels' houses in trees on my father's cardboard shirt boards, which he gave me every morning while he got dressed. (These were not ordinary squirrels: they had a community life in the tree I created for them, and they had names and personalities.)

By the time I was six I was also in a children's theater troupe, which met under the tall oaks on the Converse College campus, under the tutelage of Luellen Murray, known on the radio in Spartanburg for many years as Jane Dalton. Our troupe performed frequently on the radio with Miss Murray on WSPA and this whetted my appetite for acting. As far as being a writer, I started composing stories when I learned to write. I remember the first one was called "The Lone Ranger Captures Lanfo." It was short but had a powerful ending. In high school as a freshman I played, prophetically, the role of the Russian Countess Olga in *You Can't Take It with You,* where I learned from my coactor Sheldon Soffer, who played the Count, what blintzes were. His mother, who had a Russian Jewish background, made them for our cast party, and what a revelation they were—buckwheat pancakes I was familiar with, as a great treat, but rolling them up with cherry preserves and sour cream was totally new, and my introduction to Jewish and Russian cuisine.

In high school I went on to play the leads in *Gaslight* and *Ladies in*

Retirement. I was so smitten with the theater that I decided I wanted to be a professional actor; that would be my career. As a junior, I applied to The Cherubs, a six-week summer school for theater, radio, and debate students at Northwestern University in Evanston, Illinois. I was accepted and won an acting scholarship there and made great friends. I went back to Northwestern and studied acting there with the legendary Alvina Krause, and spent two summers at her theater in Eaglesmere, Pennsylvania, where I got to play Joan in Shaw's *Saint Joan.* All this was leading to the Yale Drama School, where I had been accepted, until *New Faces,* a Broadway revue, arrived in Chicago.

New Faces of 1952 was one of several *New Faces* Leonard Sillman produced, and it was the most successful. The cast included Eartha Kitt, Paul Lynde, Alice Ghostley, Carol Lawrence, Robert Clary, June Carroll, and Ronny Graham, who wrote a lot of the sketches in the show. I had known Carol in our freshman year at Northwestern, before she left for New York to try her luck in the theater. Carol and Paul, who was a Northwestern alumnus, urged Leonard Sillman to bring the cast up to Northwestern to see the WAA-MU Show, our annual campus extravaganza, and, sure enough, they all came. Afterward Mr. Sillman asked me to come and audition for him onstage at the theater where *New Faces* was playing in Chicago.

For my audition I sang Bea Lillie's "A Campfire Girl." I tromped around the stage in my Campfire Girl costume, singing this wonderfully absurd song, and when I got to the line "Put that cat *down,* dear! You don't know *where* it's *been!*" I could hear Mr. Sillman's laughter in the otherwise empty theater—a kind of infectious neighing sound—and I became hopeful when he said he would be in touch with me soon. I went back to Evanston and on to my college graduation the next day. My father had come up for the occasion and he drove me home to Spartanburg. I persuaded Dad to stop overnight at a motel where they had a TV set, rare in 1953, so I could watch the Ethel Merman–Mary Martin Special that night. We were in the middle of Kentucky bluegrass country when we found a motel equipped with a television set. Dad sat on the front porch and rocked while I watched the live broadcast on a flickering set in the reception room and loved every grainy minute of it.

When I arrived home that evening a telegram was waiting for me. I opened it and read it aloud to my mother and brother, who were sitting down to dinner: "Offering $110 a week in New Faces. Return to Chicago immediately to start rehearsals. Confirm by telephone to Morty Halpern, stage manager. Leonard Sillman." My head was spinning. I couldn't think. When I pulled myself together I called the theater, reached Morty Halpern, and accepted the offer. One hundred and ten dollars a week seemed like a fortune.

I canceled the typing course I was scheduled to take in Evanston and the summer-theater acting jobs and wrote the Yale Drama School that I wouldn't be attending in the fall. Were these decisions wise? I could have taken the typing course—I'm still hunting and pecking to this day—but my thoughts were elsewhere. The decision about the Yale Drama School I have often pondered. I think I would have come to New York much better prepared as an actor if I had gone to Yale. But who could turn down a chance to join *New Faces*?

After the run in Chicago the company went to Hollywood in November to make a movie of the show. Then we played Los Angeles twice, San Francisco twice, and St. Louis before closing in Detroit in April, when we were all put on a train and came to New York. The rest of the cast was crestfallen to be out of work again but I was thrilled. I was in New York at last—my dream had come true. All of us who weren't born in New York but yearn to be there as soon as we can manage to escape from wherever we come from, eventually get off some bus, some train, or some plane and shout, "Here I am! I've made it!"

I went to stay with two of my sorority sisters, Lee Firestone, a fine actress, and Lovelady Powell, who had already become a cabaret performer of note. They had been in New York for a year, and lived on West 55th Street off Sixth Avenue on the top floor of a brownstone. My theater trunk stayed in the hallway on the ground floor.

The first morning after my arrival, I walked up to 57th Street to introduce myself to the father of a friend of mine from Northwestern who had a shoe store next to the Automat. It turned out that this shoe store was the hub of gossip around the neighborhood, and while I was there another former Northwesterner popped in and and in the course of conversation told me about a closed audition to be held the next week for a part in *Ondine,* the Broadway hit that starred Audrey Hepburn and Mel

24

Ferrer. "Closed audition" meant, I found out, that it was not an open cast call for all members of Actors Equity but a private audition to which only a few actors were invited to try out. The question was how I would get into that closed audition.

Later that week my mother arrived in New York. I had not been in communication with her since my arrival, fearing she would interfere in my life. In fact I had just dropped off the map when *New Faces* closed in Detroit, leaving no traces of my whereabouts. I needed a few days to get my bearings. I knew Mother would try to get me to go to the Barbizon Hotel for Women and live in one of their dingy cubicles, and, sure enough, she found me somehow and came up to do just that. But dear Dinnie Smith, whom I had replaced in *New Faces,* had already found me a wonderful sublet at 14 East 64th Street, and my mother backed down.

She and my uncle "Dig" took me to see *Ondine,* so I had some idea what the part I wanted to audition for entailed. It was mostly moving draperies around, the draperies of a medieval court gown, wimple and all. There were only two lines to learn, besides, and to understudy the part of the Milkmaid, which had more lines.

I showed up the next day at the appointed hour at the 46th Street Theater and went backstage with the young women who had appointments to read. When the stage manager read the list of names, mine was not on it and he asked me who I was. I told him I had heard about the audition, and having seen the play the night before, thought I would be right for the part. He had a kind heart and let me read, and by some miracle hired me.

Audrey and Mel decided to close the show by the summer's end, and I was out pounding the pavement for the first time, making rounds, looking for an acting job. When the casting offices and producers saw my résumé and learned that I had been in *New Faces,* they naturally assumed I was a singer and dancer. I got in a lot of trouble when I tried to audition, because the truth was I had been hired by Leonard Sillman to do comedy sketches, understudy all the female leads, and replace them when they were on vacation, but I did not really sing or dance. The *Ondine* credit, however, helped in an unexpected way. Casting directors assumed that I had understudied Audrey Hepburn because I looked a little bit like her, so I often didn't bother to correct that impression.

Finally, that fall I was hired to be in a play called *Put Them All Together,* starring Fay Bainter, which opened on Christmas night in New Haven. What a disaster! The press agent for the show confided in me that he was leaving town and going back to New York and if I had any sense I would, too, as the producers would be looking for a scapegoat. Since they couldn't fire the star, who was indispensable, he said, they would surely fire me—I played the very dispensable maid. I didn't need to follow his advice, though, as we closed in Boston on New Year's Eve.

When I came back to New York my sublet was up and I didn't have a place to live, and a generous couple, the Stanburys, who were friends of my mother, took me in for almost four months until April, when I finally found a furnished apartment of my own.

It was then that Alan Becker asked me out for dinner for the umpteenth time, and this time I said yes.

Alan Becker worked for BMI, a company that sold composers' rights to recording companies, where I used to go to get sheet music I needed for my voice lessons. Alan, who wore a sort of permanent sheepish grin, was always behind the counter and he would give me free sheet music and ask me out to dinner. Finally one day I felt I either had to give up the free sheet music or go to dinner with him, and so I said yes.

Alan called to suggest that we meet at six o'clock and have an early dinner. He said he always went to bed early. And instead of offering to pick me up at my apartment on East 83rd Street, Alan suggested that I pick him up at his apartment on West 58th Street, and thinking this over, I decided this was not a good idea, so I called him back to cancel the date. There was no answer on his phone, alas, so I slowly got dressed and took my time about getting downtown to his building, the Coronet, just off Sixth Avenue. Even so, I was early. Then he had the nerve to ask me to wait for him in the lobby while he walked his two Labrador retrievers, and it was still only six-fifteen.

We ate at a tiny Chinese restaurant on Sixth Avenue that didn't have a liquor license, and since we didn't have much to say to each other, we found ourselves back on 57th Street, still in broad daylight, at seven o'clock, not knowing what to do. It was too early to call it a night when it hadn't even gotten dark yet, so we walked up 57th Street. Alan suggested going to see *Smiles of a Summer Night,* which was playing at the

Little Carnegie Theater, but I had already seen it. Somehow the thought of Ingmar Bergman must've given Alan an idea, however.

"I know!" he said suddenly, with uncharacteristic energy. "Let's go to the Russian Tea Room!" It was as if he had awakened from a long sleep. "I want to introduce you to the owner. I think he'll find you very interesting!"

I thought this strange indeed, but was happy to go along. The Russian Tea Room seemed to me to be a romantic place, and I thought wonderful things could happen there.

The restaurant was jammed when we arrived. It was the first time I had seen it that way, as my first visit had been in the afternoon for tea in 1949, with my mother and my cousin Carol Jones, who was making her singing debut at Town Hall that night. The only other time I had been in the Russian Tea Room was with an actor who brought me there for a drink, hoping the free hors d'oeuvres would substitute for dinner. A downpour with thunder and lightning errupted while we were there, but it did not earn me a meal—we ran out in the midst of the storm and dined at a nearby deli.

That night the bar booths were packed with couples, and the bar itself was crowded with people, both sitting and standing. I could see that the dining room inside was full, too. Two people got up from a bar booth as we came in and Alan quickly slid into it, as if he were taking first base, pulling me in beside him, before Anatole, the maître d', could get to us and send us away.

But Anatole hurried over at once. "I'm sorry, sir, but this table is reserved," he said, pulling himself up to his full six feet three inches. I started to get to my feet but Alan pulled me back into the booth.

"Ask Sidney to come over," Alan said, looking up at Anatole with that silly grin of his.

Anatole blinked down at him over his thick round glasses and said, "Mr. Kaye is very busy, but I will tell him." Anatole seemed to know who Alan was but he clearly didn't like him. I later learned that that look of Anatole's meant either that the person owed the RTR money, or worse, that they had misbehaved somehow in the eyes of the management.

Sidney didn't exactly come over to our table. He just happened to pass by on his way to see someone else, but Alan grabbed the hem of his tweed jacket and said, "Hey, Sidney! I want you to meet somebody. I think she'll remind you of—" Sidney, however, had already seen me and he stopped in his tracks. "Move over," he said to Alan, and sat down, putting out his cigarette in the ashtray on our table.

"What'll you have to drink?" he asked me and waved his hand at Anatole.

"A gin and tonic, I guess," I said, off the top of my head.

"Scotch on the rocks," Alan said, though Sidney hadn't asked him.

"The same," said Sidney, without looking up at Anatole, who went off to give the order to the bartender. Then I got my first good look at him. What struck me was his energy, which was almost explosive, and his humor, which was reflected everywhere in his face. He was a compact, athletic-looking man with a large head, a smooth, heart-shaped face, dimples, a sensuous mouth, big ears, a fringe of dark hair, and beautiful brown eyes looming behind thick glasses. He had small expressive hands with short slim fingers that were always in motion and an enigmatic grin that seemed to imply he had a secret. He was not conventionally handsome but he was vitally attractive.

Before Alan could introduce me, Sidney, who was still looking at me intently, said, "Who are you?"

"I'm Faith Burwell," I said. He laughed—at least it sounded like a laugh, but there might have been more to it than that. Anyway I took it to mean that telling him my name didn't enlighten him much about who I was.

The drinks arrived and Sidney took them off the tray and served them himself. Alan, whom Sidney had been ignoring, got up and excused himself, saying he was going to the men's room.

Sidney said to me, "What's your telephone number?"

I couldn't help but laugh. This man was irrepressible!

"I'm in the phone book," I said, helplessly.

"I don't have time to look in the phone book," he said, with that grin on his face, his dimples showing. He took a corner of a paper cocktail napkin from the table and a Mont Blanc pen from the handkerchief pocket of his jacket and waited.

I rattled off the number: "Butterfield 8-2667."

"I'll call you," he said, as Alan came back and plumped himself down again. And suddenly Sidney was gone, lost in the crowd.

"You look like his Swedish girlfriend," Alan said. "I thought he'd see that, and he did, right away."

"Where is she?" I asked.

"In Sweden," said Alan. "He just broke up with her and he's been acting like a madman ever since she left. Did he ask you out?"

"No," I said, blushing. "I don't even know him."

"You will," said Alan. "I can tell."

"You sound like you know him pretty well," I said.

"Everybody knows Sidney," he said. "If you hang around the Russian Tea Room enough, you get to know Sidney. It's one of the perks." This was the longest conversation Alan and I had had all evening, but it seemed to have come to an end. Alan looked at his watch and we both got up and left the restaurant under Anatole's critical gaze. We walked down to Sixth Avenue, where Alan put me in a taxi and said good night. It's a good thing I had enough money to pay for it. When I got home I saw that it was only nine o'clock. I thought about Sidney and the Russian Tea Room and imagined that the swirl of activity there would soon be reaching its peak.

First Date

The next day, which was Sunday, I woke up unusually early and lay in bed thinking about the night before and wondering if Sidney Kaye would really call me. Why should I think he would? We had only met in a crowded restaurant for a few minutes. "He must ask every female who comes in for her phone number!" I thought. Suddenly the phone rang. It was Sidney, at eight o'clock in the morning. I was so surprised I said, "Sidney!"

"I told you I'd call," he said.

"But it's so early!" I blurted out.

"I couldn't sleep. I have a lot on my mind. So I called you. What are you doing today?" he asked. "I'd like to see you."

"I'm going to Paul Lynde's for lunch," I said.

"Can we meet for dinner? I'm going over to some friends, the Littlers on East Ninetieth Street, around six for drinks. We could go by there and then go on to Quo Vadis."

"I'd love to," I said, not believing this conversation was happening.

"Where do you live? I'll pick you up," he said. It's funny, I thought, he doesn't know where I live and I don't know where he lives, either.

I gave him the address (1113 Madison, at 83rd). I said, "Ring the bell, third floor, and I'll come down."

"We can walk on up to Bill and Mooie's. I'll see you then."

I was struck by an edginess that pervaded Sidney's conversation. I couldn't quite put my finger on it—was it reluctance? Impatience? Or maybe a deeper sense of disappointment, almost despair. It was as if he were about to do something against his will but felt a need, a compulsion, to do it.

The day was scorching hot, unexpected in April. Everything was in bloom in New York. The tulips and apple trees on Park Avenue were at their peak as I walked down to lunch that day at Paul Lynde and Jimmy Russell's apartment in the East Sixties. Paul, who was one of the funniest people I ever met on- or offstage, shared an apartment with his friend Jimmy Russell, who had been the dance captain in *New Faces*. Jimmy was as cheerful and even-tempered as Paul was manic-depressive, and they fought a lot, mainly over Paul's jealousy of what he imagined to be Jimmy's wandering eye. Jimmy was flirtatious with everyone, but I believe he was faithful to Paul. I was tremendously fond of them both. We had bonded on the road, and they and Alice Ghostley, who was like a sister to Paul, had helped me through my difficult overnight transition from college kid to rookie professional.

I had met Jimmy for the first time when I was late to my first dance rehearsal. As I drove down from Evanston, where I had rented an apartment for the summer, the drawbridge in downtown Chicago went up and all traffic stopped for fifteen minutes while a ship went through. I was beside myself—I hadn't anticipated that! When I arrived at the theater, Jimmy was sitting alone onstage in his warm-ups, waiting for me. When I told him my story, he just laughed and patted me on the shoulder. I don't know if he believed me or not, but he was so kind it didn't matter. He forgave my tardiness and I chalked it up to beginner's bad luck. But I soon learned that in the theater being late was a severe crime, and I never let it happen again.

When *New Faces of 1952* started out, all the performers were equal in billing, but when Eartha Kitt made her first album in the spring of 1953, she became more equal than everybody else, and she often took advantage and arrived at the theater just minutes before the curtain went up. She would slip into her formal white gown—with her natural good looks she didn't need to put on makeup—and take her place behind one of the screens from which we were to appear for the opening, singing, "You've never seen *us* before, we've never seen *you* before, but before this evening ends, *New Faces* and you will be good friends!"

Leonard Sillman would get furious with Eartha and scream at her after the show, "Why were you late!" And Eartha would answer in her best "Santa-Baby" delivery, "I was *dee-layed*."

The lunch at Paul and Jimmy's went on into the afternoon. After a few glasses of white wine, I told them I had met someone special the night before but didn't tell them who it was. It was too soon to talk about it, and I felt a little uneasy, anyway, about Sidney. I knew he must be a lot older than I was, and I wondered why he seemed so unhappy. I felt I was on the brink of something slightly dangerous, which, of course, had its charms.

For our first date I decided to wear a lime green nylon wash-and-wear dress my mother had bought for me when I went to Europe in the summer of 1950. At that time we took our own toilet tissue, Kleenex, and soap with us, especially to England, where the country was still recovering slowly from the devastation of World War II, and what we in the U.S. looked on as necessities were rare luxuries there. I was also advised to take along a portable clothesline, which had suction cups at each end, to hang out my wash-and-wear dresses. In a pensione in Florence, I hung the line with all my laundry on it in the shower and the suction cups pulled all the tiles off the bathroom walls.

This nylon dress could literally be washed and dried overnight, and I had taken it everywhere with me for five years. It had short sleeves, an open collar, and a fluffy look about it, like a little girl's party dress. This April heat wave felt like the middle of summer—hardly anyone in New York had air-conditioning in his apartment, and it was so hot that people prayed for the sun to go down to get some relief. In those days women wore linen and cotton in hot weather, dresses that had to be carefully ironed. Wash-and-wear clothes were rather odd-looking, all crumply and puffy, and were strictly for travel. But I thought my green dress, which I never realized might look out of place, would be perfect to wear on such a sweltering night. I soon learned, however, by Sidney's reaction when he saw me in it, that I was wrong. It was the way he looked at me, as if he couldn't believe what he saw. As we walked up to the Littlers' Sidney didn't say much. Was he unhappy with me, or just in a strange mood? I tried to pry from him who the Littlers were, and was able to find out that Bill was a well-known hand surgeon, that he and Sidney had been in the army together, and that Sidney had been the best man at Bill's wedding when he married Mooie, who was from Baltimore, and that they had both been married before.

Mooie and Bill greeted us in the living room of their maisonette on East 90th Street, which was glamorous enough, all in beige and persimmon, but Mooie was even more so. She was tall and rail thin, with short, perfectly coiffed blond hair. She wore a sky blue Chanel suit with blue and black piping on the jacket—no blouse, but a strand of baroque pearls around her neck—and black and white sling-back pumps. She reminded me of someone out of the twenties—like Lady Brett in *The Sun Also Rises*. Her husky voice, her slow delivery in speaking, were all part of her languid charm. Bill was attractive, too. He had a chiseled face with wonderful beetle eyebrows that partly hid his narrow eyes, spiked salt-and-pepper hair, and a wonderful smile. I was definitely out of my element, but I tried. Too hard. After two drinks, Mooie made an arch reference to my dress, and I took the bait. I had felt from the outset that she disapproved of me, but I attributed that to my observation that she had a crush on Sidney and that she didn't like women much in general, both of which were true. But when she made a veiled attack on the dress I felt it as a direct hit, and the drinks having gone to my head, I said, "What's wrong with my dress?"

"Why, nothing. It's a perfectly nice wash-and-wear dress," Mooie replied, and turned away to fix more drinks. Her words hung in the air, and we were all silent. I began to realize that this was a test Sidney was giving me, consciously or not, to see if I could make the grade with Mooie, and I could see that I had failed so far. Mooie was like a tigress prowling in her lair, occasionally raising a paw to threaten a lethal blow to any female who might cross the threshold. Drink followed drink, and as Mooie and I exchanged unpleasantries, it became apparent that Sidney was mortified and that the evening was ruined. Sidney announced that we had to leave and led me down Madison Avenue in silence. I regretted the dress—I saw now that it was all wrong, but I didn't know how to confess it. I was too proud and too wounded. Sidney left me at the door, like an abandoned stray, and I went upstairs to open up a can of mushroom soup by myself, instead of enjoying dinner at Quo Vadis.

I knew that I shouldn't think anymore about Sidney. He had shown me that I didn't fit in with his friends, and his moodiness was something I didn't know how to deal with. But I didn't want to lose him without a struggle. I was intrigued and challenged by his remoteness and what I had seen of the other side of his personality, which was witty and bright and warm. More than that, I was deeply attracted to him and didn't want to let him go. I wondered if he would ever call me again.

Several days of silence followed. I found the Littlers' phone number in the Manhattan directory and tried to screw my courage up to call them. Finally, on Tuesday I phoned Mooie, thanked her for the drinks, and apologized for whatever I had said that evening. I tried to find out from her if she had talked to Sidney and if he had said anything about me, but I got nowhere, just a brusque "thank you for calling." Clearly she never intended to see me again. That was double bad news, because not only did it seem that I had lost Sidney before I got to know him, but I had also lost contact with the only people we knew in common.

I waited as long as I could and then on Wednesday I decided to take action. It wasn't so much a decision as it was a strong impulse to seek Sidney out and try to connect with him again. So while I was making rounds looking for acting jobs, I dropped by the Russian Tea Room, which was just across 57th Street from where my agent, Barna Ostertag, had her office. Barna was a saint. She took me on out of the goodness of her heart, I'm sure, as I certainly was not making money for her at this point. It was true that I had an unusually good start in the theater and showed promise, but Barna was still taking a big chance. What she gave me during those difficult days was hope. I felt like I really belonged in the theater because I had Barna looking out for me. I would go to see her in her office, she behind her imposing desk, I sitting opposite her on a tiny yellow print sofa, as she poured forth words of wisdom about the theater. When I failed to get a job or was turned down at an audition, just knowing she was there on 57th Street, a phone call or a visit away, kept me from giving up.

I peered through the glass of the revolving doors at the Tea Room entrance. It was just after lunch and I could see that the room was almost empty. I didn't see Sidney anywhere. Suddenly someone behind me pushed the revolving doors and I found myself inside the restaurant, looking up at a tall man, nearly bald, with small round glasses on his nose. It was Anatole! He glared down at me and asked, "May I help you?" I switched my pocketbook and briefcase from one arm to the other.

"Why, yes, you may," I replied. "I was wondering if Sidney is here?"

"Do you mean Mr. Kaye?" asked Anatole, who I now noticed was dressed in a tuxedo.

"Yes, Mr. Kaye." I blushed. "Is he here?"

"No, he's not, but who shall I say is calling?" he asked.

"Faith Burwell," I said. "I'm a friend of his." Anatole's eyebrows shot up. "He might want to know I'm asking for him, I mean, if he happens to be here."

Anatole disappeared through a door behind the bar where a slight, dark-haired man in a maroon Russian peasant's blouse was drying glasses with a towel and then holding them up to the light.

I took a step up to the partition that separated the bar from the dining room. I noticed for the first time the three Art Deco chandeliers in the middle of the room, hanging from the ceiling like giant upside-down cakes.

I also noticed a tall woman with long chestnut hair falling down her back arranging gladiolas in a vase on a long table in the center of the room. She was dressed in a crisp tailored man's shirt and a long full cotton skirt, which reached to her ankles and seemed to be supported by a crinoline petticoat underneath. It was cinched at the waist with a wide belt. I learned later that this was the formidable "Miss Anne," who ran the dining room during the day and put up with no one except "Mr. Kaye," with whom she was secretly in love. Today she was alone except for a couple in a corner nurturing their tea.

Anatole silently reappeared behind me, clearing his throat to get my attention. I turned around and he said, with a solemn face, "Mr. Kaye will see you now." He led me behind the bar, through a door, and down some dark stairs, between walls of solid granite, to the basement.

"What an odd place to have an office!" I thought, but it turned out that we were heading instead for the room where the air-conditioning machinery was kept. There we found Sidney with his jacket off and his sleeves rolled up, banging away on some pipes with a monkey wrench. He stopped banging for a minute when he saw me and turned his face, glistening with sweat, in my direction.

"I'll get this goddamn thing going again if it kills me!" he said, and suddenly, in spite of himself, broke into a grin.

"Hi!" I said brightly. "I was hoping you'd call sometime. I wanted to say I was sorry about the other night."

Sidney waved his arms as if to dismiss the subject. "I would've called you but I've been—" He stopped.

"Preoccupied?"

"I've been stuck with a lot of problems the past few days—like this one, for instance!" With renewed vengeance he resumed banging on the helpless machine.

We were not alone in the air-conditioning room. There was a tall, good-looking young man with rough-cut features leaning against a wall, watching Sidney's efforts in silence. He turned out to be Alex the Yugoslav, who did a hundred different jobs around the restaurant. And there was a short man with grizzled hair and glasses, looking on. This was Paul, the back manager, who had known Sidney since childhood days in the Bronx.

That day Sidney didn't comment on my dress, neither the lime green fluffy one of the other evening nor the one I was currently wearing, which was fitted and sleeveless. It had a scoop neck and was bright aquamarine, and I had bought it on sale at a little shop on Sixth Avenue. "Hmmm. It's the color of the bottom of a Hollywood swimming pool," Barna mused when I went by earlier to see her in her office.

Suddenly Sidney threw down the wrench and wiped his forehead with his shirtsleeve. "Let's get out of here," he said. "I haven't had lunch yet." He led the way back upstairs, leaving Alex and Paul to worry about the machine. He motioned to Anatole to give me a seat in a bar booth and said he'd be right back. When he returned he was spotless in a clean white shirt, a black ribbed tie, a brown tweed jacket, and gray slacks. He took me by the arm and, to my surprise, led me out of the restaurant.

"Let's go to the King Cole Bar," he said. "We can't talk in the Tea

Room." And off we went. I'd never been there but I'd heard about it and I knew it was in the St. Regis. It was elegant and intimate, and the Max Field Parrish mural of Old King Cole was a perfect touch. We had cocktails, lunch, and wine, and Sidney began to brighten. I saw more of his wit and his playfulness and his sentimental side. He told me about his family and how he grew up in the restaurant business, his stay in the army, his childhood in the Bronx, his first marriage, and his son, Joel, who was twelve and lived with his mother, Sidney's ex-wife. I told him about my life, too, and before long the lunch had made up for the lost dinner at Quo Vadis. Then Sidney said, without warning, "Here's a hundred dollars. Get your passport renewed. I'm taking you to Europe." Then we got up from the table and he walked me to the corner and said, "I've got to get back to the store," and, for the first time, kissed me gently on the lips and then said good-bye and walked away. I couldn't figure it out. Why did he want to take me to Europe? Why would it cost a hundred dollars to get my passport renewed? I was excited. I was dying to go to Europe, and I would love to go with Sidney. I walked around the block thinking about it, getting all pumped up, ready to drop everything, cancel my acting class, my dance class, my voice class, my psychiatrist, and sail off into the blue with Sidney. Suddenly I saw a vision of my mother and knew she would disapprove, and I didn't know what the consequences would be. I imagined my phone call to her: "Hi! I just wanted you to know I'm going off to Europe with this man I just met." No, I didn't have the guts to do it.

I went back to the St. Regis and sat down at one of the desks in the lobby and wrote a note on the hotel stationery:

Dear Sidney,

I can't take your $100 and I'm sorry but I can't go to Europe. Thank you anyway for asking me.

Love,
Faith

P.S. Thanks for the lovely lunch.

I put the note in an envelope with the $100, bought a stamp from the concierge, and dropped it into the mailbox in the lobby. It was one of the lowest moments I could remember. I resolved then and there to break the stifling hold my mother had over my life.

Since I couldn't find a job acting in the theater, I decided to look for any kind of employment. But what was I trained to do? Well, for one thing, I could paste newspaper clippings into Ray Bolger's career scrapbook. I was hired at a PR agency that handled Mr. Bolger's publicity, and they let me drop in and out of the office, working by the hour, so I still had time to make rounds. This was my introduction to business life—I had never had a "civilian" job before—and my introduction to inner-office warfare. I was flabbergasted at what went on. Each one of the women in the office wanted to take me to lunch so she could complain about the others to me, since I had no stakes in the game. I found out that all of them felt they were underpaid, misunderstood, and trapped in an unpromising job. I felt lucky to be an unemployed actor! And Mr. Bolger, who to all appearances was a commanding theatrical star, was, underneath, a hen-pecked husband. Mrs. Bolger was a stage wife extraordinaire, calling the agency every day to demand more and better media coverage for Mr. Bolger. Nag, nag, nag! I was glad I didn't have to take those calls. The job ended after a few weeks when I got the scrapbook up to date and I moved on.

Then I read in the paper that the Chase Manhattan Bank was holding typing tests for new secretaries and decided that I would apply. What on earth made me think I could convince the people at the bank that I could type the required words a minute, when I could only hunt and peck, I don't know, but I was quickly shown out through the revolving door.

After I knew Sidney a few months, I was desperate for a job and got the idea to answer an ad in the paper for models on Seventh Avenue. I went down to this loft building and a woman came out to the reception area and asked me to put on a yellow shantung dress and jacket she was holding and then come into the showroom and walk around, posing in ways that would show off the costume. I did this as I imagined a model would do it, using my acting "as if" to help me—as if I were a model. The woman shook her head slowly back and forth to indicate I was not moving like a model. But a man in a brown suit who was standing in the back of the room, leaning on a clothes rack, came forward.

"I'm the salesman for the company," he said. "I think you would be just fine on the road," he said. "I would take you with me as my model." He grinned and I saw his uneven teeth.

The woman looked surprised.

"Where would we go?" I asked, looking at the man looking at me.

"All over," he said. "Don't worry, you'd get home every weekend."

"How much would the salary be?" I asked him.

"One hundred and fifty a week plus expenses," he said.

I was momentarily excited, thinking of making money. And of course I had had experience on the road.

"I'll let you know after lunch," I said.

I went up to the Tea Room and told Sidney I had a job opportunity. He was in the middle of the lunch service and only halfway listening to what I said.

"What's the job?" he asked, as he shook a customer's hand.

"It's on Seventh Avenue," I said. "A modeling job."

He stopped in his tracks. "Seventh Avenue! Are you crazy?" Now I had his full attention. "They just want to get you into the sack! Call them and tell them no! You can't go! And please, Faith, do me a favor—don't ever go back down to Seventh Avenue!"

My feelings were hurt but I decided to take Sidney's advice and not get involved with the garment industry. I thought the woman was right anyway—I wasn't cut out to be a model.

Newlyweds

After all the Sturm und Drang of our two-year courtship, we were finally married, Sidney and I, and we started preparing to become domesticated, or our somewhat eccentric equivalent of it. Neither one of us had kept house with anybody, and we didn't know exactly how it worked. True, Sidney had been married before, and had a fourteen-year-old son, Joel, but he had been divorced since Joel was a baby and evidently had never gotten into the routine of married life.

Sidney found an amazing penthouse apartment in the Osborne, across the street from Carnegie Hall and the Tea Room. It was like a ship's cabin, with a view of all Central Park to the north, the Hudson River to the west, and, from the galley kitchen, which was up a flight of stairs, a view of the New York Athletic Club and points east. From the bedroom the view from the French doors was south to the Empire State Building and beyond. The terrace was much larger than the apartment (Thirty-five feet by seventy-five feet), and it became our living room and dining room in warm weather.

Sidney moved uptown from his bachelor's pad on East 22nd Street, leaving behind the murals on the bedroom ceiling painted by his friend Woodrow Parrish-Martin depicting rosy-cheeked cherubs in flight, but bringing along the practical furniture his sister, Alice, had selected for him. I left my one-room furnished apartment on Madison Avenue and

83rd Street to move in with Sidney, bringing nothing along but my clothes, some books, and my portable record player.

We were certainly not yet domesticated: we didn't even cook at home. (I remember that when Jackie Susann and Irving Mansfield moved from the Navarro Hotel where they had been accustomed to having room service three times a day to 200 Central Park South to a "real" apartment, Jackie moaned to us over lunch at the Tea Room, "What am I supposed to do with this damn kitchen!")

If Sidney and I didn't have dinner at the RTR or at another restaurant, we had food sent across the street by one of our busboys. Or Sidney ate at the Tea Room and I stayed home alone.

After we had been married several months, I was still hesitant to have people over, so one evening Sidney invited his gang of chums from the Tea Room to come for drinks to "break the ice." I never thought about buying napkins and matches (people smoked in those days) or fancy sugar for the coffee—I just used the ones from the RTR, including RTR sugar cubes wrapped in red paper with the RTR logo on the sides. Jimmy Gelb, Harold Clurman's stage manager and sidekick, chastised me for my gaucheness, and I was so embarrassed I scooped up all the matches, napkins, and sugar cubes and hid them in a drawer out of sight. I would like to have done the same with Jimmy Gelb.

Bella and Sam Spewack, the playwrights, brought flowers, and I was taken aback by their thoughtfulness (in contrast, I have to say, to the other guests).

"Nonsense, Faith!" said Bella. "That's what people *do*!" I never forgot that.

Sidney, ever the raconteur, loved to entertain his buddies at the RTR with stories of his newly formed and highly unexpected state of matrimony. He reported on, amplified, and transformed the warp and woof of our relationship into tall tales that revealed our efforts to come to grips with married life. After all, Sidney was forty-three years old, unfettered for ten years, and now starting over with a young woman from a different culture and eighteen years his junior. (Sidney's son, Joel, observed, "I'm closer in age to Faith than Daddy is.")

As my father said in his opening remarks to Sidney and me before our brief wedding ceremony in Spartanburg (reading from his prepared notes), "*Abie's Irish Rose* may have been a big success in New York, but I don't think it will go over very well down here!"

The only people who heard those remarks besides us were my mother, my father, my brother, Bobbie Lee the housekeeper-cook, and L.C. the yardman, who was serving us lunch that day. The justice of the peace arrived after my father had finished his speech, which ended on a more conciliatory note than it began. The JP's words were brief and to the point, but segued without a pause into a plea for political support for him in the next local election, so my mother got him out the door in mid-sentence, as he gripped the money my father pressed into his palm. (Sidney later did a hilarious imitation of this scene.)

Now every time I went into the restaurant, I felt like a goldfish in a bowl, as the crowd of regulars sitting in the bar booths formed a kind of Greek chorus—they came to know the most intimate exchanges between Sidney and me each day. Every development in our "domestication" process became fodder for that evening's anecdotes. When we brought home our first "child," Timmy the Yorkshire terrier, there were many stories for Sidney to tell about that, including the time Timmy had his tonsils out and we went down to the Spyer Animal Hospital and climbed into the big cage with him and sang him lullabies so he would fall asleep.

My efforts at learning to cook contributed more raw material for Sidney's stories. He couldn't understand why I wanted to acquire this skill—"Don't you like the food at the Russian Tea Room?"—but to me it was important, coming from the background I did, where cooking was relegated to servants as much as possible. Knowing how to cook was a step toward independence, I thought, an area where I would no longer need to rely on others. And then Sidney wouldn't have to eat at the restaurant and we could entertain at home!

I enrolled in a small cooking class given by Sally Hurwich, a friend of Sidney's who was a Cordon Bleu graduate. The dishes we learned to prepare in her apartment kitchen were classically French, and difficult, not the kind of ten-minute menus a working couple would scramble together at the end of a hard day.

Veal Orloff, my first experiment at home, was not a great success. In fact, after tasting it, Sidney decided to eat at the restaurant that night.

The gang was waiting at the RTR to hear the report on my first effort so I decided to stay home (and eat crow).

I mastered crème brûlée, but how much of that could we eat? I soon became discouraged with the response to my French cooking and went back to ordering from the RTR.

About that time, continuing the domestication process, I hired a cleaning woman to come in once a week. Her name was Beautiful Sun and she belonged to a religious group that had a very uplifting philosophy. She so impressed me with her spiritual strength, I felt I needed to get the apartment clean before she arrived, to show her I was not living a messy life. Unfortunately, because of my excellent housekeeping, she found little to do and gave me notice. I was devastated to lose her and it took a while for me to understand what I had done.

During the first year of our marriage, I had what I believed to be the chance of a lifetime: I read for the director Elia Kazan and he hired me to play Sister Woman and understudy Maggie in the road company of Tennessee Williams's *Cat on a Hot Tin Roof*. I raced home full of excitement to tell Sidney, only to see him perceptively upset at hearing the news. He was not at all pleased with the idea of my leaving New York, and even though I told him it was only for a few weeks and he could come to Chicago and I could fly home between engagements in other cities, he was unbending. I began to see I was up against a formidable barrier, a conflict between us I never expected. I decided I had to get out of the job somehow and stay home, to keep the marriage from falling apart.

The humiliation of having to go back to Mr. Kazan's office and turn down such an opportunity in my acting career was almost worse than losing the job itself. But back I went. The decision was so painful that I never felt the same way about acting again, and, as a person, I felt defeated. Sidney, the only ally I had, couldn't be counted on.

What was the next step, then? To have a child, of course. Someone I could count on, someone who would really be mine.

Serious domestication began when Ellen was born. It had been hard enough to leave Timmy, our Yorkshire terrier, alone when we went out, but now here was this baby who needed constant care and could not be left alone for a minute.

I worked with Sidney at the restaurant until the last day of my pregnancy, which turned out to be New Year's Eve. I started to have contractions in the office that morning and was lying down on Sidney's BarcaLounger when Joe Steinberg the accountant stuck his head in the door.

"Faith," he said, "I know you can produce this baby before midnight. Remember—it will be a big tax saving!" And I did.

Sidney brought Ellen and me home from the hospital on a snowy January morning. We had courted a lovely young nurse for months, so that she would be ready to come to us when the baby arrived, and now at the last minute she had canceled and we had to scramble around to find someone else. We ended up with Miss Beck, an older German woman who was the model of organization. Our apartment was not up to her standards, I could tell right away, as she ran down a list of the movie stars she had worked for in palatial palaces in Hollywood. Nor was the apartment ready to receive her, or Ellen, either, for that matter—no heat was coming up through the pipes when we arrived home and Ellen's nursery was freezing.

We had not used this new part of our apartment while we were waiting for the baby to arrive, and we didn't realize that the old radiators couldn't pull heat up to the penthouse until the whole building below was heated. Somehow it worked better on the other side of the apartment, where Sidney and I lived, but we never found out why. We accepted it eventually as just one of the downsides of living in a sixty-five-year-old building like the Osborne.

We had electric heaters sent up from the hardware store and did the best we could to make it warm enough for Ellen, but when Sidney left that morning and went back to the RTR, leaving me in the freezing nursery with the new baby and a new nurse I didn't like, I felt my heart sink. It was like he was leaving me forever.

I was used to going to the restaurant myself in the mornings, to have breakfast with Sidney in the back booth in the dining room, where we were joined by our butcher and our vegetable man, who waited for us after they made their deliveries to fill us in on the scuttlebutt from the restaurant world. They knew who was doing well and who was not by the amount of goods a restaurant ordered and how quickly it paid its bills. (We were paying on a daily basis not because we were doing so well, but because they wouldn't extend us credit.)

Now I wouldn't be able to go over in the mornings because I was breast-feeding Ellen and there was always something to do at home. A new life was beginning and I was unsure what to make of it.

There was no elevator in the Osborne above the eleventh floor, and we had to walk up a flight to our penthouse on the twelfth floor. To try to contain the rising heat, hoping it would reach the nursery, we decided to enclose the stairway, giving us a private entrance at the bottom of the stairs on the eleventh floor.

We had a warm relationship with our neighbors, the Dahlrups, who lived below us on the eleventh floor, from the day I went by the open door of their apartment and saw the Baroness Dahlrup stretched out on the dining room table. I thought she might be dead but Ida Gro, the baroness's daughter, came out and reassured me the baroness was only taking her daily nap. After that we became good friends, and it was unfortunate that Sidney and I chose to enclose our stairway on the day the baroness, unknown to us, was expecting Isak Dinesen for lunch.

FOUR

New York Restaurants

When I met Sidney New York was not as great a restaurant town as it is now, not by a long shot. The places we went to were mostly steakhouses like Al and Dick's, Gallagher's, the Pen and Pencil, the Press Box, and the Palm, or Italian restaurants of the old school, that is, southern Italian, where the food was usually ordinary (and heavy). Camillo's, an attractive place on Second Avenue in the Forties, was an exception, but the maître d' made himself so intrusive with his boozy chatter that we began to steer away from it. The other Italian restaurants that made a mark were Romeo Salta on West 56th Street and the San Marino on East 53rd. Both had a big following, but I always liked the San Marino, its owners, its bar, its atmosphere, its food. (What else is there, after all?) We also liked Sardi's before a show, Dinty Moore's, P.J. Clark's, the Gloucester House, Fornos, and the Blue Ribbon.

We enjoyed nightlife the most: the Little Club, the Blue Angel, the Bon Soir, Gogi's La Rue, Goldie's New York, the Embers, Café Society Downtown, Upstairs at the Downstairs, the Stork Club, El Morocco, the St. Regis Roof, and the Maisonette Russe at the St. Regis, where Peter Duchin played the piano.

There were great restaurants, too: The Pavillon and the Brussels, both started at the New York World's Fair; the Colony, where Sirio Maccione, later of Le Cirque fame, was the maître d'; the Chambord, the Voisin, the Marguery, Quo Vadis, and the Valois, where my friend Stacy and I, both in the cast of *Ondine,* would go every week, saving money from our paychecks for one great meal.

I will always remember one lunch at the Colony with my old friend Sally on a Saturday, our favorite day to go. It was the morning after Sidney and I had our only physical battle. My father and stepmother were in town, and my father had put Sidney through an afternoon of horrors the day before, shopping at the men's department of Saks Fifth Avenue. Why Sidney went on this expedition I can't imagine. He was so definite in his taste for clothes, and so finicky about the way he shopped. My father must have talked him into it.

Sidney came back home and fell, pale-faced, onto the sofa.

"What happened?" I asked. "Did something go wrong?"

"Your father!" he cried. "What he did to me!"

"I thought you just went shopping," I said.

"Oh, yes, that's what we did. We went to the shirt department and Ernest said to the clerk, 'How much are these white short-sleeved shirts?'

"The clerk told him and Ernest said to him, 'How much do you want for a dozen?'"

"What did you do?" I asked.

"I wanted to disappear right through the floor, I was so embarrassed. I thought the clerk would just turn away or maybe call the cops, but guess what? The clerk gave him a discount!"

"You know that Dad likes to do his shopping at Benny's Discount House on the Asheville Highway. You know, that funny place with a Ferris wheel in the front yard? And he's a great salesman, don't forget that. Was that all that happened?" I asked.

"Oh, no. Then we rode down in this crowded elevator and Ernest said in his loud Southern voice, 'You know, Sidney, when I was young and setting out, my father said to me, "Wherever you go, son, don't settle where there aren't any Jews [he seemed to stretch the word *Jews* into five syllables], because if *they* couldn't make it there, you *sure* can't make it!" ' And he laughed that hearty laugh of his, totally enjoying his own story. I broke out in a sweat and kept my eyes set straight forward until we finally got to the ground floor. When the elevator door opened, I expected to fall on my face, but somehow I managed to keep walking. Everybody was tittering and staring at me, not at Ernest. I guess they were wondering what in the world I was doing with this guy!"

That wasn't the end of it, either. That evening, we had dinner with Dad and Ethel and there were other comments from my father, voicing sentiments Sidney and I found abhorrent. The evening was so tense that Sidney and I drank more than our usual share, and after saying good night to Dad and Ethel, came home furious with each other and with my father and stepmother, all at the same time. The next thing I knew, Sidney was throwing our Portuguese wedding china around the living room (we didn't have a dining room), breaking several plates and cups and saucers, denouncing the South and in-laws and the state of marriage in general. Then he stomped off to bed. I was enraged. It wasn't what he said, it was the china—our wedding china—the only semblance of propriety we had! I followed him into the bedroom and, thinking he was asleep (and not being myself), sat on the edge of the bed and put my fingers around his throat and squeezed as hard as I could. Sidney easily broke loose from my grip and sat bolt upright in bed, put his hand out, and socked me right in the eye. We looked at each other, suddenly cold sober, and broke into laughter. We fell into bed and slept soundly through the night.

The next morning, we were hungover but cheerful. There were no signs of violence except, yes, the broken china spread around the living room and my, by then, colorful eye. Sidney got off easy—you couldn't even see the red marks on his throat after he put on his shirt and tie. I went off to the Colony to meet Sally, my face carefully made up, and, much to my surprise and disappointment, she didn't even notice my black eye. We had our whiskey sours and enjoyed our lunch, as always. Sidney came by later and joined us, which made the occasion complete. We were finally domesticated.

When Sidney's mother met my mother—well, that was an entirely different kind of encounter from Sidney's trials with my father. The two mothers met only once, before we got married, but it was an historic meeting. Telling about it has to be prefaced by the discussion Sidney and I had with his mother before I took him South to meet my parents.

I had already had the traumatic phone conversation with my mother, when I told her that Sidney and I planned to get married. She said, or I thought she said, "Then you'll be living a sexual life!"

I was standing in the bookkeeper's office, all eyes upon me. "No, no, Mother," I said. "Of course we won't!" What was I talking about? Of course we would be living a sexual life! What was *she* talking about?

But what she really said was "You'll be living a *secular* life!" which meant nonreligious, I guess, because in her eyes Sidney's being Jewish meant that I would leave the Faith, i.e., the Presbyterian Church. She must've forgotten that I wasn't religious, anyway. (I had never heard anyone use the word *secular* in a sentence before, and that distracted me. It was a pretty strange comment and an archaic way of expressing it, I thought. Sidney thought it was hilarious.)

So after two years of trial and error, we were getting married. We told Sidney's mother and she was very happy for us. Then Sidney said, "Mama, I have to go down South to meet Faith's parents."

"So?" said Mama. "What's so bad? That's what you should do."

"Well," I interjected, "you know, Mama, it's a different culture, and they don't . . . well, Sidney's Jewish and . . . they're Christian and . . ."

"So?" she said.

"Mama," Sidney jumped in, "they don't have any Jews!"

Sidney's mother took a long pause. "No *Jews?* Where are you *from,* my darling!"

"It's in the South, Mama," I said. "They're different down there. They might be hostile."

"Well," said Mama, "if you think they might *stab* Sidney, I don't think you should go!"

The subject of religion was never far from Sidney's mind, one way or another. It seemed to follow him like a dark cloud he could never shake. When he went to Wittenberg University in Springfield, Ohio, for instance, he was asked to fill out a personal questionnaire. When it came to "name your religion," Sidney wrote "Zoroastrian." The next question asked was "name your parents' religion" and he again wrote

"Zoroastrian." Finally they asked him to "name your grandparents' religion" and Sidney, giving up, wrote "Jewish."

Mama and Mother met later, when the religious question had been resolved as best it could be, and, I must say, they were both at their very best. They ended up talking about cooking, and Mama described how to prepare gefilte fish, mixing and seasoning it.

"What is gefilte fish?" asked my mother, finally.

"It's buffala," said Mama, which didn't answer the question for my mother, but they both moved on with their conversation.

Alice and Mama

Sidney's mother, Mrs. Kalmanowitz, came to New York from Russia when she was a young woman and married the man who had been sent by relatives to take her off the boat. She was without any formal education and her command of English was basic. She was, however, a shrewd and able self-taught investor who made decisions based purely on intuition—for instance, she kept all her money at the Irving Trust Company because she thought, with the name Irving, it must be a Jewish bank. She had built her portfolio from scratch over many years of saving and scraping, and she advised me right after Sidney and I got married:

"You should take the change out of Sidney's trouser pockets every night and, when you save enough, you should buy a share of IBM."

"But Mama," I said, "IBM is five hundred dollars a share!"

"You'll be surprised how quickly it adds up," she said.

"Mama," as we all called her, was my ally from the beginning of our relationship because I brought Sidney back to her, in a way. He hadn't spoken to her in years until he and I met and I urged him to make up with her. I knew he was unhappy about the estrangement, though he was still angry with her for something or other, and he did finally agree to go to see her when we were up at Grossinger's in the Catskills, where Jan Peerce, Sidney's brother-in-law, was singing and Mama was staying at Kutcher's, a nearby resort hotel.

Jan Peerce, who was married to Sidney's oldest sister, Alice, had just drummed his son, Larry, out of the family by saying the Jewish prayer for the dead for him because he had married a Catholic girl. Jan was an

Orthodox Jew, and very religious. In spite of Alice's pleas Jan didn't speak to Larry for two years. It was Alice who finally broke Jan down and got him to communicate; he wanted to do it, he was just too proud to take the initiative himself. But Alice was never able to heal the rift between Jan and his brother-in-law Richard Tucker. The fact that they were both great tenors and great rivals had a lot to do with it, I imagine, but there was something else, too, now lost in the clouds of family history, and they never spoke for the rest of their lives.

Jan didn't hold the same demands of religious compliance for Sidney. On the contrary, he urged Sidney to marry me. After all, Sidney, though he was like a kid brother to Jan, was not his son, and besides, we had gotten to know and like each other, Jan and I, and he thought, I believe, that it would be good for Sidney to settle down.

Alice was my best friend of all the family members. She was like a mother to me, and helped me through many hard times.

When I first met Sidney I was having difficulty making ends meet. My father was sending me $100 a month but I had a psychiatrist's bill of $100 a month to pay, so I had to make another $100 at least to keep going. I didn't have a job except for work in an industrial show as an automaton, demonstrating tractors, which didn't last long, so I decided to sell some things.

I looked around my apartment for salable goods and found only the set of Great Books of the Western World, a collection put together by Mortimer Adler of the University of Chicago. I had asked my father for these books when I graduated from Northwestern, thinking that if I managed to read them all I would become well educated, maybe even an intellectual. I sent to Spartanburg for them when I got settled in my first real apartment, and I had been looking at them in their special bookcase for several months but hadn't made much headway in reading them. It was time to let them go.

Then one day I decided to sell the diamond and emerald ring my father had brought me back from Australia when he was there during the war. Emerald is my birthstone and the ring was beautiful and special. But I decided it, too, must go. I asked Alice, who loved jewelry and bought a lot of it, if she knew where I could sell the ring, and she took me herself to a wholesale jewelry store on 47th Street in the diamond district. The salesman offered me $300 for it and I thought, painful as it was, that I was doing the right thing to sell it, though I knew my father would be terribly hurt when he found out the ring was gone. I accepted the offer and we walked out of the store.

The next time I saw Alice in the Tea Room she asked me to join her for a glass of tea and we sat down in the back booth, which we called the "Stammtisch"—German for a table reserved for regular customers. As we talked, Alice suddenly reached into her pocketbook and pulled out a small package, which she laid on the table between us.

"Open it," she said. I did, and it was the ring.

I couldn't say anything—I just looked at it.

"I want you to have it back," said Alice. "It belongs to you." She had bought it so I could keep it. I never forgot that kindness, and when much later I gave the ring to my daughter, Ellen, who had been close to Alice since she was a baby, I felt the ring had ended up where it belonged.

The Kosher Chicken Story

But what about the kosher chicken, which caused another rift between Sidney and his mother? It started with Mama wanting Sidney to cook her a kosher chicken in the RTR kitchen. Sidney was eager to do it, but Mama reminded him that the chicken had to be cooked in a separate pot and handled with separate utensils, so Sidney went out and bought the kosher supplies, and saw to the ordering of the kosher chicken itself. Then, with some disruption to the kitchen, he gave our Russian chef, Gary, instructions on how the chicken had to be prepared. Then he had the chicken wrapped up and delivered to Mama at her apartment on West End Avenue and 90th Street.

About an hour later Sidney was up in his office when he got a call from Mama.

"Thank you for the chicken," she said. There was a long pause.

Mama was being unusually reticent. "Is that all? Is there something wrong with it?" asked Sidney.

"It's a beautiful chicken," she said. "But I don't think I'll eat it."

Sidney was getting upset. "You don't think you'll eat it? Why not?" he shouted into the phone. "I ordered a special kosher chicken from the kosher butcher. He brought it over himself. I went out and bought a kosher pot and kosher knives and forks and had the chef cook the chicken just the way—" He stopped to catch his breath.

"Thank you, thank you," said Mama. "I like the chicken very much. It's a very nice little chicken. But I don't think I'll eat it, anyway."

"*Why not?*" yelled Sidney. "*What's the matter with it?*"

"I don't think it's kosher," said Mama.

Sidney took a deep breath and forced himself to ask quietly, "Why don't you think it's kosher, Mama?"

"Because it doesn't have those little panties on," said Mama. "You know, those little frilly panties they put on the legs of kosher chickens."

"Mama! Those little frills have nothing to do with the chicken being kosher!" said Sidney. "*The chicken is kosher!*"

"Maybe so, maybe so, but I don't think I'll eat it," said Mama. "Just in case."

Sidney pulled the phone out of the wall and threw it through the closed window, breaking the glass and bouncing it onto 56th Street. And he didn't speak to Mama until Alice and I finally persuaded him to drop the case many months later. Mama always had her finger on the pulse.

Sidney and I used to go to every new restaurant whenever it was possible, and Sidney would usually come away downhearted, thinking they were doing things better than we were, which wasn't usually true. But I remember one experience when I was the one who felt downhearted, a moment that stuck with me through the years as a kind of warning. We had heard about the Absinthe House, how popular it was at lunch, and how unusual, in that a group of people had formed a syndicate to put up money to open it, and they all ate there frequently. I wasn't sure that that was such a good deal, having all those investors eating virtually on the cuff, but anyhow we decided to go by there one day for a late lunch. When we walked in, the tables were clearing out and the owner, an attractive middle-aged woman with long red hair, sat in a booth by herself, drinking. She motioned us over and eagerly asked us to join her, and as we sat there, I became transfixed. I knew her husband had died and left her the restaurant, and I could see that she was lonely and, I thought, "She's trapped." She was already well away in her cups and it was still only early afternoon. I made a silent prayer not to let that happen to me—to be sitting some day by myself in my own restaurant, Sidney gone, drinking the hours away and longing for company.

Downtown the best restaurant was the Charles, on lower Sixth Avenue. We went there the night Kafka's *The Trial* opened at the Provincetown Playhouse on MacDougal Street, where I played the role of Fraülein Bergner, one of the three women surrounding K, the antihero. I was nervous at the opening and afterward felt I had given a bad performance, so I pulled Sidney away from the cast party and asked him to take me to the Charles. The meal was good, as always, and we headed back uptown in a taxi. By that time I was distraught about my part in the play, and as we rounded the corner of Fifth Avenue and 57th Street, I took off my silver high school "Teena Club" ring, shaped like a short silver tube, and threw it out the window. I seemed to be trying to say good-bye to childhood, or something heavily symbolic. Whatever it was, I regretted this dramatic gesture the next day, and went back to that corner, where phalanxes of people were crossing the street, to look for the ring, but of course it was gone forever.

By the 1960s, Restaurant Associates was leading New York restaurants in a different direction by creating theme scenes like Forum of the Twelve Caesars, La Fonda del Sol, the Tower Suite, and the one that lasted, The Four Seasons. Maxwell's Plum was another kind of innovation—it offered three tiers of service and menus, all encased in an Art Deco setting with Warner LeRoy's stained glass ceilings and a jazzy atmosphere he created that broke down social barriers. The restaurant as theater and entertainment was beginning. So Le Cirque, for instance, when it opened in 1973, chose an apt name to describe what went on there: it was a social circus with Sirio Maccioni genially cracking the whip.

There are principally two kinds of restaurants: the formal, which feature haute cuisine, and the casual—brick walls, wood floors, and café chairs like Mortimer's, which was the home of socialites who wanted to "dine down," a haven with no frills and low prices. Most contemporary restaurants fall into the latter category. The RTR fell somewhere in between. Endeavoring to keep a café atmosphere, we continually played with the look of the RTR to make it more accessible. "Changing without seeming to change" was our goal, without losing the "pizzazz."

Howard Kissel, feature editor of the New York *Daily News,* frequently lunched at the RTR, often with Jean Dalrymple, who, he says, gave him his introduction to the restaurant. "I have always been a timid person, and would never have the nerve to make a reservation for myself, but I could ask if Jean was coming that day, and if she wasn't I would usually get her table, which was in the front where she could see everybody go in and out. She knew so many people from different worlds, it was the perfect place for her to be."

Howard has strong opinions about New York restaurants. He told me three years after the RTR closed:

> One of the hilarious things about them is Who Controls Where You Sit. I'm speaking of fancy French restaurants (and certain others). These people who tell you where to sit—back home in France they would be peasants! And usually they are from Brittany, one of the poorest regions in France. But here they are, experts at making you feel uncomfortable. It is a great privilege for you to let them take your money! And New Yorkers love it! They love to be intimidated!
>
> The Russian Tea Room didn't make you feel that way—it was much more welcoming, and unlike any other of its caliber. It represented a certain idea of New York: the New York of cultured immigrants, most of them in the arts, from the '30s on.

FIVE

Isaac

In the early days of my getting to know Sidney, a character appeared who would have a strong influence on my life: Sidney's controversial cousin Isaac Chertok, a Russian émigré who was related through Sidney's mother, who came from the intellectual side of the family. Isaac's appearance belied his power to cause trouble among the tightly knit Kalmanowitz clan: he was small and frail with bristling gray hair and close-set eyes partly obscured by wire-rimmed glasses, which he wore on the end of his nose. His suits were frayed and hung loosely from his bony frame. His stiffly starched white shirts with rumpled collars and cuffs were too big for him, making him look like a Russian intellectual in a Chekhov play. He was, in fact, a Russian intellectual, as well as a Japanese scholar, an engineer who helped design the Trans-Siberian Railway, a diplomat, artist, linguist, teacher of Russian at the U.S. Naval War College during World War II, and translator of Chekhov stories.

In 1930 Isaac (pronounced "eet-sok") left Russia to join the staff of the Soviet Embassy in Tokyo, as a diplomat and architect. His assignment was to design the new Soviet Embassy, and while he was there he became immersed in the life and culture of Japan. It suited his nature— his love of structure, formality, and mystery, his focus on simplicity and the meaning of details. As he became proficient in the intricacies of the

Japanese language and its accompanying class structure, he became more Japanese than Russian.

One day while he was stationed in Tokyo, he was ordered to go on board an arriving passenger ship to welcome a visiting Soviet official to Tokyo. As soon as formalities had been exchanged, the official took Isaac aside and warned him to stay on the ship and leave Tokyo when the ship sailed, as the Stalinists had marked him to be purged and killed. Hiding on the ship until nightfall, he set sail for parts unknown, leaving behind the young Japanese woman who was the love of his life. In Istanbul he escaped from the ship and found his way to Israel by a circuitous route, and lived there for several years, until the war came and he made his way to America, under the sponsorship of his cousin Alice Peerce, Sidney's sister.

Life was not easy for Isaac wherever he went, as he had a confrontational personality. His brusque manner made him seem rude and he seldom formed close relationships. It was hard enough to understand him when he was calm, because of his strong Russian accent and his high-pitched nasal voice. But when he was excited, which was often, he had a way of speaking rapidly, agitatedly, the words tumbling over each other so fast that they came out in a breathless hiss. To many people he seemed like a creature from another world.

Isaac brought with him to America a metaphorical sackful of family skeletons, which he would eagerly unpack and display to anyone who would listen. Old never-to-be-forgotten betrayals and dark secrets reaching far back in time, into long-ago Russia, were his specialty. Like some strange wizard he would pull from his sack a daughter's broken love affair or a brother's stolen inheritance, laying it out in the cold light of day. He kept the family members wondering what his next awesome revelation about their past would be. They feared him because of the illusions he shattered, illusions they had carefully constructed and maintained since their arrival in the New World, not wanting to remember any of the unsavory parts of their past, now mercifully cut off by the wide expanses of the Atlantic Ocean. They wanted to avoid Isaac, too, because he was penniless, never having valued money or its acquisition. This fact made him suspect among this group of people who had struggled so hard to get to this land of golden opportunity and who valued nothing more earnestly than making money.

But avoiding Isaac meant risking his wrath, so he was inevitably invited to dinner. Besides, he did have wonderful stories to tell, and his erudition was astonishing, so it was not surprising that when he appeared at the Tea Room one day in 1955, I fell quickly under his spell.

When I met Isaac he was, as usual, down on his luck, but his pride prevented him from taking a number of unsavory jobs, and, since he wouldn't accept charity, he hardly had money to live on. To illustrate his point he told me one of his favorite stories.

It was about an old man, poor, sick, and out of work, who one day, while sitting on a park bench reading the want ads in a newspaper, finds an ad looking for a weight lifter. He tucks the newspaper under his arm and limps slowly to the address listed in the ad and painfully climbs five flights of stairs to the weight lifter's office. Out of breath and exhausted, the old man approaches the desk, where a muscular, bare-chested man is seated. He leans over to him and says in a barely audible whisper, "I just came to tell you—I can't take the job!"

Isaac lived in a tiny garage apartment in Nyack, a town about an hour north of New York on the Hudson River, where he had friends in the Russian colony there. He took a bus every day to New York to have a meal at the Tea Room at Sidney's ongoing invitation. He could somehow justify accepting this because Sidney had given him a commission to redesign his office. Not really wanting Isaac to do it, he just wanted to help Isaac save face so he could get enough to eat.

But in spite of Sidney's generous gesture, he had a temperamental dislike for Isaac and didn't want to be around him. "It's his incessant chattering, his gossiping, and that false pride of his," Sidney would say. Isaac reciprocated Sidney's feelings. He felt Sidney was beneath him in class on Sidney's father's side, and therefore insensitive to the finer things of life.

Meanwhile Isaac, in his wily way, had befriended me and invited me to join him in his daily repast at the RTR. I, too, was down on my luck, and had no immediate prospects in the theater, so I was happy to spend time with Isaac and learn about his life and his philosophy, which he was eager to share with me. Besides, it was a way for me to be near Sidney, who seemed preoccupied in those days and paid me little attention. I wondered if he was still carrying the torch for his former girlfriend in Sweden. The thing that sustained me during those dark days was Uta Hagen's acting class at the Berghof Studio.

I auditioned for Uta with a Dorothy Parker monologue, and she won my heart forever when she laughed out loud during the reading.

Uta was a charismatic teacher, full of warmth and encouragement. She was vivacious, seductive, regal, and earthy—all at the same time. (Of course, she has these qualities on stage, too.)

Uta inspired an energetic approach to acting: "Acting is human behavior in action," she taught us.

Our class was a great mix of actors, some already established, like Geraldine Page and Jules Munshin, some blossoming, like Anne Meara and Jerry Stiller, and others, like me, who were aspiring. The result was dynamic and, to me, an unforgettable part of my coming-of-age.

Isaac's philosophy had an incendiary quality: I think he was an anarchist at heart. He began to school me in the treacheries of governments toward their citizens, and made me aware of the callous manipulations of politicians and businessmen.

His educational technique was to clip articles from the *New York Times* and underline the theme and the key statements the writer made about the issue. Then, in the margins, he would explain the subtext, what the article was really about. Sometimes the most important and revealing statements would be hidden at the end of the article and Isaac would ferret them out. He called it "learning to read between the lines." Isaac's exposé journalism has since come into fashion; he would probably smack his lips over today's constant disclosures of the underbelly of the news.

I did my homework, and tried to see the meaning that lay underneath what the writer was saying. "Never trust anyone in power," Isaac would say, and I would nod in agreement. It fit in so well with my natural skepticism and rebellious nature. He also introduced me to the writings of Knut Hamsun and Hermann Hesse and advised me, when I was depressed, to go home and soak in a hot tub.

One aspect of our lunch meetings I found disturbing, however. Sometimes Isaac would refer to Sidney in a slighting way as if Sidney were a philistine and Isaac and I sensitive intellectuals, poor and unappreciated in a world ruled by greed. I may have felt unappreciated but I was young and didn't think this would last forever, and the kind of poverty Isaac was referring to I didn't understand. And Sidney a philistine? Something was wrong here. Wasn't he feeding Isaac every day? It made me uncomfortable to hear these things, and I knew that Sidney, knowing Isaac as well as he did, must have guessed that Isaac was criticizing him behind his back. When he walked by our table, I sensed Sidney increasingly resented Isaac's presence at the RTR.

I didn't speak up on Sidney's behalf to Isaac because I had a bone to pick with Sidney, too. I could talk to Isaac about Sidney's neglect of me, and my fears that he didn't care, and even share secretly in the sharp criticisms he made of Sidney. It gave Isaac and me a bond. We both felt like outsiders in the whirl of life inside the Tea Room, both of us without a base and without a job. The fifty years between us in age and the stark differences in culture, religion, and language faded beside our shared pain.

Meanwhile the design Isaac was to make for Sidney's office was slow to be completed, and only after much prodding from Sidney was it finally done. Then there was a question of what would happen next. Isaac had no resources for hiring workmen, so Sidney had to do it, and he had to pay them, too, above the contract fee he had already settled on with Isaac. Sidney's growing irritation mounted as he was inconvenienced by the work going on in his office. He moved out of it and went back into the bookkeeper's office, and seemed to revert more and more to his military days, wearing his old WW II uniform and barking orders at everybody. He didn't want to see Isaac or what Isaac was doing and sent me in to look at the work in progress from time to time, but my reports were tentative. I didn't want to compromise Isaac's position and I honestly couldn't tell what he was doing, anyway.

When the carpenters and painters had finished "making a mess," as Sidney said, he could no longer postpone looking at it and went in to see the results. The room was now totally Japanese in feeling, with framed vertical panels around the walls in colors alternating from beige to yellow to orange to brown. The only decorative touch was a portrait Isaac had painted, in Japanese style, of his Japanese girlfriend in a classic kimono. Sidney's office had been transformed into a Japanese teahouse.

The "unveiling" ended in a shouting match between Sidney and Isaac. What was this Japaneseness all about? Why had it taken so long to finish? Why did it cost so much? Underneath those questions were other, deeper matters—old grudges from the past. Isaac referred to his own superior intellectual and social background, and Sidney lashed back with accusations that Isaac was a pretentious ne'er-do-well who liked to bite the hand that fed him. Threatening to throw him out of the office, Sidney instead walked out himself, slamming the door behind him. Isaac was thereafter banished—not from the Tea Room, where he continued to enjoy his daily meal—but from Sidney's presence. The Russian language lessons Sidney and I had begun with Isaac, another way Sidney found to funnel money to Isaac without allowing him to lose face, were canceled, and though he didn't actually say so, I knew Sidney didn't want me to fraternize with "the enemy" any longer.

I was heartbroken. It's true that the Russian lessons had not been successful thus far, partly because Sidney and I both lacked the patience to wrestle with the Cyrillic alphabet, the numerous conjugations of verbs, the endless declensions of nouns. It didn't seem fair that the Russian language would not meet us halfway, when every day we were trying to keep the old Russian traditions alive in the restaurant! And the lessons didn't progress partly because Isaac managed to turn our lessons away from basic grammar study into an intricate study of Russian root words. Bad enough that they were in Cyrillic, but each word was a treasure trove of etymological gold to Isaac, and he would pause over each one like a gourmet digging into a spoonful of Beluga caviar. Even harder to digest were Isaac's digressions about family roots, and his jokes. Oh, his jokes.

His favorite pedagogical story was about the little Jewish boy in czarist Russia who is asked to stand up in class before the teacher.

"Who wrote *Eugene Onegin*?" the teacher bellows at the boy.

"I swear I didn't do it, sir!" cries the terrified boy.

"Well, who wrote it then?" shouts the teacher, getting impatient.

"Well, sir, I didn't do it. But if I did do it, I swear I won't do it again!"

Recounting this would send Isaac into uncontrollable laughter, which sounded more like a loud wheeze. Then he would delve further into family secrets, and, as the stories grew longer and darker, I could tell by Sidney's squirming that he was planning his escape and the end of our studies was approaching.

After Sidney and Isaac had the scene about the office design, Isaac didn't come into the restaurant as much. He turned more to Alice, who had always been his ally, and went often to Alice and Jan's in New Rochelle for his meals until he fell ill and couldn't get out anymore. Some of us took turns taking food to him in Nyack for a while, but then he became too sick to eat and had to be taken to the hospital.

He had the last word with Sidney, though. At the end of his life he hired an ambulance to take him to Mount Sinai Hospital in New York, and charged the bill to Sidney.

Dear Isaac. We understood each other, but now I understood Sidney better, too. He was jealous of the old man he thought was undermining my affections. But in the end Isaac brought Sidney and me together. Sidney began to notice me more when he saw Isaac's attentions to me. And he began to see that Isaac accepted me as a member of the family long before I *was* a member of the family, which reassured him. Still Isaac advised me not to marry Sidney. "You're much too good for him!" he would say. I wonder if he really meant it or was it just another way he had of getting even with Sidney?

But wouldn't he have laughed—that rasping, shallow laugh of his—to think his final role had been to play not Polonius, not Iago—but Cupid?

Hungry Artists

Isaac was not the only recipient of Sidney's largesse. There was almost always somebody sitting in the Tea Room eating happily away at Sidney's expense, be it struggling relative or impecunious friend. The hungry friends were usually artists of some sort, trying to make ends meet, and Sidney was sympathetic to them and let them build up large tabs. The only requirements were that Sidney like the person and believe in his talent or at least his need.

A dramatic instance in point was Dalmatov, a Russian character actor who had been a member of the company of Le Chauve Souris (The Smiling Bat), a famous Russian revue that played in Paris during the 1920s and '30s. Dalmatov, who, like many Russian artists, was always referred to by his last name, had come to New York with the show and had stayed on. Now old and almost destitute, he lived at the Wellington Hotel, two blocks down Seventh Avenue from the Tea Room. His main source of sustenance and diversion was his two daily visits to the RTR, where he knew many of the other Russians who treated the restaurant as their club. Of course, he was always Sidney's guest. As he grew older, Dalmatov began to lose track of time, and he would appear at the restaurant in the middle of the night, trying to push through the revolving doors, and, finding them locked, would bang on the panes until the night watchman came to see what the noise was about. The watchman would gesture to the big Belle Epoque clock on the back wall of the dining room and wave Dalmatov away, but in an hour Dalmatov would reappear, still looking for his breakfast, and would continue to come back on the hour until the restaurant opened at 11:30. Often I would arrive at eleven and find him already sitting alone in the empty restaurant, finishing up the last drop of his borscht, which the chef had sent out to him, and the last crumb of his pirojok, before pushing his bulky frame away from the table, but all the time waiting to tell theater stories to any of us who would give him our time. If no one came over to him he would leave, but he would return for his dinner promptly at five.

Danny Stern was a young writer with cherubic cheeks and the eyebrows of a basset hound who was having no luck selling his novels to the American public. Fortunately for him he belonged to the special Russian Tea Room "club," and Sidney endorsed his eating habits because he believed Danny was going to make it someday. And he did, but Sidney never got to enjoy Danny's success, which came after Sidney was gone. It was a joke among the regulars in the bar booths: Jerry Lurie, Bob Hector, Jack Sachs, Gina and Hy Hollinger, Jimmy Gelb, and their leader, Harold Clurman, that Danny's books kept getting published but they didn't sell enough copies to keep a bird alive. But Danny was always cheerful, and always hungry, as far as I could tell. Maybe he knew he was going to be successful someday, and would have the last laugh.

There are two kinds of hungry artists: the kind that doesn't have enough to eat and the kind who, like Harold Clurman, has plenty to eat and isn't in financial need but enjoys food and is knowledgeable about it. Harold was a very special member of the RTR club. An eminent director, teacher, and theater critic for the *Nation,* he was a delightful raconteur and a warm human being, who, unlike some of his contemporaries in the Group Theater, had spent time abroad, especially in Paris, which gave him a panache and urbanity the others lacked, except, of course, his exotic ex-wife, Stella Adler, the celebrated actress and acting teacher. He wore a fedora and smoked big cigars, and always had a story ready that would reveal character, maybe about something that happened at a rehearsal, always about the foibles of ego and pretension, even his own.

Harold lived at the Osborne, across the street from the Tea Room, where Sidney and I lived from the time we were married in 1957. Though Harold was married for a time to a wealthy actress named Juleen Compton who lived separately in a town house in the East Sixties, he didn't bring her to the Tea Room and I never saw him with her around town. Harold, when he wasn't directing a Broadway play, taught his acting and directing classes at night in a Carnegie Hall studio, and would come into the Tea Room after class with his students and Jimmy Gelb, his stage manager and sidekick, who had a wild Trotskyesque look about him, his wiry hair standing on end, his bushy eyebrows raised in a perpetual question. Most every day Jimmy or the actor Joseph Wiseman, a protégé of Harold's who was usually in a state of panic, would come through the revolving door and ask anybody standing near the door, "Has Harold been in yet?"

It was always fun to watch Harold when Stella appeared: Harold sitting in one of the bar booths up front, surrounded by students, Stella sweeping by in her grand style. Then, spying Harold, she would do a classic double take and come to a dead stop, staring at him in silence. Harold would look up, paling at the sight of her, and stop talking, sometimes his arm caught in a gesture in midair. Then Stella would rise up to her full height, rearrange her fur stole, and continue her sweep through the bar and into the dining room. Once, I remember, she stopped and did a little dance in front of Harold, twirling and bowing and lifting her diaphanous skirt to some imaginary Gypsy tune before she swept off. Once, when Stella passed Golda Meir in a bar booth, I overheard Stella say, "Well, *that's* no raving beauty!"

Years later, after Harold died, a writer called me and said he was writing a biography of Harold Clurman, and asked me if I would talk to him. After an ordinary exchange, he seemed to be probing for something. Finally he said that someone told him that Harold said I had asked him to marry me and he had turned me down! I was too stunned to comment. What could Harold have had in mind, to say that? We were good friends, never anything more. Maybe he *didn't* say it, that could be the answer!

Jules Munshin, called Julie by everybody, was a wonderful comedian and one of the three sailors, with Frank Sinatra and Gene Kelly, in the original *On the Town*. A great friend, he loved to play the hungry artist with Sidney and knew how to get Sidney apoplectic: He would come into the Tea Room and, standing at the entrance to the dining room, take a hard-boiled egg out of his pocket, crack it against the back of the nearest booth, and proceed to eat it, as everyone in the restaurant watched. Then Sidney would throw him out!

SEVEN

Location! Location! Location! Real Estate

From Goat Hill to Carnegie Hall

The 1870 brownstone that housed the RTR had a rich history of its own, corresponding neatly with the story of nineteenth-century New York City's continuous move uptown. In order to arrive at the year 1870, a little background history will be helpful.

By 1811 the city was moving away from its origins in Wall Street, Greenwich Village, and what are now SoHo and TriBeCa. That year, the city fathers created a gridiron plan, mapping out all the city's future streets that started above Greenwich Village in a checkerboard pattern running north, south, east, and west, unlike the crooked lanes—really expanded cow paths—that made up the old Dutch and English settlements at the bottom of the island in the early seventeenth century.

By 1844, New York had moved so far north that Edgar Allan Poe, then in New York editing *Broadway Journal,* was horrified when he took a walk in Jones Wood, an area between Third Avenue and the East River extending from 65th to 70th Streets, that had been set aside for a city park until the idea of Central Park replaced it. That was one of the ongoing problems with New York's development back then: real estate interests, i.e., greed, always won out over public interest when it came to creating space for public parks. Light, air, and greenery always fell before almighty mammon.

Poe observed, "The wonderful mansions here are already neglected: those magnificent palaces doomed by the spirit of improvement, which has withered them with its acrid breath. The streets are already mapped through lawns and in 30 years the whole island will be densely desecrated with enormous buildings."

It therefore seemed like a miracle when, in 1859, the construction of Central Park began at 59th Street and Sixth Avenue, eventually extending to 110th Street. At last the city would have a permanent park! This massive commitment in the middle of New York City not only created a vast green haven but also sealed off upper Manhattan from all future commercial development.

In 1863 row house construction was moving uptown by increments of three blocks each year. Row houses were blocks of joined brownstones, usually five stories high, fourteen to twenty-five feet wide (anything wider was called a mansion) and sixty feet deep, built on lots one hundred feet or two hundred feet deep, leaving room for a garden and a stable behind the house. In front of the house was a stoop, a tradition introduced by the Dutch—*stoep* means porch—one flight up from the street, at the main entrance to the house on the parlor floor. This floor contained a small front parlor—the "waiting parlor"—and a larger parlor and a dining room in back. The kitchen was on the floor below, and food was brought up to the dining room in dumbwaiters, small "elevators" lifted and lowered by pulleys.

In 1870 the population of the city reached one million. That was the year the row house that later became the Russian Tea Room was built on Goat Hill, called that because that was who lived there—goats! Soon the elevated railway began to push its way up Central Park West, paving the way for Upper West Side development, and the grazing goats were replaced by horses and carriages. About that time, Mrs. Eustiss Monroe's School opened in our brownstone at 150 West 57th Street, promising "chaperonage, home social life and special instruction for backward girls."

Along with the steady movement of New York farther uptown there were other innovations changing the city. In the 1880s the use of steel construction and the invention of the elevator made possible a new kind of city dwelling: the luxury apartment building. The fashionable set moved out of brownstones and into these buildings, which supplied maid and laundry service and public dining rooms for their inhabitants. The first of these buildings was the Dakota, which went up in 1882 on 72nd Street and Central Park West and was given that name because that's where people thought it was—in Dakota! It was followed in 1885 by the Osborne on West 57th Street and Seventh Avenue. Both are still in existence and remain coveted and colorful addresses in New York, along with the Alwyn Court, built in 1909 at 58th Street and Seventh Avenue.

Other memorable buildings went up on West 57th Street: the Art Students League of New York, in 1892, home of the Ashcan School, also known as the Eight, which included Robert Henri, the inspiration for the group, George Luks, John Sloan, William Glackens, and Everett Shinn; then the first General Motors Building—two more GM buildings were to follow—and Carnegie Hall in 1890, formerly called the New York City Music Hall until it was discovered that classically trained European musicians refused to play there, thinking "music hall" meant vaudeville house.

The 1890s were a golden age in New York, brimming with prosperity. The rich built mansions on Fifth Avenue's "Vanderbilt Row," as far north as 59th Street and around the corner on West 57th Street, where Franklin Roosevelt was born. It was the world Edith Wharton lived in and wrote about. Her aunt, Mary Mason Jones, built a white marble mansion on the corner of 57th and Fifth, which little Edith traveled to for visits from her family's home in the East Twenties, and which she later wrote about in *The Age of Innocence*.

Fifty-seventh Street was the Last Frontier—the last two-sided street below Central Park where commercial construction was allowed. When the park was built, upper Fifth Avenue was zoned for residential construction only, a plan made to keep bars from springing up near the park, where drunks might wander in and disturb the peace. The rich were buying lots along upper Fifth Avenue by this time, but no one actually had the courage to move up that far yet.

By the early twentieth century, the music world had moved uptown from Fourteenth Street, art galleries came up from 23rd Street, and fashion relocated from the Ladies' Mile on lower Sixth Avenue, placing 57th Street in the center of the city's activity.

When the Volstead Act, introducing Prohibition, was passed by Congress in 1919, New York's character underwent a dramatic change. Many restaurants were forced to close because of lack of business, and nightlife moved underground. It was the end of the golden age, when men dined with their "fancy women" at elaborate restaurants called "lobster palaces," or gave white-tie dinners on horseback. Ward McAllister's list of New York's Four Hundred (the number of guests who could fit into Mrs. Caroline Astor's ballroom) was becoming O. Henry's "four million" and the beginning of speakeasies and tearooms.

Louis Sherry, until Prohibition a successful restaurateur, said at the time, "Two things closed me down—Bolshevism and Prohibition: Prohibition with the clientele and Bolshevism with the waiters."

A new trend began with Alice Foot McDougal's coffeehouses. Here women appeared in public, often without men, and they were allowed to smoke. The artsy Bohemian atmosphere—shawls thrown casually over the backs of chairs, enormous jungle plants reaching to the high ceilings—gave women a seductive taste of the exotic and formerly forbidden. Ms. McDougal's favorite of all her coffeehouses—each one had a theme and a unique decor—was the Sevilla on West 57th Street.

Nineteen twenty-seven, the year the RTR moved to the south side of West 57th Street, and two years before the Crash, was a pivotal year in America: the postwar boom creaked to a stop. It was the year Babe Ruth hit sixty home runs, the year that brought the first national radio networks and New York–to–London telephone service. (Noël Coward wrote a hilarious short play about it entitled *London Calling*.) Streamlining became the rage in design for trains and autos, and Art Deco began to replace the Victorian and Edwardian styles in interior design. And it was the year of Lindbergh's historic flight.

On West 57th Street many new buildings were going up: Chalif's

School of Dancing across from the Russian Tea Room, later to become the Columbia Artists, or CAMI Building, Steinway Hall and Chickering Hall down the block, and Jay Thorpe and Milgrim's stores between Fifth and Sixth Avenues.

In 1932, three years after the Crash, in the midst of the Depression, Prohibition ended and Sasha Maeff, the new owner of the RTR, had a kitchen put in where the garden behind the brownstone had been and added a long bar in the front of the dining room, and suddenly the RTR became a real restaurant. The stable in back was enclosed and, after being a frame shop for many years, became the Tea Room's storage area, preparation station, and steward's office. The second floor of the stable later became our bakery but continued to be listed on the city's books as a stable up to the end.

That year, the Casino Russe, a Russian nightclub, opened under the same management in the Rembrandt Building, between the RTR and Carnegie Hall. Yul Brynner played the balalaika there, accompanying his sister, a famous Russian cabaret singer, and I once saw an old photograph of him seated cross-legged at her feet, playing away. The Casino Russe had a back entrance that led into the RTR's Boyar Room, a small private dining room used for parties and later for Sidney and a few cronies to watch the World Series on a set Sidney rented every year for the length of the baseball season.

The Beginning of Lincoln Center

In a radio commercial I wrote and recorded some years later, I said:

At 11:00 A.M. on May 14, 1959, twelve thousand people gathered out of doors in what is now Lincoln Center Plaza to listen to Leonard Bernstein conduct the New York Philharmonic. Surrounding them was a vast clearing resembling a bomb site, relieved only by the presence of a huge orange bulldozer. Suddenly the orchestra struck up "Hail to the Chief," announcing the arrival of President Dwight D. Eisenhower, who with a wave and a characteristic grin lifted aloft a silver shovel and broke ground for the new Lincoln Center complex. Here where squatters had huddled in frame shacks, where the Ninth Avenue "El" had run high over the heads of grazing goats, in this area long lost to the rhythm of rapidly expanding Manhattan, rose an architectural phenomenon containing New York's opera, ballet, theater, and orchestra. For the creators of Lincoln Center and for the people of New York, this was a Promethean moment. The Russian Tea Room—six minutes and twenty-three seconds from Lincoln Center and sixty years in the heart of New York. (Recorded 5/2/86.)

In 1959 something was developing before our eyes, which was to change the life of the Tea Room ever after—and that was the creation of Lincoln Center. By 1960 the huge project was well under way with the construction of the Metropolitan Opera, the New York State Theater, Philharmonic Hall (later renamed Avery Fisher Hall), the Vivian Beaumont and the Mitzi Newhouse Theaters, the Lincoln Center Library for Performing Arts, and the Juilliard School of Music.

When Lincoln Center was still on the drawing board there were already invitations to the Russian Tea Room to move and become part of the new complex. Brendan Gill wrote in the *New Yorker* in the 1950s that without enticements like the RTR the Lincoln Center environment would be barren.

As the land was cleared and the buildings began to rise we were shocked to learn that the New York Philharmonic would be leaving Carnegie Hall and moving its home ten blocks northwest to Lincoln Center. And not only the Philharmonic would be leaving—there was the likelihood that all the other principal orchestras and concert artists would move up to the new location, too. No longer would Carnegie Hall hold center stage in the music universe, which included jazz, with the New York Jazz Festival, and popular music, with the great one-man shows featuring Frank Sinatra, Judy Garland, Tony Bennett, and many others. The pop artists turned out to be faithful to Carnegie Hall, believing the cachet of performing there was far greater than at the upstart location uptown. Just the name *Carnegie Hall* on a poster or in the newspapers—"Frank Sinatra at Carnegie Hall"—still implied the zenith of achievement.

Then there was the City Center on West 55th Street. It would no longer be the venue for the New York City Ballet or the home of the New York City Opera, which would both move uptown. So would the Metropolitan Opera, then on West 39th Street in a building that would be destroyed and would vanish without a trace. Among the reasons given for abandoning the wonderful old building to the wreckers' ball was that it had become outmoded: it had insufficient space onstage and backstage, and the location, since New York was always moving uptown, had become inconvenient. I remember Jan Peerce's sadness at saying good-bye to the old Met, where he had had many triumphs. His good friends, opera stars Roberta Peters and Robert Merrill, felt that way, too.

This leave-taking of artistic institutions in our neighborhood made the Russian Tea Room, up to then the hub of that special universe, less closely connected, we feared, to the future of New York's artistic community.

The ties were not completely severed, of course, and not forever. Carnegie Hall would regain some of its status later, especially when the acoustics at Philharmonic Hall initially proved to be disastrous, but it would never be the same.

It was in that period of upheaval that the RTR clientele began to change. The regulars were no longer a primarily musical crowd but were becoming predominantly theater and movie oriented, along with artists, fashion designers, media and publishing people. It did not happen overnight, of course, but gradually and imperceptibly, just as the old Russian crowd did not go away all at once but began to thin out as its members grew older and disappeared from the scene.

In June 1959 Sidney and I took a trip to the Soviet Union, and saw for ourselves the Russian roots of the RTR—the history, the arts, and especially the cuisine. It was difficult to ferret out the great classic dishes like Beef Stroganoff and Chicken Kiev on the menus, and when we did we found them transformed and distorted, but still visible beneath the surface. Nineteen fifty-nine was the first year tourists were allowed into the country, and the year Vice President Nixon had his "kitchen cabinet" meeting with Khrushchev at the Moscow Agricultural Fair. Sidney declared on his passport that his occupation was "restaurateur," which led our Russian guides to ask, "What do you restore?" This was not such a foolish question when I thought of it: the French word *restaurant* originally meant and still means a place to become restored.

It was the year of the first thawing of the Cold War, and the impresario Sol Hurok seemed to bring it about himself single-handedly. He brought over the Bolshoi Ballet and the Moiseyev Dancers, among others, and the Tea Room was once more bustling with Russian artists. PepsiCo, with exclusive rights to soft drinks in the Soviet Union, brought Stolichnaya vodka to the U.S., which became an enormous success at the RTR and all over the country. For a while it was OK to be Russian, but it didn't last long. Soon politics and international conspiracy took a turn to the right and we had to deemphasize "Russian" and focus on the New York qualities of the Tea Room.

The year 1959 was important in still another way: it was the year the Diners Club was launched, which had a profound effect on the restaurant industry. People would no longer have to carry money—they could carry plastic instead, and they would also have a record of what they spent. Even tips could be added to the bill, paid out by the employer to the waiters, and later reimbursed by the Diners Club. The carrying charge to the restaurant ranged from 3.5 percent to 5 percent according to the volume of business the restaurant did with Diners Club. To most restaurateurs it was worth paying this heavy expense to bring in the new customers that the Diners Club promotion and advertising provided, and, best of all, it was harder for the waiters to steal food checks and pocket the money.

In 1959 the Boyar Room, our private room in the back that we rented from Carnegie Hall and which had once led through to the Casino Russe, the nightclub on 56th Street, was torn down to become part of a Kinney parking lot, occupying the old Rembrandt Building site at 152 West 57th Street. It was the first of several demolitions to follow in that block.

Lincoln Center planners came to Sidney that year and invited us to bring the Russian Tea Room up to join the new complex and become the principal restaurant there. We were excited beyond our dreams.

At the time, however, the success of Lincoln Center wasn't yet a sure thing. The plan had detractors. Some people felt the city would be better served by keeping music, dance, opera, and theater spread out in different locations around the city, not concentrated in one place. By diversifying the art centers, restaurants had grown up around each one, providing variety and avoiding the serious traffic problems that were bound to result from the concentration of simultaneous performances at the Lincoln Center complex. There was much grumbling, too, from the people who loved Carnegie Hall, the old Met, and even the City Center, which had been built as a Masons lodge and never accommodated itself very gracefully to theater and dance. Even its admirers had to admit it was a terrible stage to dance on, raked (that is, slanted at a steep angle toward the audience) as it was to the point where dancers almost fell off the stage.

This flattering offer to the Russian Tea Room to become an important part of Lincoln Center from its inception turned out to be a difficult one to accept. First of all it would mean changing our location and leaving 57th Street for an area that, at that time, was a wasteland. There were few good restaurants there, and most of the population was far from affluent and were not regular restaurant patrons. And where would our clientele come from when there were no performances? Sidney was concerned that there would only be pre- and postconcert business and little else at Lincoln Center—that our regular business throughout the day and evening would be lost. And how would our regular customers from 57th Street find their way to Broadway and 67th Street? Our location was so much better, near the theater district and surrounded by movie houses, the City Center, and Carnegie Hall.

The idea of running two restaurants didn't appeal, either, as we didn't have the kind of money needed to invest in a new location, even with support from Lincoln Center, or the staff to operate it. Shortly afterward, when our landlady, Mrs. Axe, sold us our building, we decided to stay put, and Lincoln Center faded from our horizon.

In 1960, right after Ellen was born, the Russian Tea Room lease was running out at 150 West 57th Street. Sidney tried to contact Mrs. Axe, who had promised to sell us the property when the lease was up because she liked us and thought we deserved to have it. She was an unusual woman who owned, with her husband, the Axe-Houghton Mutual Funds, based in Tarrytown, which operated from a castle visible from the New York Thruway. I believe they were computerized before we even knew what the word meant. Mrs. Axe also had wine holdings in Bordeaux, and spent a lot of time traveling there, and she owned several pieces of land on our block on West 57th and West 56th Streets. She was fond of the Tea Room because, as a child, her mother had brought her there after ballet classes next door at Carnegie Hall, and she remembered the tuna fish sandwiches she always had when she came in. Then later, as an adult, often wearing her clear plastic raincoat and hood, she would come in alone and have her usual tuna fish sandwich. We would sit with her and she would reassure us about the future—the RTR would be ours. But now Sidney couldn't find her, and he was becoming anxious, as only Sidney could be.

Sidney, in panic, decided we had to move the Russian Tea Room before the lease was up. We had bitter arguments about this, because I felt Mrs. Axe's intentions were good and she would turn up in time. Then someone offered Sidney a restaurant on Central Park South called Monte's on the Park, in the Navarro Hotel, between Sixth and Seventh Avenues. It was already in Chapter 10, that is, on the verge of bankruptcy (there is a Yiddish expression for it, "Eriv Mehulah," translated "Eve of Bankruptcy," a takeoff on the words "Eriv Shaboth," "Eve of the Sabbath"). Chapter 10 is the step where the creditors are settled with, before bankruptcy, which is Chapter 11. It would mean that Sidney would have to take over all the outstanding debts of Monte's and try to make it go as the Russian Tea Room. We would have to take over room service for the hotel, too. I didn't like the restaurant's layout or its location. Central Park South was not a busy pedestrian street and because it bordered on Central Park, only one side of the street had buildings, and no stores or theaters, only hotels.

I don't suppose there can ever be a final answer about Sidney's decision—whether he was right to buy Monte's or not. What would we have done if Mrs. Axe hadn't come through? The Russian Tea Room had to go somewhere. But in light of everything that happened to us afterward, I still think it was a mistake.

The bankruptcy proceedings over Monte's were very upsetting to Sidney. I remember when he came home distraught after the judge asked him to remove his cufflinks and any other jewelry he had on, as they would be held in court against what he owed the suppliers. These companies turned out to be connected to the Mafia, and one dealer called Sidney and threatened him, saying he would kidnap Ellen if he didn't get his money.

At this Sidney went over the top. He wanted me to stop taking Ellen, who was six months old, to the park and to keep her at home. But I didn't believe the threats were serious and I continued to take Ellen out. Nothing happened. I was angry about these threats, and indignant: how dare those hoodlums threaten us? Then, sure enough, Mrs. Axe reappeared and offered to sell us the property, "as I always said I would."

Now we were stuck with Monte's—it was too late to get out of buying it, but if we bought the Tea Room property we could stay on 57th Street where we belonged, and somehow we would just have to come up with the money for both, and keep Monte's going until we could unload it. Mrs. Axe took back a first mortgage and, at a tremendous interest rate, Sidney found somebody to take a second mortgage. I remember every month sitting with the checkbook—Sidney was teaching me to write checks "the right way" and had me in tears because I kept getting it "wrong." I was making out checks for the two mortgages, the unions' pension and welfare funds at Monte's (these had to be personal checks— not from the RTR account), and to Gertrude, Sidney's ex-wife, for alimony, and seeing that we had just enough in the bank to cover them and that's all. Two of our friends each personally lent us five thousand dollars that summer, which saved our lives. One of the friends was Jerry Lurie, who ironically was a lawyer for those same unions. The other one, Jean Thomas, was my agent for commercials.

Maybe we would have gone up to Lincoln Center if we knew then what we know now. In contrast to Sidney's decision in 1960 to stick with one location, today many restaurateurs feel that the only way to make their business viable is to acquire and operate several restaurants, in order to keep purchase costs low and sales volume high. Even with only one restaurant, we managed to make that principle work: we could only stay successful utilizing those two ingredients—low costs and high volume—and we were able to do that for many years, thanks in part to the careful purchasing scheme Sidney had worked out: for instance, utilizing every part of the lamb to create different dishes, like all the cotelettes. Later, in boom times, expanding our dining room space enabled us to increase our volume, so that even though our costs were climbing, we could make up the difference by serving more people. Of course, there was a downside to this, which worried me from the start: when times turned bad, what would we do with all that space?

In 1960, Carnegie Hall was saved from the wrecker's ball through the valiant efforts of a committee led by Isaac Stern, and the city bought the building and made it a landmark. The New York Philharmonic stayed on at Carnegie Hall until 1962, when its new home in Lincoln Center was finished, or they assumed it was.

In fact, soon after the opening concert there was an uproar over the acoustics. The press reported the angry comments of irate music lovers who said they couldn't hear in some parts of the hall, that the sound was tinny and generally unacceptable. The Philadelphia Orchestra announced it was going back to Carnegie Hall for the next season and Isaac Stern reportedly said that now that he had saved Carnegie Hall, it looked like his next task would be to save Philharmonic Hall!

Eventually the 136 golden "clouds" on the ceiling created to give perfect sound were taken down, and a series of structural changes that continued on and off for seven years finally brought the acoustical complaints to rest. It would be twenty years before Carnegie Hall, during an enormous renovation, would face similar acoustical problems and cause an equally shrill outcry from concertgoers until a solution was found.

We made some questionable real estate decisions along the way, and there were some sins of omission, too: for instance, we never utilized all the space we had in the five-story brownstone on 57th Street, costly real estate that could have been income-producing. Instead, we used the entire third floor for offices, and the top floor for storage of everything from china to broken samovars, discarded ballet murals, worn waiters' blouses, and boxes of family photos and souvenirs. The fourth floor contained our only remaining tenant, whom we tried for years to evict. Only the second floor, where we built the Café and the New York Room, were profitably realized.

The top floor contained, besides the large storage area, a two-room apartment, where, in an unlikely scenario, Arthur X, Sidney's psychiatrist, lived for a short time while he was trying to escape from his wife. By some strange coincidence his real residence was next door to Sidney's brother, Walter, in New Rochelle, and Walter, knowing Sidney saw Arthur professionally, would ask him, "What happened to Arthur? He doesn't seem to go home anymore!" Of course Sidney was sworn to secrecy, so he couldn't tell Walter that Arthur was living on the fifth floor of the Russian Tea Room.

There was one real estate decision I made that has been hard for me to live with. A month after Sidney died, Mrs. Axe suddenly died, too, and I received a telephone call from her estate representative, who told me Mrs. Axe's property next to ours at 148 West 57th Street was going to be sold, and they wanted to offer it to me first. They were asking $325,000 for the 25-by-200-foot property. I was standing at the front of the restaurant by the checkroom when I took the call, and after I hung up I saw one of Mrs. Axe's lawyers, whom I knew, sitting at the bar. I went over and asked him what he thought I should do. He told me he thought it was a great opportunity and I should buy the property. But I was afraid of overextending and I turned it down. Today I wonder how I could have been so shortsighted, but I did not then realize that having no money was not necessarily an obstacle to expansion. Sidney's accountant had told me I was in deep financial trouble when Sidney died, and I believed him. But I'm sure the money could have been raised. I should have taken Mrs. Axe's lawyer's advice.

"This is about a piece of America called West 57th Street, about real-estate speculators talking routinely in multi-million-dollar terms and about the power play to force the celebrated Russian Tea Room to sell out."

That was the way Owen Moritz opened his column in the New York *Daily News*, December 29, 1982. By then the West Side building boom, which Mayor Ed Koch had encouraged by giving air rights privileges to builders in what was then a dormant and underdeveloped part of the city, was in its ascendency. The zoning changes went into effect in May

1982, allowing taller buildings to be built on the West Side and encouraging mixed residential and commercial use in new construction. There was a lot of pressure to complete the projects quickly as the liberalized rules were to be rolled back in 1988.

The RTR building became a target for development on both sides. Carnegie Hall owned the parking lot to our west, which had formerly housed the Rembrandt Building, and the Carnegie Hall management wanted to acquire our site, and more important, our air rights, to make it easier for them to put up the skyscraper that became the Carnegie Hall Tower.

To the east, Harry Macklowe had assembled 142–148 West 57th, and he wanted 150, our location, to complete the package in order to build another skyscraper, the Metropolitan Tower, or, as we referred to it because of its ominous appearance—triangular in shape with black glass walls from top to bottom—"the Darth Vader Building." Yet another skyscraper, the City Spire, was going up directly behind us on 56th Street, next to the rear of the City Center, where problems with the city arose when the builders topped the structure with a Moorish tower that was lofted above the zoning limitations. This tower caused attention in another way. It "sang" in the wind, and had to be silenced.

Harry Macklowe offered to purchase our property, move the RTR somewhere else temporarily, and then put it into his new building when construction was completed. He was especially interested in acquiring the air rights to 150 West 57th Street. But what would have happened to the restaurant? It belonged in its old building, just the way it was, I thought. I felt strongly that restaurants don't "travel" well. The RTR in a brand-new building was not a concept I could accept, and the idea that in the interim period we would be in some no-man's-land really gave me pause.

In a *New York Times* article in the "About Real Estate" column on April 23, 1982, Lee A. Daniels wrote, "The belief that progress in real estate does not automatically mean demolishing older buildings and replacing them with new ones has become an article of faith in the development process. Brendan Gill, chairman of the New York Landmarks Conservancy, believes that the broader interest in preservation stems from a recognition of the role older buildings play in maintaining the character of neighborhoods and of a newfound value in the physical and psychological links with our past."

There was a lot of pressure from the Macklowe group to sell. I felt we were standing at a crossroads, and it came down to a David and Goliath situation. What could they offer me that I didn't already have? I kept asking myself. We had a flourishing business, the people who came to the RTR were by and large the people I enjoyed seeing most, and it was a tremendous challenge for me to keep the place going and to be innovative and try to see beyond the next curve in terms of what the public wanted, without changing the much-loved traditions we had preserved. And why should West 57th Street be turned into a parade of giant steel monoliths, anyway?

My then-husband, James Stewart-Gordon (Jim), got into the fray by sending up a trial balloon in the form of an announcement to the media: not only were we not going to sell—we were planning to add floors to our own building, three in the front and five in the back, where there were only three stories, to create an eight-floor building to accommodate our flourishing business. Lawrence Josephs printed a rendering of the new Russian Tea Room facade in the *Daily News,* a design by our architect, Millard Breslin, which looked surprisingly like Warner LeRoy's 1999 plan for the RTR.

Another reason for Jim's trial balloon was to scare off our last hold-out tenant, a woman who lived on the fourth floor of the RTR building. We had constructed the Café on the second floor even though she continued to live upstairs, but while she remained in the building our hands were tied as far as any further expansion was concerned, and she was an anachronistic presence during business hours. It was especially eerie to see her wandering through the hallways at night like Grace Poole in *Jane Eyre.* The only thing missing from the picture was a long white nightshirt, bare feet, and the flicker of a candle held aloft in the dark.

Eventually Jim's ruse worked on the tenant, and we did negotiate her out and began to proceed with our renovations—but not Jim's concept of constructing up to eight floors.

Lawrence Josephs wrote, "Exactly how the new space will be used is still being debated. Mr. Stewart-Gordon wants an open-air garden on the roof." It never happened.

I don't think Macklowe was affected at all by Jim's announcement. He went right ahead with his own plans for his Manhattan Tower.

Paul Goldberger, then architectural editor of the *New York Times,* put it succinctly in an article on January 27, 1985, entitled "The Tower Blight Has Struck West 57th Street." He said, "What seemed inconceivable was that entirely separate towers would go up virtually side by side on either side of the Russian Tea Room. But that is precisely what [happened], and it has turned West 57th Street into a horror of urban non-planning."

I could have taken the money and run, of course, when Macklowe made his first offer, and I would have put $12.5 million in the bank. But what would have happened to the RTR, and what would have happened to me without the RTR? Money couldn't buy the life I had there. I got to see my friends, hear the gossip from the Rialto, watch the celebrities come and go—in fact, it was my living room. I had come to realize, in spite of all the headaches, that I had a challenge and a goal that gave my life meaning. It was an important discovery, and I acted on it and kept the RTR intact for another thirteen years.

Meantime we made overtures to Macklowe and to Carnegie Hall to purchase our air rights together and join forces to build one big building on top of ours. But the timing never worked out. The Carnegie Hall group took too long getting their plans together and Macklowe began construction of his building without them. He withdrew his offer for our air rights when I refused to sell him our building. And by the time I decided I should sell our air rights to Carnegie Hall it was too late. Their plans were already under way.

In 1983 Andrew Alpern and Seymour Durst published a book entitled *Holdouts!* The Russian Tea Room was pictured in a two-page spread on the frontispiece, and described only as "This nineteenth-century holdout structure is flanked by the vacant property of two different developers. It houses a venerable restaurant and is six minutes and twenty-three seconds from Lincoln Center and slightly to the left of Carnegie Hall."

Following a foreword by former Mayor John V. Lindsay, the authors describe in the introduction "the different types of holdouts." Among those listed as "the most pathetic, the frightened type," was "the successful restaurateur who is afraid of failure at a new location." It no doubt referred to the RTR, and there was truth in that, though it was not the only reason we wanted to stay where we were. At least we were not put in the list of "greedy types" or "foolish types." And Andrew Alpern inscribed the following in the copy of the book he sent me: "For Faith Stewart-Gordon, Keeper of one of the more civilized traditions of New York, and a Holdout that offers delicious compensations."

During the construction of the Macklowe building, the RTR was pummeled and pelted with flying glass and debris and blasting, which caused considerable damage to our property. The most dramatic exterior incident was the collapse of a crane on the building site on September 8, 1984, when it swung out of control and headed directly toward the buildings across 57th Street. Instead of jumping out, the driver stayed in the cab of the crane, steered the crane back onto the building site and saved the day. But in the process he lost several fingers and part of his foot. Those years of construction were not for the faint of heart.

During that time, Mayor Koch gave a fund-raising breakfast at the RTR, and all the time he was speaking, the Macklowe crew was blasting next door every few minutes. Tom LoSquadro, our comptroller, went next door and asked them if they would stop blasting for an hour until the mayor had finished speaking, but the only response was an acceleration of blasts, the disturbance aimed at the RTR, not the mayor. Macklowe was expressing his annoyance that I didn't sell.

I have always been sentimental about Carnegie Hall, not only for the reasons so many of us share about its history and its mystique as the symbol of perfection in musical performance. It also reminded me of Twitchell Auditorium at Converse College in my hometown of Spartanburg, built at the same time as Carnegie Hall and resembling it in style. Throughout my childhood I attended concert recitals of the greatest musicians there. My mother was a music lover and had majored in voice when she attended Converse College, and her older sister Gertrude, who preceded her there, later sang with the Paris Opera.

My favorite part of the concerts was intermission, when I would run

around the auditorium and greet my teachers and other adults I knew
and a few of my friends, who, like me, had been allowed to come out on
a school night. Whenever I entered Carnegie Hall, I was drawn back to
that time, and I felt a strong sense of nostalgia just being there.

So it was painful to me when, in 1987, the RTR became embroiled
in a most unlikely and unexpected legal battle with Carnegie Hall. The
Hall was moving ahead at that juncture with its plans to build on the
Rembrandt site and was expected to have its property lines cleared
with the city, which Rockrose, as the builder, needed before construction began. I believe that the Hall was negligent in pursuing the search,
because, after the building plans were already completed, the engineers
came up with the discovery that part of the RTR building jutted twelve
to eighteen inches over the property line of the Rembrandt building
site, Carnegie Hall's property. This was unknown to us or, evidently,
to the Hall. Twelve to eighteen inches is quite a lot on a sixty-story
building!

Without any warning Norton Belknap, then managing director of
Carnegie Hall, whom I looked on as a friend, came out with all guns
blasting: the Russian Tea Room would have to get off Carnegie Hall's
land! Our wall would have to come down, meaning our building,
attached to the wall, would have to be demolished!

Jim at this time jumped again into the fray, bringing in Bill O'Conner,
our lawyer, to answer the Carnegie Hall attacks. Bill was the soul of
diplomacy, but when subsequent meetings brought no results and the
threats persisted from Norton Belknap and the Carnegie Hall lawyers,
Jim and I agreed it was time to call in some heavier ammunition. We
decided to ask William A. Shea to help us work this problem out.

I went to meet with Bill Shea, whose reputation as an arbitrator had
attracted me to him back in 1975. Bill was once described as "a power
broker who is well connected in a city that puts a premium on political
clout." He was a heavy-hitting lawyer well known in New York City
Democratic politics and in sports—especially baseball, though he made
a reputation at Georgetown University as a great lacrosse player. It was
he who inspired Shea Stadium when he led the drive to bring a replace-
ment team to New York for the departed Dodgers and Giants. Naming

the Mets' new stadium for him in 1964 was Mayor Robert Wagner's way of saying thanks.

The first time I met Bill I was ushered into his paneled office at Shea and Gould, filled with baseball trophies and souvenirs and lacrosse sticks hanging on the walls.

Our conversation that day was mostly about baseball, but I felt an immediate rapport and thought I could count on Bill for help as the real estate assemblage on 57th Street became more imminent.

The next day, September 1, 1975, I wrote Bill a letter:

Dear Mr. Shea,

I enjoyed our first meeting enormously. I hope it is the beginning of a long relationship which will benefit all of us.

Since our meeting something new has developed: the lease on the Rembrandt property next to us, where the Kinney parking lot is now, is up, and I would like to acquire that lease and build a sidewalk cafe across the 50 foot frontage on 57th Street between the RTR and Carnegie Hall, and behind the cafe build a dining room, offices, restrooms and a kitchen. Julius Bloom at Carnegie Hall is enthusiastic and wants us to have plans ready within a month. Can we get together about this as soon as possible?

Cordially,
Faith Stewart-Gordon

That plan never got off the ground but Bill and I became friends from the start. He had an infectious personality—he was the personification of the brash straightforward New York Irishman from an era that had almost passed. In the next few years I spent many evenings with Bill and his wife, Norrie—so different from Bill but just as strong in her own way, and wry down to her fingertips—enjoying dinners around town and baseball games together. Bill was like a father to me, and I felt protected knowing he was on the scene. When he died in 1991 at age eighty-four, I felt a big loss, as I did when Norrie died a few years later.

"How can we tear down 'part' of our wall?" I asked Bill in reference to the Carnegie Hall threat. "Our whole building will be destroyed!"

Bill organized a meeting between the RTR and Carnegie Hall to get to the heart of the matter, and he immediately calmed the waters. He must have waved his magic wand because the Carnegie Hall people backed off and left us alone.

"Carnegie Hall owes you something, anyway," Bill said. "You've been giving them free advertising for years with 'Where does the Russian Tea Room stand? Slightly to the left of Carnegie Hall.' And I'll bet they've never even acknowledged it."

When the tough reform administration of Mayor Ed Koch came to power, Bill Shea's old-line Democrats were left out in the cold. I was conflicted because, loyal as I was to Bill personally, I liked Ed Koch immensely and supported him from the time he was a congressman. It was the changing of the guard, and many of us thought it was healthy for the city.

The Carnegie Hall incident did not improve our relations with them or vice versa. Jim, ever contentious and litigious, had already soured our connection with the Hall by withholding our air rights from them. Gradually we mended our fences, helped, no doubt, by the fact that I had legally separated from Jim. It was a relief when the unpleasantness died down and we began to have an exchange with the Hall again, which traditionally ranged from our paying for the printing of the Hall's ticket envelopes to their giving dinners and receptions at the Tea Room.

Later it was a pleasure to deal with Judith Arron, the executive and artistic director of the Hall, who had talent, musical knowledge, tensile strength, charm, and grace. Her premature death in 1998 was a great loss to the music world.

In Russia the term *Russian tea room* (*Russkaya chainaya*) is generic and describes a popular place where people meet and sit around the samovar and exchange gossip. Our Russian Tea Room, however, was a valuable commodity, and in order to protect the name we went to a lot of trouble. After all, if there were Russian Tea Rooms all over America, our Russian Tea Room would be devalued, sort of like what happens when you print counterfeit money. So when a little restaurant in the back of the Carnegie Hall building on 56th Street opened and called itself the Chinese Tea Room, we took up arms. It was an obvious rip-off of our name, and being right next door to the RTR we felt it was unfair competition. Eyewitness News interviewed Tom LoSquadro, our comptroller, about our efforts to get the Chinese Tea Room to change its name, and it became a brief cause célèbre, not to mention a tempest in a teapot! We finally threatened them with a lawsuit, and they changed the name to the Chinese Tea House and subsequently went out of business.

More serious were the "Russian Tea Rooms" that opened in Chicago, Los Angeles, and Washington. When we found out about these places we asked them nicely to change their name and then, if they refused, we sent them a lawyer's letter. (Tom used to call around to the largest cities in the country and ask information for the phone number of the Russian Tea Room. If one existed, he would follow up with a phone call, and sometimes one of us would pay a visit.)

Flying home from Rome among a group of people who had been guests at a weeklong birthday party given by Susan and Bob Summer in May 1992, Alan Grubman, the high-powered entertainment lawyer, started giving me advice about the Tea Room.

"You should utilize the whole building," he said. "After all, you've retained the air rights and you're not using them. I think you should build a very chic hotel on top of the restaurant with the lobby on the second floor, entrance on 56th Street. . . . Listen to me—you couldn't afford this advice!" My friend David Beer, a well-known architect (and man about town) was one of the party, too, and was listening to Alan Grubman's ideas. The next thing I knew, David was drawing up plans for the RTR Hotel, and we were talking to Alan Grubman and Marvin Josephson, head of ICM, who had been in on the initial conversation, and my lawyer Bob Cohen. There was one problem: where were we going to get the money? The name Rosewood came up, the Texas firm that developed and managed luxurious boutique hotels. I had a promising talk with one of their executives, but it turned out that, with money tight, they now only managed hotels, so would not be interested in developing the RTR Hotel themselves. Gradually the idea died for lack of nourishment, and David Beer got the worst of it because he never got paid for his plans. That's show business, I guess. But the plans were beautiful!

EIGHT

RTR Divas and the Art of Having Lunch

The Russian Tea Room was blessed with a series of unusual women who ran the dining room, each with her own definitive style, each establishing her own imprint on the restaurant. Though these maîtresses d' all worked principally during the day, they set the tone for the evening as well. Their job was a combination of sergeant-major, field strategist, public relations specialist, psychiatrist, police officer, and children's nanny. It was they who decided where customers would sit. It was a high-wire act—and there was no net!

The only time I ever attempted to seat anyone during my entire career at the RTR was one day early in my RTR life, when Miss Anne, our maîtresse d', was on vacation and I thought it would be a lark to show a few customers to their tables. It looked easy enough: just pick up some menus, walk the customers down the aisle, and pull out a chair.

In walked Mr. Goldwurm, a longtime customer, an elderly man with a pince-nez and a heavy Dutch accent, who owned the Little Carnegie Theater next door. In fact, the RTR and Mr. Goldwurm's theater shared a common wall, and if we hung a picture on the east wall of the Tea

Room, Mr. Goldwurm's movie patrons would hear the sound of our hammer, and Mr. Goldwurm would come running over to complain. If water overflowed in our kitchen, Mr. Goldwurm's patrons would see it creeping slowly across the stage in front of the screen, and we knew we could expect to see Mr. Goldwurm momentarily. Ours was a sensitive relationship. On that day, Mr. Goldwurm was accompanied by Mrs. Goldwurm, of the flaming red hair, and their nephew and heir apparent Felix, who always wore a crew cut and was always in tow. I picked up three menus from the captain's desk and, with an encouraging smile, motioned them to follow me. They seemed surprised to see me in my new role. I led them to a nice table in the middle of the restaurant, and was about to pull out a chair when Mr. Goldwurm turned on me with a viciousness I could not have imagined. "This is not our table!" he screamed at me in his heavy accent. He had always treated me with the utmost cordiality, but my mistake caused him to suddenly turn into a viper. I was so shocked I could only stand there, holding the menus, unable to speak, as customers piled up behind the Goldwurms and Felix, waiting to be seated. Finally Sidney saw the commotion from the other side of the room and came to my rescue, putting the Goldwurms at their proper table, which was the front booth (I should have known!), and I retreated to the sidelines, where I stayed, happily ever after. In a few seconds my respect for seating captains had increased enormously.

But that was not the end of my relationship with Mr. Goldwurm. We resumed our mutual cordiality soon after, and he and I later became coconspiritors when Harry Macklowe was trying to assemble most of our side of the block as a building site. Mr. Goldwurm and I would meet in the "stammtisch" (the back booth) after lunch and keep each other apprised of what we'd heard about Mr. Macklowe's progress in his efforts to buy us out. Mr. Goldwurm tried to protect me, but eventually he sold his holdings to Macklowe and left me all by myself, squeezed between Macklowe and Carnegie Hall.

I had a similar coconspiritorial relationship with Julius Bloom, then the Hall's managing director. Julius would call me and say he had some important news about the Hall's plans to build on the Rembrandt property between us and the Hall, which was, at that time, a Kinney parking lot. Julius, of whom I was very fond, was an artist at heart, a musician who had stepped over the fence into the business side of things and straddled it as best he could. But he was still a dreamer and a romantic, despite his somewhat comical appearance. He had a receding chin and bristling mustache, uncontrollable waves of brown hair, and popping eyes, which made him appear to be constantly surprised. I never knew what to believe in the "news" he reported to me, though I think he genuinely wanted to help me save our building, but he called our meetings so frequently that I came to suspect that he also just enjoyed having lunch!

My fondest memory of Mr. Goldwurm had nothing to do with real estate. It took place one day when he came over out of the blue not long after Sidney died, and formally invited me to accompany him to the Cannes Film Festival, which, like many of our other "movie" customers, he attended every year. Ide Halpern, Sidney's cousin, who was still working for me as a bookkeeper, nearly collapsed when I told her about Mr. Goldwurm's offer.

"Why, that dirty old man!" said Ide, no spring chicken herself. "What happened to Mrs. Goldwurm?"

"He says Mrs. Goldwurm doesn't want to go," I said.

"Well, I bet she doesn't know he's invited you to go in her place!" said Ide. Of course I didn't accept, but I thought it was a hilarious idea. It was not easy to conjure up the image of Mr. Goldwurm as a lothario, but, you see, you never can tell! (And what would he have done with Felix?)

P.S. Not long after the demise of Mrs. Goldwurm, Mr. Goldwurm remarried, this time to a much younger woman, and took an extended honeymoon in Europe. The couple's first stop on their nuptial trip, he told me, was, of course, the Cannes Film Festival.

Lunch at the Tea Room took place in the short space of time between noon and 3 P.M. Evenings were different. They were divided into pre-theater dinner, served from 5 to 8 P.M.; dinner for serious diners from 8 to 10 P.M.; and after-theater supper—10 P.M. to midnight—for night owls, concert- and theatergoers and Europeans and South Americans, who dine later than most New Yorkers. Downtown dining in SoHo and around Union Square had not yet become the rage, and the Greenwich

Village choices were limited—Mama Bertollotti, the Granada, the Charles, and Joe's, all in the West Village, were the ones I knew. In the 1940s and '50s there was much more activity in Midtown at night, with most theater curtains going up at 8:30, and nightclubs and late-night eateries abounding. The RTR was open then—and busy, too—every night until 1 A.M., and 2 A.M. on Saturdays.

Lunch, which every New York businessperson knows, has the blessed asset of having a definite beginning and end. At lunch you can be more adventurous with your choice of partners because you know you won't get stuck for more than two hours. Say, for example, you had a lunch date at the RTR at 12:45. By a quarter to three you or your lunch partner, looking up at the big Belle Epoque clock on the wall, would be sure to announce, "Well, time to get back to work!" (even if you had no intention of going back to work and planned to go straight home to walk the dog) and the diplomatic check-scrambling would begin.

Many of the regulars had RTR charge accounts. The RTR did not encourage this because it cost too much both to carry the accounts and to pursue the deadbeats. Ide and I once had a few scary moments in front of a grand jury because of a collection problem in which she innocently became entangled. So it was considered something of a status symbol to have a house account, and if you had that privilege you could sign, like Sam Cohn, the agent, in a scratchy hieroglyph and quickly make your exit when you had to, sometimes leaving your guest to finish coffee alone. But it wasn't just the time limitation that made lunch so appealing—there was a spirit of gratitude and lightheartedness in the air. After all, the workday was already half over, and for those who still drank at lunch it was almost as good as finished! The beneficent reprieve from a tedious morning's work celebrated with guiltless companionship, a glass of white wine, and a salad—yes, you could get a salad at the RTR (nobody could eat caviar every day, though some tried). The salad was enjoyed while plying one's trade and being seen by Those Who Count. All this was about as close to happiness as most people would get before Friday afternoon arrived and the jitney carried them off to the Hamptons to recover from their harried workweek.

I remember days during lunch when the whole room seemed to vibrate with intensity, everyone seemed to be on the same wavelength, and there was a hum of good feeling and laughter that made its way around the tables. How it started was hard to say, but sometimes it could center around a person—for instance if Jackie Onassis was spotted in the front booth on the left, where she always sat, often with Mike Nichols. But the hum would really start before that, upstairs at the reservation desk when the call came in that Mrs. Onassis was coming for lunch. The reservationist would breathlessly call Ona de Sousa, the maîtresse d', in the dining room and she would alert the staff. Meantime someone would bring me the reservation list in my office and I would join in the excitement. Sometime during lunch everyone in the office would find an excuse to walk through the dining room to catch a sideways glance at "Jackie." Our policy was "do not disturb" for celebrities, and they were seldom interrupted, unless they wanted to be, but everyone could look!

It was the maîtresse d's job to control the room with charm, wit, and quick-stepping flexibility. If all else failed, muscle might have to be brought into play.

What to do, for instance, when Paul Newman arrived unannounced, as he often did, and stood in line, blue eyes dancing? The game of musical chairs would begin, as Ona moved people around until she could find a way to make everybody happy.

Only a few things could throw Ona into turmoil in her effort to seat "the famed and famished." One was if a well-known person didn't show up, either because he or she couldn't make it and nobody bothered to cancel (celebrities never make phone calls themselves) or because the reservation was a misrepresentation: someone extremely unknown would arrive and say, "But my name really *is* Jack Nicholson!" Or if a well-known person came in with someone else who had made the reservation in his or her (unfamiliar) name and the well-known person ended up sitting in no-man's-land, smiling bravely while Ona shot daggers at the culprit who hadn't had the good sense to use the well-known person's name to make the reservation in the first place. It was painful for all, but for Ona it would be a three-Advil morning from the start!

Physical disasters could have even worse consequences. One of the longest-lasting of these occurred during the period when Harry Macklowe was building the Metropolitan Tower next door, to the east of us.

We pleaded with the foreman on the construction site to stop drilling and blasting during the lunch hours, but we managed only to get him to give us a warning before every blast. (Some of us suspected that Mr. Macklowe was not eager to help us after I refused to sell him the building.) The routine began when the foreman called Ona. Then she and her captains would scurry around to all the tables on the east side of the dining room and say in a low voice, "Blast in five minutes!" and sure enough, the blast would come with a tremendous boom, shaking the building and all its inhabitants, especially those on the east side of the dining room. The regulars got so used to it that they hardly noticed when the blasts went off and they were raised out of their seats, but it was harder on newcomers, who were shocked out of their wits. It was amazing to me that during all those months, none of our customers complained, nor did they abandon us, either, which really gave us heart.

But along with the blasting and drilling we had another problem—the front of our building was under scaffolding for three years while the Metropolitan Tower was being built to the east and three more years while the Carnegie Tower was being built to the west. As a result we were totally invisible from the street. It was during that period that I started thinking about selling the business. I spent one Christmas alone with my dogs, trying to decide what to do. There was an interested buyer in the wings, but a lot had to be worked out, and, hardest of all, the deal had to be negotiated in secret so that our business wouldn't be hurt. If people found out I was about to sell, it would create panic in our key staff members and they would start leaving, our customers would look for new haunts, our suppliers would demand cash for their deliveries—not a pretty picture.

The only person I talked to about my predicament was my friend Helen Gurley Brown, who kept counseling me not to sell. "You'll lose your base! Nobody in New York will know who you are anymore!" she warned me. (That seemed to be the worst thing that could happen to a New Yorker.) As much as I cared for Helen I couldn't get it out of my mind that I wanted out. Operating the business had become too hard, and maybe I was running out of steam. Still I couldn't make up my mind. I stayed in this agonized state for months, waiting for some small incident to push me over the edge one way or another. But "the deal" was not as simple as I thought. In fact, it turned out not to be a deal at all, as the money had not yet been raised, and the potential buyer would have to make public the name of the restaurant in order to get backers. At that point I decided not to sell. The moment had passed and I realized that I was not ready to leave the Russian Tea Room yet. When I made the decision I felt a great sense of relief. It renewed my spirit and I was ready to go back and give myself to the work at hand: dealing with the tightening economy and trying to make the Tea Room better in the process. Suddenly I began to enjoy my work again.

My rededication did not affect the ongoing construction problems, however. Lumber and debris continued to fall on our roof from the new building, and when it rained, clogged up our drains. One day at lunch I was sitting with a friend in the midst of a summer thunderstorm with torrential rain and flash flooding, when part of the ceiling of the dining room caved in before our eyes. Water gushed down the walls and over the banquettes, but our staff, trained for disasters, leaped into action and began taking down the paintings and putting them away where they wouldn't be damaged. Our manager was already examining the roof and our comptroller had already called the plumber. The strange thing was that none of the customers noticed what was happening! Ona had to go around to the tables where water was beginnng to trickle down from overhead, and ask the people to move to "drier land." They did so, but without interrupting their conversations or even wondering what was taking place. They just got up and moved over to the next table, as directed.

When the scaffolding finally came down after six years and the huge buildings on either side of us were completed, we threw a party on 57th Street in front of the Tea Room to celebrate. Anne Meara and Jerry Stiller, dressed in Russian waiters' blouses, handed out blini and caviar to passersby, there were balloons and balalaika music and much revelry, thanks to our staff and especially to Anne and Jerry's generosity and spirit of fun.

Then there were the bomb scares. They started with crank telephone calls, and two of them ended with the evacuation of the whole building. One occurred in the middle of lunch and people didn't want to move.

Some of the customers took a piece of bread with them, or whatever food they could carry when they were finally persuaded to leave, and then came right back after the building was checked out and finished their lunch, cold or not.

During the other scare, the police came in response to our call about a bomb warning and found a black bag containing metal parts in the checkroom, so they called for an evacuation of the premises. I had been off recording a commercial, and when I pulled up in a taxi in front of the restaurant, there was my daughter, Ellen, opening the door for me!

"Mom, don't be alarmed! Don't be alarmed!" she said, and as I got out of the taxi I saw, across the street in front of the Fontana di Trevi restaurant, the entire RTR staff, standing in a group as if posing for a class photograph, waving at me.

"I didn't want you to walk into an empty restaurant," Ellen said. "You would have gone bananas!" By the time I recovered from the shock, the police had discovered that the black bag belonged to a cash register repairman who had gone out to lunch and the "bomb" was only a collection of metal computer chips.

Summer

Summer was a difficult time in the restaurant business in those days. Business was usually slow and the suppliers got nervous as their checks were held back week after week. The RTR never closed in the summer, or any other time, nor could we have even if we wanted to. The cost of closing and reopening was more expensive than staying open and taking in the few dollars that we did. It took two days to get the kitchen running again after a closedown.

One hot summer day, when Sidney was going crazy with the broken-down air conditioner and the empty dining room, his good friend Zero Mostel, surely one of the funniest and wildest of comedians, came in. "This place would make a great bowling alley!" Sidney said to Zero. Zero, without further ado, went outside and got down on his knees on the sidewalk, and raising his outstretched arms to passersby, cried, "Please come into the Russian Tea Room! The Russian Tea Room needs you! The boss is going broke!"

Another time, Zero was passing by Harold Clurman's booth in the bar of the Tea Room while Harold was discoursing on the theater, about which he was passionate, oblivious of everyone around him. The booth was packed with his students. Zero stopped and waited for Harold to acknowledge him. Nothing. Harold continued his discourse without noticing Zero at all. Finally, in desperation, Zero suddenly unzipped his fly and let his trousers drop to the floor, revealing red, white, and blue striped boxer shorts. Harold still did not notice, so Zero, furious, pulled his trousers back up and moved on into the dining room, looking for greener pastures.

Sidney got some momentary pleasure out of summer when we played the "pigeon game." This game could be played only when the air-conditioning was not working (which was often enough) and the revolving doors were opened to let in a little (hot) air. Then some of the local pigeons, out of curiosity, would come waddling into the restaurant one by one, step by careful step, then stop, look around, and slowly turn and walk out again. Sidney would break up with laughter. "You see, nobody wants to come into this damn place!" he would say. "Not even the pigeons!"

My worst memories of summer were when I was making theatrical rounds in the broiling sun, wearing high heels and burning my feet on the sidewalks of New York, all the time encased in a rubber Playtex girdle, which stuck to my skin, creating my own personal sauna. How did we put up with those things?

One summer we closed the RTR for four weeks to renovate the kitchen. It seemed strange to have the Tea Room dark after all those years of never missing a day. Anne Meara wrote a poem about it:

July Is the Cruelest Month
BY ANNE MEARA

A poem for all those who are experiencing withdrawal symptoms from the Russian Tea Room's being temporarily closed.

Famous faces are streaked with tears
Living legends weep in their beers

Actors and writers feel great deprivation
There's nowhere to go for a mid-day libation.

The cream of the crop, the tiptops in taps
Are screaming and wailing and gnashing their caps
They just want to eat, to discourse and dine
On Shashlik Caucasian and imported wine.

Wheelers and dealers are slightly dyspeptic
Agents and managers near cataleptic
Production is halted on all series mini
Deals aren't valid unless eating blini.

Sylvia Miles is beating her breast
Milton Goldman is very depressed
Ruth and Gar, Woody and Mia
Sneak out for lunch to a cheap pizzeria.

There's moaning from Dustin and Meryl and Tammy
There's groaning from Whoopi and Raoul and Sammy
"Where can we go?" sob the talented many
While Sam Cohn longs for a plate of pelymeni.

These delicate psyches are hurt and abused
By Faith Stewart-Gordon most sadly misused
They need to be nurtured, to be praised and be seen
They need reservations and Slavic cuisine.

But no joy will they have this hot muggy July
The reason must make all celebrities cry
Fifty-seventh Street's undergoing great tribulation
The Russian Tea Room is closed for slight renovation.

At the conclusion of the renovation, we gratefully opened for lunch—
almost. Just as the revolving doors were opened to let customers in, a fire
broke out in the ducts over the new stoves. The automatic sprinkler system went off and dumped fire-resistant powder all over the food, which
had just been prepared and was sitting on the steam table waiting to be

served. I had just sat down in the back of the dining room, heaving a big sigh of relief, when the news arrived from the kitchen. Customers were already seated, so we couldn't close down and start up again later. The chef decided the only thing to do was make sandwiches, and so everybody had a cold lunch for the "grand reopening." Well, it was a very hot day.

My favorite summer story is not about the Tea Room, though I heard it there. It concerns John Barrymore and the Players Club, a distinguished hangout for thespians in New York for well over a hundred years. In Barrymore's day, before air-conditioning was born, the theaters closed during the hot months of summer. One torrid summer day in the 1920s a fellow member showed Barrymore with pride the newest acquisition of the club, a handsome painting by Childe Hassam entitled *Summer.* Barrymore studied the picture carefully and stepped back. "Ah, summer!" he exclaimed. "The lay-off!"

In the November 7, 1988, issue of *New York* magazine, Michael Gross wrote a cover story entitled "Table Envy: The Best Seats in Town, How to Get Them—and How to Avoid Siberia." The restaurants critiqued in the article included the Russian Tea Room, the Four Seasons, Le Cirque, Mortimer's, "21," Elaine's, La Grenouille, and La Côte Basque (and three more that no longer exist). The article included floor plans of the dining rooms of each restaurant, the tables marked in pink for "best seats" and in green for "Siberia." Pale lavender indicated "next best" or "neutral territory." An RTR regular, Susan Blond, described in the article as running a "music-business P.R. company," was quoted about the Tea Room:

[She] goes to the Russian Tea Room several times a week. She usually gets one of the small booths that line the aisle leading to the dining room. Both her faithfulness and the stars she brings—Boy George and Julio Iglesias, for example—helped her gain status. And status is a lot to the point, she thinks. "You go so that whoever you take can see how many people say hi to you," Blond says. "There are also people you're excited to see. Lunch becomes an event. It doesn't seem like business because it's so much fun. And when Jackie O. is waiting for her coat, you get a long stare. You can examine her shoes and her pocketbook."

But Blond knows she has a way to go. The booths she covets are just inside the dining room, occupied by agents like Sam Cohn or by stars like Michael Douglas. "That's what you aspire to," Blond says. "I hope some day I get one of those booths. Whoever's in them must be very important."

Could this actually happen, grown people attaching so much importance to where they sit for lunch? Well, of course it could! In the palmy days of "Masters of the Universe" on Wall Street, of power-brokerage, expense accounts, and omnipotent gossip columnists, status was the most important way to show riches and power, and what more graphic way to test it out than to enter the competitive restaurant sweepstakes?

None of the restaurant spokespeople in Michael Gross's article wanted to talk about special tables being held for special people—it's against the code of fair play and "equal distribution" that restaurants give lip service to—it would be too discouraging to potential diners, who would feel they'd never have a chance to get a good table.

At the RTR I held out at first against the policy of promising specific tables to people. I used to chastise Ona about it, and Rosa before her. "Who wants to see the same people sitting at the same tables every day?" I complained. "Let's give some other people a break!" But what were our maîtresse d's to do? The star regulars came in nearly every day and because they did, they expected special treatment, and the truth was they were the hub of our universe—they brought in other people who lit up the sky, too. When they weren't in residence the tables went to "civilians" and somehow that happened often enough to keep most people who were looking for those top tables happy. And many people looked forward to walking in and seeing the regulars there. They seemed to be comforted and reassured to find "Sam" and "Robby" and "Sylvia" in place. It meant all was right with the world.

Sam Cohn was the best sport about taking any table offered him, in spite of the fact that some people considered him temperamental. Robby Lantz said you could tell Sam's mood by the color of the sweater he was wearing: dark colors were fine and meant smooth sailing, but pink was like a red flag that indicated danger. Too bad Sam's clients didn't have Robby's information!

Sidney Poitier was the same way, one of the most unassuming people I have ever met, and one of my favorite people, too—someone I have known and cherished since the 1950s. Sidney always preferred sitting in one of the back booths of the restaurant, where he could have more privacy. For years he and Harry Belafonte would sit back there and have a hilarious time, catching up with each other's lives and breaking each other up over glasses of freshly squeezed orange juice.

Not surprisingly, you can tell a lot about people from their behavior in a restaurant. Sidney used to say we saw the world from the point of view of the *Police Gazette*. Sidney put his philosophy of the restaurant business into one succinct Freudian phrase: "It's the mother's tit." People's basic needs do seem to become exaggerated with hunger and thirst and the ancillary needs for recognition and comfort, or, to put it simply, people can be testy until that first drink and the bread and butter arrive.

Ruth Gordon and Garson Kanin always sat in D1 when they came to the RTR, which was several times a week. When Garson died, his full-page obituary in the *New York Times* on March 15, 1999, said about him and Ruth: "They became a fixture at the Russian Tea Room—first booth on the left—where they had lunch together almost every day." After Ruth died I asked Garson for a photograph of Ruth to hang on the wall back of their booth; he gave me one of her in her dressing room during the run of *The Country Wife* (1937). I had it framed with a small plaque with her name on it, and we had a dedication ceremony one morning before the restaurant opened. A small group of Garson and Ruth's friends came, and Marian Seldes and I each said a few words about Ruth.

Marian and I had been friends since we were actors together in *Ondine*, when she had taken me under her wing. The most fun of that production for me was when Marian invited me to her dressing room for tea on matinee days between shows. In spite of the fact that the beautiful and delightful Audrey Hepburn starred in the show, the play was heavy going. Based on a German fairy tale, it consisted largely of Audrey disporting in a sea nymph's costume, flanked by the Seitz twins, Tani and

Dran, dressed as mermaids. The show was overproduced and must have cost a fortune, because there was a large cast with a number of well-known featured actors, none of whom had much to do. Audrey's husband and costar, Mel Ferrer, was unhappy in the show and, evidently, with their marriage, as we would hear sounds of unhappy verbal exchanges between them from their dressing rooms. Playing the part of a maid in the court, my most challenging task was getting up and down three flights of steep iron steps to and from our dressing room in my wimple. Alfred Lunt directed the show, but because I came in after the opening I never worked with him. He did come back to see the show while I was in it, however, and left a note with the stage manager asking, "Who was the Lady in the Court who looked as though she had got caught in a washing machine?"

Some time after Ruth's death Marian and Garson announced they were going to be married and I was thrilled for them both. Marian had been a longtime friend of Garson and Ruth, and had helped Garson take care of Ruth in the last years when she was ill. I went to their wedding at the Players Club, the second time I'd been through that with Marian. The first time, when she married Julian Claman, I wondered if it would ever happen to me. Would I get married and be happy and go away on a honeymoon like Marian and Julian? Marian assured me I would. The second time, thirty years later, I didn't even want to get married again, but their happiness was something I envied and rejoiced in at the same time.

There were other pictures on the wall behind D1: it was sort of my private collection of people I had known, which I started in the 1960s and added to spontaneously, without much rhyme or reason. The other pictures on the dining room walls, eclectic in style though they may have been, did have themes relating to the restaurant. "Every picture has a story!" I read somewhere. Certainly our pictures did.

There was a color photograph of Sol Hurok I saved from a magazine and framed—the best likeness of him I ever saw. He was grinning with that "I-know-something-you-don't-know" grin of his, and sporting a top hat and white tie, which said a lot about where he spent his evenings. Mr. Hurok's granddaughter, Nessa Hyams, felt the booth belonged to her whenever she came in because her grandfather's photo was on the wall behind it, which sometimes caused a problem for Ona when she had promised it to someone else. Nessa complained, too, when the photo of her grandfather was moved up a few inches to make room for Ruth Gordon's picture. Who says people aren't—observant? I remember Nessa's mother, Ruth, who was married to the conductor Arthur Lief, showing me the photograph her father had inscribed to her: "To my daughter Ruth. Sincerely, Sol Hurok." Ruth said, "Now you understand my life."

I put Fran Allison's photo there, too, with Kukla and Ollie. I get weepy when I think about Fran, who was one of the dearest, sweetest people I ever knew. I met her in Chicago when I was in *New Faces* and she was the star of "Kukla, Fran, and Ollie," Burr Tillstrom's wonderful puppet television show, which originated there. Chicago was in the forefront of early TV, which was televised live in those days. Dave Garroway and Steve Allen started there, and, along with "Kukla, Fran, and Ollie," were big successes, though I don't think there were any sponsors then, so the successes have been mostly of esteem. I watched "Kukla" fanatically and knew all the characters—Madam Ogglepuss, Cecil Bill, Fletcher Rabbit, Beulah Witch, and the other beloved creatures Burr created. They were to their fans what the Muppets became to a later generation. Fran had an amazing ability to convey to the audience her belief in Kukla and the other puppets, and she treated them with the same love and respect she did the "real" people in her life. And what a great sense of comedy she had! We were always excited when Fran came to town, and missed her greatly when she could no longer pay us any more visits because of declining health.

Anne Meara and Jerry Stiller were on that wall, too—a cover from *Cue* magazine in the 1960s, which I had framed. They are both friends of mine going back to the 1950s. Jerry and I used to make acting rounds together. (Anne says she wasn't with us but I'm not sure about that. I believe she just wants us to think she was working, and didn't need to make rounds.) We would go every day to this casting agency, a real mass production outfit where they cast extras for movies, TV, and commercials. You'd stick your head through this little window and somebody in the back would take a look at your head, poised as if waiting for the guillotine to drop, and the voice would say, "Nothing today—Next!"

and you'd pull your head out and move on to the next public humiliation. I have been lucky to have Anne and Jerry as friends all these years. It's given me a lot of pleasure to follow their successes and to watch Ben and Amy, their children, grow up and find their successes, too.

Jerry told me, in that confidential tone of voice he has, "We were not like those people who came to the RTR. We were not famous. But because we knew you and Sidney, and you made us feel at home, we began to feel we belonged there. It was a mood set, a warm atmosphere, elegant but casual at the same time—it was like a family, not a biological family but a theatrical family. You felt free to walk from table to table and you were greeted in some wonderfully ingratiating way by Garson Kanin, Jackie Susann, those people you'd idolized—and you thought, 'If I'm already here I must be somebody! I couldn't be nobody!' "

One of the most compelling things to me about the theater, and which I miss the most, is that feeling of having found a family, which Jerry talks about. Every show brings a new family and a new breakup at the end, which are among the chief joys and pains of the theatrical life. The Tea Room fulfilled a great part of that for me, as it must have in a small way way for Anne and Jerry and many others.

Jerry continued, "And Woody Allen, sitting quietly in his corner, pretending not to want to be seen. But if he didn't want to be seen, why was he there? Usually it would be the day after his picture opened."

Anne says it was always the place they celebrated everything good that happened. I remember when they did their first *Ed Sullivan Show* and invited Sidney and me to come over to the theater on Broadway and 55th Street, now the Ed Sullivan Theater, where the show was being televised. And it was live! Anne said later, "How did we have the chutzpah to invite you to our first live network show? Suppose we had bombed?" But they didn't. They were a big hit and came back on the show many times.

I also had a photograph of Clive Barnes up in my little section of the wall. It was a picture taken in the Tea Room one night for an article about him in *New York* magazine. Clive was drama critic for the *New York Times* then and chose the Tea Room to be photographed in because it was his favorite restaurant. I stayed for the photo shoot after we closed and Clive had come from the theater, and we plied him with caviar and champagne, so the night wouldn't seem so long. In the photo he looked quite mellow.

Clive, who had formerly been the dance critic for the *New York Times,* knew all the principals in the ballet world, and helped me initiate a reunion between two former ballet stars—Alexandra Danilova (George Balanchine's first wife) and Freddy Franklin, who had often been her partner. Danilova had always frequented the Tea Room, and now she also walked past it every day on her way to teach her ballet classes at Lincoln Center. She kept this up into her eighties and I used to go out and watch her go by, because the way she walked—"turned out," like the great ballerina she was—was wonderful to see. At that time, the Tea Room's walls were covered with murals painted in 1939 of popular ballet dancers of that day, including Danilova and Franklin in a pas de deux from *Les Sylphides.* Clive Barnes and I arranged a reunion luncheon, and we took photos of them standing beneath their mural. I took advantage of the opportunity to get Danilova to take me around the room and identify the dancers in each of the murals. We stopped in front of *Swan Lake,* a large painting with Danilova in the center foreground and a number of "swans" with drooping wings hovering around her. "Who are all those other ballerinas?" I asked, knowing that one of them was Balanchine's second wife, Tamara Geva. "Nobody!" she answered in her heavy Russian accent, turning away abruptly to look at the next mural.

George Balanchine had three other wives after Danilova and Geva, all ballerinas (I understand they had an ex-wives' club): Vera Zorina, who later became a Hollywood star, and whom I am fortunate to call a friend; Maria Tallchief, who was a good friend of Sidney's; and Tany LeClercq, who contracted polio and had to give up her career. Of course there was Suzanne Farrell, Balanchine's protégée, who made her impact, too. Knowing Mr. Balanchine—"Call me Georgi"—was an exciting experience. My favorite Balanchine story was told in Gold and Fitzdale's cookbook. It seems that Mr. B. was cooking dinner, which he loved to do, when a pushy friend called. "You're cooking dinner? May I come?" "Do you like leftovers?" asked Mr. B. "Oh, yes!" said the pushy friend. "Then come tomorrow!" said Mr. B., and hung up.

When Mr. B. was dying, his close friends called the RTR and asked us to prepare a Russian meal for him with all his favorite dishes: borscht, blini with caviar, Chicken Kiev, and Cranberry Kissel, and we sent it over to his apartment. Everyone hated to see him go—it made us feel at least we were doing something to make him feel better for a little while.

The last picture to be added to the wall was a cartoon of Cindy Adams, gossip columnist for the *New York Post,* drawn by herself. It was in red crayon, and it was a wonderful likeness—whimsical, humorous, even glamorous. Lionel Larner, the agent and my good friend, won it at one of the "Doodles Auctions" that we gave at the Tea Room every year to help New Dramatists, on whose board I sat, which sponsors young playwrights. Famous people in the theater or related fields would draw a "doodle" of their choice and the doodles would be auctioned. Abbott Van Nostrand, president of Samuel French and Company, the theatrical publishing house, and another great friend, had an extensive collection of doodles, which he added to every year; he papered his guest bathroom with them. Lionel very kindly gave me the doodle of Cindy Adams and I decided to put it up with the other "mug shots" on that little section of the east wall. Cindy was a good friend for many years, and she and her husband, the comedian Joey Adams, spent a lot of time at the Tea Room. Cindy is one of the smartest people I know, not to mention her everlasting good looks, and her dry sense of humor used to have me convulsed, especially when she and Virginia Graham had lunch together. Virginia and her husband, Harry, were friends from the 1950s on, and I learned quickly that to be Virginia's friend you had to take it when she dished it out. It was a great education to be on the receiving end of her razor sharp tongue, and worth every twinge it caused.

There was a lot of flack about putting up Cindy's cartoon, which puzzled me. Radie Harris of the *Hollywood Reporter* told me she wouldn't come back to the RTR as long as Cindy's picture hung on the wall— imagine how high feelings can run! I left it up, of course—after all, it was my wall, and I wanted it up there. Things quieted down after a while and people took up other, more important causes, thank goodness.

Anne Messavage, the first of the RTR divas who commanded the room, was hired by Sidney in the late 1940s, when she left her hostess job at the White Turkey restaurant on 38th and Madison and came to work at the

RTR. "Miss Anne," as she was always called by the staff, was not a tall woman but she gave that impression in the dining room because of her regal, imposing manner. She had the look of an old-fashioned school-marm in a John Wayne movie. But there was mystery about her, too, an undecipherable something that made one think of the still missing Anastasia! She had strong features—eyes wide apart, high cheekbones from her Polish ancestry, a full mouth around the edges of which a faint smile always played, as if uncertain whether to break out or not. Though she could be stern, she was also shy, and could be girlish, even coquettish, especially around "Mr. Kaye," whom she adored.

It was my luck, upon tentatively entering the RTR world, to become, in Anne's eyes, a rival for Sidney's affections. Hers was a romance that blossomed in only one bosom, but it was strong and fiercely loyal, and had no room for competition.

Anne always called me Faith from the beginning of our relationship, and treated me like the young fly-by-night she thought I was. Actually, our mutual fondness for Sidney gave us a bond that grew over the years into friendship, making it all the more difficult for me to say good-bye to her when she decided to leave two years after Sidney died.

I had a lot of difficulty trying to take control of the restaurant, and to try to clear away the many obstacles in my path. It was evidently hard for the staff to accept me as the new owner. Who could blame them, in a way? A young upstart—and a woman!—tries to take over from a much-loved and respected man with experience and know-how. Still, life goes on and Sidney was no longer there, but Anne Messavage didn't feel comfortable with the new "regime," because, as loyal as she was to the restaurant, she was more loyal to Sidney's memory. Anne never got over Sidney's death and just couldn't be happy at the RTR without him. Also she liked doing things her own way.

Paul, the back manager, was another person who made my life difficult. Paul knew he had a safe job and that Sidney had a soft spot for him, because they had known each other in the Bronx when Sidney was a kid, twenty years younger than Paul. Sidney wanted Paul to stay with him as a kind of security blanket when he bought the restaurant and the other partners moved on. So he gave him 12.5 percent of the Tea Room shares, worth nothing at the time but later they cost me a lot of money. Paul was a fixture, and spent most of his time sitting in the "stammtisch," chatting with the waiters, who took their breaks and ate their meals there in those days.

Then there was Marcel, the waiter appointed by Sidney to act as maître d' "until we find the right person." This was a phrase that would have been emblazoned on our coat of arms, if we had had one, we said it so often. We always seemed to be so desperate to hire someone to fill a key role quickly that we often hired people who we knew were not quite right for the job but could use "until we find the right person," which could be never!

After a short time I knew that Marcel was not going to be strong enough to run the dining room and control the "hanky panky," as Mama would say, of the night waiters, who were particularly adept at legerdemain. But solving the problem with Marcel was, in a way, the easiest, because he really did not want the job of maître d', so I decided to address his case first. But I was terrified to tell him in person that it was not working out. I had visions of Marcel leaning over my desk, as I cringed in my chair, saying to me, "No, I refuse to step down!" And then what would I do? (He was actually very mild-mannered and shy.) I decided to write him a letter, enclosing a large severance check, and send it to him while he was on vacation. I almost didn't have the nerve to go through with it—who was going to replace him? Since Anatole died we had been unable to find anyone to fill his shoes, but someone had to assume the role. Sidney had asked Marcel, because he was personable, to help us out "until we find the right person" and he had reluctantly accepted. Now, who else among the crew could I get to fill in or take over permanently? "Permanently" is not in the restaurant vocabulary— let's say for a reasonable amount of time.

The maître d's at the RTR did not make much in tips—they were really glorified seating captains—and took home much less than the waiters, which meant that they did not command the waiters' respect. We, as management, even had to supplement their incomes. Yet they played a very important role, fronting the restaurant, and we needed someone who, like the maîtresse d's at lunch, could attract customers and make them feel at home. It was an irony, and seemed to be an unsolvable problem.

The logical candidate would have been Chris Zoas, an unusually handsome waiter who was a natural leader. Chris and I came to the RTR about the same time and were about the same age. He was the best waiter we had then—handsome, soft-spoken, attentive, and knowledgeable. He was the favorite waiter of Salvador Dalí, who used him as a model in his biblical painting of the fishermen pulling Christ in a boat to shore. The waiters divided themselves according to their ethnic groups—Hungarian, Greek, African-American, Hispanic, and whatever others there were at the time. Chris became the mouthpiece for the Greek contingent, then later for all the waiters. But he turned down the offer to become a maître d' because he didn't want the responsibility and because he could make more money as a waiter. He never realized his natural talents and became instead just one of the crowd.

The Greeks at that time also included Gregory, a dead ringer for Mussolini, who no doubt would have won if he had run for office in Italy, though his girth exceeded the former dictator's by several inches. Gregory was famous for having chased a customer, his enormous stomach leading the way, down 57th Street, looking for a tip—and he got it, too!

How to handle tipping was an ongoing problem in the restaurant. The good waiters wanted to keep their tips because they made more than the slow waiters, but the slow waiters wanted to pool their tips so they would get part of what the good waiters made. Management had no control over the situation. The waiters voted among themselves and pooling (or keeping the "kitty") always won out because there were more slow waiters than good waiters. The "kitty" was bad for management and for the customers, too, because it meant that the slow waiters had no incentive to be faster and better. The RTR had been a union house from the beginning and there was no way to "deunionize," which was unfortunate for us because we were competing with restaurants that were nonunion and were better able to control their staffs and payroll costs. Nor could we fire a waiter without going through a tortuous procedure, and even then, it was very unlikely to happen.

Annette, who was Miss Anne's assistant (we referred to her as "Miss Anne's slave"), took over from Anne when she left. Annette didn't have the strong personality Anne had brought to the job and, having been a waitress, she always struggled with the mentality she had acquired being part of the crew, but she was kind and conscientious and had a soothing effect in the dining room. She retired because of a heart problem and was much missed when she left.

Enter Rosa Forand, better known as "La Bomba" (the Brazilian Bombshell), a four-foot-eleven-inch (in high heels) dynamo who came as a cashier and ended up running the dining room with great panache. In spite of her thick Brazilian accent, Rosa was able to make herself understood in any language. When she started at the RTR she was living in one room with her husband, a typewriter repairman, and fifteen typewriters, all laid out on the floor. But Rosa was indomitable—she was determined to make a career for herself. She came at a pivotal time, when the Tea Room was beginning to buzz with excitement, and she added her own Latin buzz to it, too.

It's interesting to note that the first two RTR Divas could speak in Russian and other Eastern European languages. By the time Rosa arrived, the Russian clientele had aged and dwindled and a knowledge of Spanish was much more important. The kitchen had for many years been manned (certainly not womaned) by Spanish-speaking people, in the intensive labor categories at least, and by the late 1970s we were beginning to see Spanish-speaking waiters, captains, bartenders, and hatcheck personnel, too. Rosa's Portuguese was close enough.

About that time, Jack Martin, then gossip columnist for the *New York Post* (before gossip became an intensive industry), started coming for lunch and reporting about all the well-known people he saw there, and this caused a lot of attention. Liz Smith, then writing every day in the *Daily News,* commented that she was sorry to see that the RTR had become so popular because now it would be difficult to get in. When I read that, I figured we were on our way! It began to look like the RTR had joined the ranks of those memorable lunch spots like Sardi's, "21," and Le Cirque, where the atmosphere and the crowd were as important as the food.

Liz Smith was a great friend to the Tea Room and gave some wonderful parties there—a great one for Helen Gurley Brown, and the best of the best, the party she and Joe Armstrong, Texans to their souls, gave for Ann Richards, then governor of Texas. For the occasion the name on our canopy was changed to "The Texas Tea Room" and *everybody* came—politicians, artists, society people, most of the State of Texas, and, of course, myriads of the press. It was a hoedown!

Rosa eventually left to open her own restaurant, so I couldn't be angry with her for abandoning ship, even though she left in the middle of our accelerating popularity. I am proud to watch her success at Rosa's Place, her Mexican restaurant on the corner of Eighth Avenue and 50th Street.

Rosa was a hard act to follow, but all the time there was somebody in our midst who surprised us all with her ability. When I hired Ona de Sousa, an African-American who originally hailed from Panama, as a cashier, I asked her if she had any dining room experience. It turned out she had run the restaurant at the Top of the Sixes, and before she knew it Ona was whisked out of the cashier's booth and was training to take over Rosa's position on the floor. Ona has short reddish hair and, like Rosa, is not prepossessing in stature. Meeting her, you wouldn't necessarily think of her running a dining room. Ona in repose could look almost expressionless, but when she swung into action she became animated, laughing, moving swiftly around the room, her eyes darting everywhere, seeing everything, pausing to give instructions and corrections to her waiters and busboys and seating captains. She was at the same time busy answering the telephones, looking at the latest revised reservation list (which resembled subway graffiti), and filling in wherever she was needed. Her presence was magnetic, and her voice unique. She spoke with a touch of a Caribbean accent, just enough to set it off from any other.

By the time Ona was put in charge of the dining room at lunch, the RTR was much in the news and the maîtresse d' was in a sensitive position, having to learn the names and faces of so many celebrities, as well as all the old-time regulars, the tables they wanted, and the foods they preferred. All this Ona was able to absorb and then added her own flavor. She could joke around with the customers, but she always maintained her natural dignity, which inspired respect, and everybody wanted to please her. Even when Archer King, a theatrical agent who made the Tea Room his home, got out of line with his wisecracks and impatient demands, Ona stayed serene, at least on the surface. She was den mother to us all, through good times and bad, and I wouldn't have wanted to continue at the RTR if I hadn't had Ona to give me her emotional support and to share her sense of humor.

Another side to Ona was her tenacity. "Once," she told me, "two women came in and said they were looking for someone and wanted to walk through the dining room and see if they could find the person. I took one look at them and knew they were no good, but the manager took them right in and showed them around. As they came back up to the front I heard a woman customer in the back of the dining room call out, 'My purse has been stolen!' and I saw the two no-goods running out. I ran after them and followed them down 57th Street and grabbed the pocketbook from one of them, but she wouldn't let go. I dragged her and the pocketbook, the other one following, back to the RTR, and I kept telling them, 'This is not your pocketbook!' When we tumbled back into the restaurant I wrenched the bag away from the no-good who was hanging on to it, and waited to see them both arrested, but the manager said, 'Ona, let them go!' I said, 'What! What did you say?' and he said, 'Let them go! There'll be a big mess and when the police come there'll be a lot of attention for the wrong reasons—just let them go!' I couldn't believe it. The customer got her pocketbook back all right, I gave it to her myself, right from the no-good's clutches, but can you imagine that we let them go—to do it all over again somewhere else?" As a matter of fact, the same two women came back to the Tea Room not long afterward, but Ona recognized them and when they saw her they ran out as fast as they could run.

Lunch Characters:
Sylvia Miles

Through the years, the actress Sylvia Miles was a consistent RTR star. Dustin Hoffmans and Meryl Streeps could come and go, but Sylvia was with us always, and she brought something special to the Tea Room that nobody else could: she brought her downtown, off-Broadway, Village style uptown and saved us from becoming too mainstream and bourgeois. She dressed eccentrically, and developed it into an art as the years went by—beaded dresses, feather boas, turbans, and medallions—a look that never failed to raise an eyebrow and often got a round of applause. Sylvia's costumes were works of art, carefully assembled for effect. She was a downtown person who happened to be based uptown.

She and I first met when we both lived at the Osborne and she was married to Jerry Price, an actor, and was playing off-Broadway in a famous revival of *Threepenny Opera,* as was another friend of mine, Jo Sullivan, who later married the composer Frank Loesser. I had just married Sidney and he and I were busy collecting tchotchkes (little playthings) to hang on the walls of the Tea Room. We felt we needed a little more of "the light touch" to brighten up the "shabby gentility" of the restaurant's decor. It was a counterculture thing, like so much else in the 1960s, our tiny rebellion against the staidness of the 1930s ballet murals that pervaded the dining room, and Sidney's rejection of the unadorned bareness of Art Deco in a room that he thought cried out for rococo.

At Christmastime we also decided that the Art Deco chandeliers in the dining room needed a lift, and we went out in search of gold tinsel to drape around them and bright red Christmas balls to hang from the tinsel, and we bought wall sconces at Macy's to replace the Art Deco sconces that had been on the walls since 1932. Later we would have been thrilled to have all that Art Deco back, but in the 1960s it was "out." We browsed up and down Third Avenue, which was still old-fashioned and pleasantly run-down, still looking the way it was when the "el" was dismantled a few years before. There we found some "objets" to hang on the walls in between the murals and the samovars and behind the bar.

We already had a crowded area in the front, around the checkroom and the cashier's booth next to it, where we pinned up theater posters and concert posters from Carnegie Hall and Town Hall. They were brought in by PR people who were anxious for their shows to be represented at the Tea Room. Many of these posters had to be updated every week, and it was my job to get up on the ladder and rearrange them, taking down and putting up whichever ones needed to be changed. There were also little wire baskets on one wall of the checkroom where music PR people put flyers for programs to be given in the different smaller halls, as well as at Carnegie Hall, the City Center, and later, Avery Fisher Hall.

Sylvia Miles appeared in the movie *Midnight Cowboy* at that time, and was nominated for Best Supporting Actress. Sidney said, "If you get nominated you can have anything you want off the walls. You can take your pick," never thinking she had a chance. But sure enough, she was nominated! Sylvia came running across the street from the Osborne to tell us, and immediately announced what she wanted from our walls—a huge pair of spectacles with wire frames and blue lenses, which originally decorated an optician's shop and now hung behind our bar. It was one of our favorite acquisitions, but Sidney kept his word, and off went Sylvia with her prize. I think she enjoyed getting it almost as much as the nomination!

Sylvia liked to sit at the second table, 32, right behind the first booth in the middle row, where Sally Lefkowitz sat, and next to the second booth, where Robby Lantz sat, on the right as you walked in. It was a clever choice, because she would never get "bumped," as she might have sometimes from a booth, and she was in the thick of the action, could see everything from where she sat, and, more important, she could be seen, too. "And the lighting was perfect," she told me.

How to describe Sylvia? She is a personage who has been around so long and been a part of so many of the most interesting developments in pop culture in our generation that she has become a legend. She was part of the Warhol Factory and starred in *Heat*, one of his best movies. She won another nomination as Best Supporting Actress in *Farewell, My Lovely*. She was also in the first American production of Genet's *The Maids*. Her New York accent, her rasping delivery, her self-presentation, have all singled her out. And her indestructibility! She has become an icon for all that went on, especially downtown, in New York in the 1950s, '60s, right up to the present.

Sylvia said about the Tea Room:

> I got a lot of jobs at the Tea Room (I made forty-eight films). I'm famous so I want to be in a place where I can see my peers and be among them. The RTR was an extended family and a grapevine for everybody. Now the only place you see people is at memorials!
>
> A great many highlights happened in my life at the RTR. I was there when I heard I got the Oscar nomination for *Farewell, My Lovely*. Carol Kane was there, too, and she got nominated at the

same time. We called up Anne Meara, and she came down to the Tea Room and took us to lunch to celebrate.

What the Tea Room meant was—we always think we have a community in the theater, but the Tea Room *made* it a community and now that community has fallen apart. There are only disparate places to go and nobody knows actually where to find *anybody*. It wasn't just a question of seeing everybody you knew. It was a question of feeling that you *belonged* when you were there.

The Tea Room was elegant and funky at the same time. Imperfection is in all great art. If you don't have imperfection you don't have it, and the RTR had it.

And everybody who worked there—I've run into practically every one of them, working at some other place or on the street—Wiley, Ted, this one, that one—and you get so excited when you see them because they're like the best old friends. And now all that is *gone*.

Every city, every great metropolis in Europe had *one* place that the cognoscenti went to—not the people with a lot of money, not the hucksters, not the phonies, not the Henry Kravitzes of this world—I don't know why I'm picking on poor Henry Kravitz—but the people who made up the artistic underbelly of the whole city, who made up the fabric of what's unique about New York. And we all went to the RTR and we belonged there, we felt we were *wanted* there. And that's gone. And that to me was one of the most upsetting and disappointing things in my whole life. You gave us that and we had that and it's gone.

[Faith] I felt that way, too.

[Sylvia] Oh, I didn't mean to make you cry!

Leonard Bernstein

Leonard Bernstein was a regular at the Tea Room when he was conducting the New York Philharmonic at Carnegie Hall. At that time he lived at the Osborne, too, and used to cause quite a flurry in our gilded, Byzantine lobby when he passed through with his entourage on his way across the street to Carnegie Hall to conduct. Dressed in white tie and tails, his long black cape with a Carmen red lining sweeping behind him, his wavy silver hair glistening from the shower, he was a sight to behold. Behind him followed a little boy holding his music, and behind the little boy Miss Coates, Bernstein's former teacher, now his secretary, fluttering to catch up, and lastly, Felicia Montealegre, Mrs. Bernstein, slinking along in a gold lamé gown and looking like a million dollars.

Here is the transcript of a tape Bernstein recorded on WNCN on November 11, 1980, discussing the Russian Tea Room and Carnegie Hall:

One of the most exciting aspects of remembering Carnegie Hall is that it wasn't just the hall itself, or even just the studio in which I lived, because it was home and my office and my workspace and all that, but it was also the drugstore on the corner which was part of it, and everything else connected with it, including the Russian Tea Room, which I have always thought of as part of Carnegie Hall. Of course one ate very often in the Russian Tea Room just as one had breakfast very often at the drugstore. I will never forget the moment, having lunch at the Russian Tea Room with Sol Hurok, when the opening bars of *Fancy Free* came to me, in the middle of conversation, in the middle of borscht, and I wrote it down fast on a napkin, not stopping the conversation, and stuck it in my pocket, and after lunch ran up to my studio in Carnegie Hall and wrote it down and the next day I had the first five minutes of *Fancy Free*. [Someone in the background says, "which were a magical five minutes." Bernstein then concludes,] Russian Tea Room—magic Russian Tea Room!

Just as Leonard Bernstein felt that the Russian Tea Room was a part of Carnegie Hall, I felt the Osborne Apartments were a part of the Russian Tea Room. The Osborne Apartments were built in 1883, soon after the Dakota on West 72nd Street and Central Park West. Though *Rosemary's Baby* was filmed at the Dakota, the book, by Ira Levin, was written about the Osborne. Sidney and I lived there for ten years, until he died, and I continued to live there another nine years. The years with Sidney were the best. I had for the Osborne a feeling something like the one I had for our community at Fair Harbor on Fire Island. Everybody knew everybody else, and there was much socializing from apartment to apartment among the tenants. And most of them were RTR habitués, so we saw them there, too.

Sidney, the opera diva Blanche Thebom, and Judge Joseph Proskauer got a group together when they learned that Mrs. Korein, the owner of the Osborne, was planning to take the building down. She told Sidney, as spokesperson for the committee, that if the tenants could raise the money she would sell the building to them instead of demolishing it. (That was before the Landmarks Commission came to the rescue of buildings like the Osborne, so rich in architecture and history.) And so they did, spearheaded by Sidney. (It had only been two years since Isaac Stern saved Carnegie Hall from demolition by getting the public's support behind him.)

Who lived in the Osborne when we were there? Leonard and Felicia Bernstein; Miss Coates; Van Cliburn; Andre Watts; Gary and Naomi Graffman; Bobby Short; Hortense Calisher and Curtis Harnack; Leo Lerman and Gray Foy; Maude Franchot; Shirley Booth; Mrs. Olin Downes; Larry Blyden and his two children, Ellen and Josh; Lynn Redgrave, her husband, John, and their two children; Judge Joseph Proskauer; Blanche Thebom; Tom Poston; Gig Young; Harold Fonville; Eva Brown (the latter two singing teachers I studied with); Caroline Bell (Ellen named her favorite doll Carolina Bella after her); Mike Mindlin; Sylvia Miles; Louis Dalmeida; the Baroness Dahlrup and her son, Just, daughter, Ida Gro, and granddaughter Karen; Rose Tobias; and Dane Clark.

Marjorie Morrison, a striking platinum blond with milk-white skin who wore cherry red lipstick, lived on the floor below our penthouse and had a vent in her kitchen ceiling that opened onto the roof. Our dogs loved to stick their heads into the open vent, sniffing all the good things she was cooking—she usually cooked while consuming a few vodkas—and when she saw their faces peering down at her, she would let out a terrified scream. Then, when she had sufficiently recovered, she would yell up through the vent to anyone who would listen, "Get those troops off the cockamamy roof!"

Sidney put in a lot of time and energy getting the building co-oped, and, as with most things he got involved in, he worked himself into a state of exhaustion. We did buy our apartment, and later Ruth Gordon (another Ruth Gordon, the sister of Eliot Janeway, the financial pundit) moved out of her apartment across the hall from us and we were able to join the two together in time for our daughter, Ellen, to be born.

That same summer (1960) Sidney went to see his friend Bill Littler, the surgeon, about a small lump he had discovered on his left cheek. Bill removed it, but in doing so, found that it was malignant. This was the beginning of Sidney's seven-year bout with cancer.

The next seven years of highs and lows we spent together, Ellen and Sidney and I, on our private emotional roller coaster, hanging on for dear life. The RTR public and employees helped foster the illusion that we were living a normal life, at least part of that time, but most people were undoubtedly aware there were constant eruptions and interruptions: Sidney in and out of hospitals, taking series of radiation treatments, having remissions and resuming his hectic schedule, falling ill again, finally being riddled with disease, unable to walk, going into Memorial Sloan-Kettering Hospital, having chemotherapy, coming home one last time, and finally dying in the hospital of pneumonia, on August 7, 1967. (The last time he had to be taken on a stretcher in the Osborne's antiquated service elevator, the "Cage," because the front one was being automated, and it was so narrow that Sidney had to be tilted upright to fit in. He said as we left, "This is my last trip. I know I'm never coming home again.")

Up until the last days, Sidney received a lot of visitors, whom he entertained and kept from feeling sad—a steady stream of family and friends. These friends were not all the "friends" who had hovered around Sidney in life. The hospital friends were the real friends, those who were not afraid to look at death.

Those last months took their toll on everyone in Sidney's life. Alice, Sidney's sister, startled me by telling Sidney and me one day in the "stammtisch," when Sidney had gotten out of the hospital after a week's stay, that she wanted to give us a tenth-anniversary party on April 10. I didn't want to say anything in front of Sidney, but it seemed unlikely to me that he would be able to get through a party. He could barely stand up and he might well be going back to the hospital momentarily. I knew Alice meant well—I think it was her way of denying the awfulness of the facts—but it was too painful to contemplate an anniversary party, such a sentimental occasion, full of hope for the future, when Sidney was struggling to sustain himself. But I saw that Alice was determined to do it, so I tried to go along, and went to Henri Bendel's to look for a dress to wear. Then, in the dressing room, I broke down. I must have stayed in there a long time because the salesperson called in to see if I was all right. When I came out I said that I was sorry, I had made a mistake, and I wouldn't be needing a dress after all. I went back home and called Alice, asking her to cancel the party, and tried to make her understand. In fact Sidney would not have been able to make it, as he was in the hospital on our anniversary.

Seeking some kind of distraction and something to occupy my mind, I enrolled that spring at NYU to finish my undergraduate history requirements so that I could start graduate school in American intellectual history in the fall. Reading English parliamentary history (deliciously dry) and American ideas at the beginning of the twentieth century kept me from going off the deep end. Trying to give Ellen some home time, looking after the RTR, and visiting Sidney in the hospital was exhausting, and the books and classes gave me a glimpse into another world and gave me hope.

The pull of life is stronger than death. Near the end for Sidney, on a hot Sunday morning at the beginning of August, I went to see him in the hospital before I left to visit Ellen at Camp Trywoodie, for Visitors' Day. It was important for me to reassure her and to be reassured by her that we would not be totally alone when Sidney was gone. I also wanted to alert Morris, the camp director, that he might be hearing from me very soon to make arrangements to bring Ellen home, and that I would tell Ellen the news myself when I came to get her. But Sidney grabbed my hand and wouldn't let go. He had got to the point where his speech was not clear, but I could tell he was saying, "Don't go!" and though I explained to him that I was going to see Ellen, that I would be back in the afternoon, it didn't matter. He was in a panic, so afraid he was dying. I didn't know how I could leave him when he needed me so much. But I felt compelled to go. Finally I wrenched my hand free and kissed him on the forehead—his skin had a cool, sweaty feel to it—and I told him again I would be back that afternoon, and left. I think I gave Ellen some indication of what was happening with Sidney without telling her straight out. When I returned to the hospital late that afternoon, Sidney was sleeping and the crisis had temporarily passed.

During those seven years I began to grow up. At the beginning of the period I was twenty-eight, still studying acting with Lee Strasberg and musical-comedy acting with David Craig, performing in the theater occasionally. Then I began to do commercials and found that I looked like a typical young housewife and even became the Chesterfield Girl, and so made some money, which we needed at that point. Most of all, it gave me a feeling of financial independence for the first time, which I really enjoyed. At the end of the period, my acting days were over; I was a thirty-five-year-old widow with a seven-year-old daughter and a restaurant I had to learn how to run.

In the early 1960s Sidney's nephew Larry Peerce, Alice and Jan Peerce's son, who was an actor and a television director, decided to become a movie director and came to New York from California to raise money for his first film, which he and his partner, Sam Weston, were going to produce. They set up their office in the "stammtisch" at the RTR, with Sidney's encouragement, and began to cast the movie, which they entitled *One Potato, Two Potato.* They got Barbara Barrie to star in it with Richard Mulligan and Bernie Hamilton. I hadn't known Sam Weston before, but I was fond of his actor brother, Jack Weston, who was a frequenter of the RTR, except when he was dieting, and whom I thought—along with Zero, Jimmy Coco, and Jonathan Winters—to be one of the funniest people I knew.

Sam was to play the Polish-American who befriends Barbara and her African-American husband, and, to my delight, Larry and Sam asked me to play Sam's girlfriend (later his bride, in a Polish wedding ceremony) and Barbara's sidekick. "You have the Eddie Albert part," Larry said to me with a straight face. After a strenuous period of money raising, in which Alice played a big role—after all, she had raised millions for Israel bonds—the movie was under way. (Sidney used to say, "Don't scratch your ear at an Israel bonds rally because Alice will put you down for a pledge of a thousand dollars!")

The movie was shot on location in Euclid, Ohio, a suburb of Cleveland. Except for the movie of *New Faces,* it was the only time I had watched a movie being made from scratch and I was in awe of how Larry pulled the whole thing together on a shoestring. Barbara Barrie shared the Best Actress Award with Anne Bancroft for *One Potato, Two Potato* at the Cannes Film Festival and Larry's career was launched. He went straight on to direct *The Taking of Pelham, One, Two, Three* and *Goodbye, Columbus,* which hit the jackpot.

Meanwhile I was gradually becoming a part of the Russian Tea Room backstage. Sidney had taught me to do the payroll, keep the corporate checkbook, and reconcile the daily figures from lunch, dinner, and supper. Everything was done by hand, with some help from the calculator. The payroll, especially, was complicated: we had to add the taxes, meal allowances, workmen's compensation, and overtime straight across the page, to get the total for each employee. Then we would make out a payroll check, cash it at the bank, and put each employee's salary into a small sealed envelope. They were constantly being stolen from lockers, these envelopes, but everybody insisted on being paid in cash. The waiters' and busboys' tips from house account charges had to be added up by the cashier before the close of every meal, and each waiter and busboy was paid in cash before he or she left the shift. The hatcheck money had to be taken out of three metal boxes every morning and counted, too. There was a lot of cash around until credit cards and automated payroll checks made our lives easier.

So now I was sitting in the bookkeeper's office on the second floor with the two bookkeeper's assistants and a part-time helper, not every day, but more and more regularly. Sidney was in the back of the building in his office overlooking 56th Street, which had been a storage area until 1960 and a stable before that. Underneath his office was a frame shop and next door on 56th Street was the Balalaika restaurant, where the Casino Russe, once part of the Tea Room, used to be.

One of the part-time office helpers was a beautiful young woman from North Carolina named Miranda, a model married to a well-known actor. One morning we were all working on our respective tasks when the door flew open and Miranda's husband burst in, followed by Alex the RTR back steward, who was Sidney's man Friday.

"You are having an affair with my wife!" the husband shouted to the steward as he pulled him into the room by his shirtsleeve. I looked up, dumbfounded. Miranda looked terrified and stood up, shouting, "No, no, no!"

Alex didn't deny it but just stood there, his head bowed. Sidney heard the noise and came out from his office, dressed in his old WW II uniform. "What's going on?" he shouted above the exchange between Miranda and her husband. When he pieced the story together he sent Alex out and tried to calm the husband, who was a friend and customer. Eventually Sidney got him to leave with Miranda and told her not to come back to work at the RTR anymore. He knew we could easily do without Miranda, but not without Alex, who was irreplaceable. I felt somehow betrayed by Miranda and Alex, as if they had spoiled the innocence of our relationship, but then, I was very young and impressionable and had a lot to learn.

That fall, Sidney put me in charge of managing the checkroom, which I found out was one of the least gratifying jobs in the restaurant. The hatcheck girls didn't make much at all, and so they were constantly moving on to better-paying jobs elsewhere. Also they were usually singers or actresses who didn't show up if they got a job acting in a play, often at the last minute. I wanted to bring some organization into that chaotic department. I wanted to get them out of their T-shirts and blue jeans and into some kind of uniform, but in our meetings (I was constantly calling meetings with them, which most of them didn't show up for) nobody could agree on what the uniform should be. And how would we be able to measure everybody, especially if they were constantly leaving? So the girls continued to dress any way they wanted to and I eventually gave up.

Footnote to History: Madonna was an RTR hatcheck girl, and I was told she was fired because of her daring costume, but this was after I had gone on to other projects, and, alas, I don't remember her being there, and I don't know what her daring costume was.

Our main source for hatcheck girls was the Rehearsal Club on West

54th Street, housed in a brownstone where MOMA now stands. This was a residence for young, aspiring actresses—the play *Stage Door* was based on it—and most of them were short on money and looking for part-time jobs. We would call up and ask if anyone was free that evening to hatcheck, and usually got somebody to run up to the Tea Room. I also called them to baby-sit with Ellen, so I got to know some of them pretty well. My heart went out to them, as I had been like them only a few short years before—so full of hope for a future career.

My favorite hatcheck girl was Anne Cannata, whose stage name was Anne Torre. She was as big as a minute, and as loyal and hardworking as anyone I knew. She was not hard up like most of the girls, but she was totally unspoiled, and great with Ellen, too, which won my heart. Annie was in love with Sidney, of course, but in a father-daughter way, and that was fine with me.

Many people thought I started out in the RTR as a hatcheck girl. It was assumed because the legend was that Sidney dated all of them, but I don't know if that's true. I only got into the checkroom after we were married, if nobody showed up on, say, a rainy night in November.

The most "famous" hatcheck girl was the last one, Iris. She saw so many celebrities over the years that she took it all very much for granted. Iris at first glance looked like a teenager, except for her raspy voice and her long gray hair, which fell around her shoulders or was piled high on top of her head. She was small and sometimes it was hard to find her under the heavy coats jammed into our tiny checkroom. But she was dauntless and friendly to all. Someone said, "You never know if Iris is going to take your coat, read your palm, or tell you her life story!" She had something Dickensian about her, a sense that there were things going on in her life beyond her control. Iris would come to see me in my office to tell me about some new domestic tragedy—and there were many—and we would cry and then I would give her a bonus and she would go back downstairs to man the checkroom. She was a brave person and a great character and I would have missed her if she hadn't been there, the first person who greeted me when I came into the restaurant every day. Everybody else who frequented the Tea Room, I know, felt the same way.

N I N E

Tall Tales

The Pope's Visit

In 1965 Pope Paul VI came to town, the first Roman pontiff to visit New York. The *New York Times* reported that his route through Manhattan would take him across West 57th Street, and large throngs were expected to line the sidewalks to welcome His Holiness.

When Sidney, who was excitable, to say the least, read that, he had visions of mobs stampeding in front of the Tea Room, the weight of their packed bodies causing them to crash through the plate-glass windows and into the restaurant. His take on the event sounded a little bit like the storming of the czar's palace in St. Petersburg at the start of the Russian Revolution. Sidney sprang into action and asked Lyro DeFanti, our cabinetmaker, to board up the front windows to protect them from the impact of flying glass, and then waited anxiously for the big event.

"Of course the pope will ruin our lunch business," Sidney said, taking the short view. "How will anyone get through the crowd?"

Just before the pope was to appear, Sidney and I went to the RTR to check out the windows. When he saw them, Sidney fell back in horror. Lyro had gone upstairs to the fifth floor, our attic storeroom where we kept supplies, lumber, and paintings, searching for lumber with which to board up the front windows. It happened that our private dining room, the Boyar Room, which was in the Rembrandt Building next door, had been demolished just a few months before and the mural by Arbit Blatas, who also painted the mural in the front bar, was being stored on the fifth floor out of harm's way. Lyro saw the mural only from the back and thought it looked like a good frame to protect the windows, so he proceeded to cut it up into small pieces to fit the space. The Blatas mural was no more. The fragments were neatly nailed into the windows and you could see them clearly from inside the restaurant. I must admit I thought it was hilarious, but I had to laugh alone. Sidney was furious with poor Lyro, and Blatas, the artist, when he heard about it, didn't think it was very funny, either.

But Sidney hardly had time to recover before we heard on our portable radio that the pope was on his way. "The pope is passing through Central Park. . . ." But where were all the people? Only a handful of meek souls drifted around in front of the Tea Room. "The pope is leaving the park. . . . The pope is traveling down Seventh Avenue. . . . The pope is turning onto Fifty-seventh Street. . . ." The announcer's voice got more and more excited, as if he were following the Kentucky Derby, and then rose to a crescendo as he shouted, "The pope is passing the Russian Tea Room!" With that I broke up completely and had to sit down to collect myself.

The funny thing was that Sidney had complained to Blatas about that mural from its inception, and always referred to it as "Arbit's slap-dash mural." So finally even Sidney started to laugh, and, looking outside at the quiet street he said, "That mural deserved to die, and it died in a good cause, anyway!" Lyro removed the plywood and canvas from the windows as customers started arriving for lunch.*

Hello, Dolly!

Dolly Parton was sitting alone at a table one day, waiting for her lunch date, when Ona said I should go over and introduce myself. It was the first time she had been to the Tea Room. I was reluctant to approach her.

---

*Arbit Blatas, who died in May 1999, was one of the stalwart regulars at the RTR over many years. He was not only a world-class artist and sculptor but a flamboyant personality. He and his equally talented wife, Regina Resnick, the opera singer and director, lived in Venice, Paris, New York, and at the Russian Tea Room.

Being such a great fan of hers for so long made me shy, but Ona was watching me, so I went up to Ms. Parton and said, by way of explanation, that I owned the restaurant. She looked up and smiled that great smile of hers and drawled, "Nice little place ya got here!"

Hello, Carol!

Enid Nemy began her interview with Carol Channing for the *New York Times* on November 29, 1995:

> Where else would she be seated but in the first booth to the left in the Russian Tea Room, which in the world of celebrity and status means you are a top-ranked someone. It also means no one can miss you, and if you are Carol Channing, once again the "Hello, Dolly" toast of Broadway, that translates into a busy lunch.
>
> The tourists and even the theater people are nudging each other and trying not to look as though they are not looking, and the waiter is already hovering, seemingly enchanted at her ordering hot coffee.

Carol Channing for many years brought her own lunch to the RTR in a silver lunch box. She was supposedly on a permanent diet of mysterious grasses. But, as Enid reports, it turned out that Miss Channing was allergic to tap water! So then, after her discovery, she could eat from our menu, but she didn't find this out until near the time of the restaurant's demise. Her former husband, who was her manager, usually accompanied her and he ordered from the menu like everybody else.

Miss Channing's costumes more than made up for the fact that she never ate our food. They were wonderfully theatrical, usually white, sometimes a sailor outfit, sometimes a Peter Pan collar, sometimes polka dots, but always noteworthy. She was extremely gracious to all the people who paid homage to her, as long as they didn't overstep the undefined barrier of keeping a respectful distance from a star. Once, in an exchange about planning a lunch with mutual friends, I made the mistake of calling her Carol, and the icy stare that greeted me was palpable. (We never had the lunch.)

My favorite story about Carol Channing is one that Richard Stein, hairdresser, wizard of intuition, and good friend, told me. He was having an early lunch meeting in the first booth and suddenly spied Carol Channing at the front of the dining room, about to make an entrance. She looked quickly around the room and, seeing that it was still quite empty, beat a hasty retreat to the front end of the bar, where she seemed to disappear, not an easy thing for Carol Channing to accomplish.

Then, when people started flooding in, she reassembled herself and made her entrance again, drawing the undiluted attention of everyone in the restaurant, including Richard Stein, who completely lost track of what his meeting was all about!

"It"

Vanessa Redgrave has that uncanny quality, too, of attracting attention. Who could take her eyes off Vanessa when she was sitting among us? Ruth Gordon had that quality, Jessica Tandy had it, and Jackie O., and Elizabeth Taylor. Uta Hagen has it, too. It isn't just beauty—it's radiance. Believe it or not Marilyn Monroe did not have it, at least not when she used to come in with Lee and Paula Strasberg after class for lunch. I was studying with Lee at the time, too, and was friendly with him and Paula, going to some of the informal get-togethers they gave for their students in their Central Park West apartment.

Lee and Paula liked to come into the Tea Room after class and one day they invited me to join them and several others they had brought along. We sat at the back center table in front of the mirror, which I was facing, and as I looked in the mirror I saw sitting next to me this pale blond woman, obviously shy, her face almost ashen without makeup, quietly sipping her borscht. It was MM herself. I never would have recognized her, but realized then I had seen her before with the Strasbergs, and never knew it was she.

Legend in a Cloche

Anita Loos, the author of *Gentlemen Prefer Blondes,* preceded Carol Channing in the Tea Room by many years. Perhaps it was because of her that Ms. Channing discovered the RTR. Ms. Loos lived across the street, also home to Charles and Barbara (Siman) Strouse, Barbara Walters, and my friends the Silversteins, whose daughter grew up with my Ellen and married Zolt, one of the RTR waiters. Earl Blackwell also lived there in the penthouse, which had a ballroom where many wonderful parties took place. Not only was Earl the center of showbiz society with his "Celebrity Service," through which, for a fee, you could find out where everybody in the theater and moviedom was at a given moment, but he was a true Southern gentleman, much loved and respected by his friends and clients. His perennial date was diminutive Eugenia Shepherd, a doll-like columnist who wore Mary Janes and short white socks and, like Earl, who was two feet taller than she was, hailed from the South.

Anita Loos, in her perennial bobbed hair framed around her face under a cloche, preferred the bar booths, where she and Helen Hayes wrote their book, *Twice Over Lightly,* over a continuing lunch.

Sally Lefkowitz, whose husband, Nat, had headed the William Morris agency for many years, came in almost every day in her wheelchair, bringing four or five guests. She always sat in the front booth in the center, which often placed her between Sam Cohn on one side and Garson Kanin and Ruth Gordon on the other. If the service wasn't fast enough for her, or if she had other complaints, Sally would honk the horn attached to her wheelchair, not once, but several times. It sounded like a gaggle of geese heading south. Guests unfamiliar with the sound would be startled out of their wits, which added to the tumult of a busy lunchtime, and would bring Ona over to remonstrate with Sally in her gentle way. (Sally insists that the "new" front center booth was built expressly for her and her wheelchair. She may be right, and it's foolish to argue with Sally, anyway!)

Thornton Wilder

Thornton Wilder used to come in with his sister, and I was privileged to sit with them on several occasions and listen to Mr. Wilder talk about his life and work. Sidney Blackmer, whose role in *Come Back, Little Sheba* with Shirley Booth was a personal triumph, sat with him sometimes, too, and they both invoked the great days of the theater, now past.

You think, in those magic moments, listening to fascinating people talk about their lives, that those moments will be repeated, but chances are they only come once.

Life at the Tea Room often reminded me of Wilder's one-act play *The Long Christmas Dinner,* in which the characters enter, one by one, sit down at a long table for a while together, and then, one by one, get up and go out. Birth, life, death, the passing parade—it's all there, and beautiful.

William Faulkner

William Faulkner came often in the evening for dinner, sitting along the side of the room on the banquette, sometimes with an attractive woman, sometimes alone, always enjoying a few drinks—a very quiet, very private person.

Obits

As soon as the *New York Times* arrived every morning, I always read the obituaries first, not only to learn about well-known people's lives but to see if any of our cherished customers had died overnight. It was important to know those things already when I arrived at the restaurant before lunch.

One morning I read that Eric Sifton, a prominent perfume manufacturer, had died the day before. His office was near us on 57th Street and he came almost daily to the Tea Room for lunch. I knew that Annette, our maîtresse d', would be devastated, as she had taken great personal care of him and conversed with him in Russian, which he especially enjoyed. When I got to the restaurant and broke the news to her as gently as I could, her reaction surprised me. She did not fall into a weeping fit, as I thought she would, but instead seemed annoyed.

"He can't be dead!" she exclaimed, poring over her seating list. "He has a reservation for lunch!"

Unfortunately, however, it was true. Lunch goes on.

Chiquita the Roller Skate Queen

Annette, our maîtresse d' at that time, was Polish, as was her predecessor, Miss Anne, which bonded them against the Russian wait staff in subtle ways, not only as their superiors but as their ethnic rivals as well.

The Russian Tea Room, 1926 (then located at 147 West 57th Street).
(RTR Archives)

Interior of the Russian Tea Room, 1926. *(RTR Archives)*

Faith and her father, Lt. Comdr. Ernest Burwell, 1942. *(RTR Archives)*

Betty Logue, Polly Ward, Ronny Graham, Virginia De Luce, Faith, Carol Lawrence, *New Faces* movie, 1954. *(Courtesy of 20th Century Fox)*

Faith and Jonathan Bush in *Bus Stop,* Southbury Playhouse, Southbury, Connecticut, 1956. *(© Peter R. Lucas)*

Waiter John Ost, Blanche Thebom, Paddy Chayevsky, Faith (at cash register), Sol Hurok, Patricia Morrison, three dancers from the Moiseyev Ballet, 1959.
(Hans Namuth, Holiday Magazine)

Sidney Kaye and
Sidney Poitier, 1962.
(RTR Archives)

Peter Duchin, Sidney, and
Faith, 1964. *(RTR Archives)*

Sidney, Faith, and Ellen, 1964.
(RTR Archives)

Faith, Sylvia Miles, Carol Kane, and Anne Meara, celebrating Sylvia's and Carol's Academy Award nominations at the RTR, 1967. *(Bela Cseh)*

Faith in front of the RTR canopy, 1968. *(NYT Pictures)*

Al Bensusen, Chef Gary Siderenko, Faith, and Allan Glass in the RTR kitchen studying Caucasian Shashlik for the full-page ad series in the *New York Times*, 1968. *(Edward Ozern, NYT Pictures)*

This page is for people who've never been to The Russian Tea Room and would rather not let their dinner companions know about it.

Just where does the Russian Tea Room stand? Slightly to the left of Carnegie Hall.

150 West 57th Street. CO 5-0947

New York Times ad: Al Bensusen, artist, and Alan Glass, account executive. Part of full-page ad series, *The New York Times*, 1968. *(RTR Archives)*

Rudolf Nureyev, Cynthia Gregory, and Lucia Chase,
celebrating Russian Orthodox Easter at the RTR, 1971.
(© Tim Boxer)

Freddy Franklin and Dame Alexandra Danilova
in front of "their" mural, 1972.
(RTR Archives)

Faith, Dame Irene Worth, Raul Julia, *The Cherry Orchard* party (Lincoln Center Production) at the RTR, 1977. *(© Bill Mark)*

Shirley MacLaine, Anthony Zerbe, Leslie Browne, Phillip Saunders outside the RTR in the movie *The Turning Point*, 1977. *(20th Century Fox Film Corporation/Archive Photos)*

Raquel Welch, Kathleen Turner, Helen Gurley Brown, Liz Smith, and Barbara Walters, celebrating Helen Gurley Brown's twentieth anniversary with *Cosmopolitan* magazine at the RTR, 1977. *(© Helen Gurley Brown)*

James Beard presenting Faith with an award at the RTR, 1979.
(Martin H. Schreiber)

The Russian Tea Room viewed from the front, with bar booths on the left, the bar on right, and the dining room behind the partition, 1979. *(Scher, RTR Archives)*

Faith in bar booth at the RTR,
1981. (© People Weekly)

Isaac Stern and Faith at
the RTR, 1981.
(© *Arthur Schatz*, People Weekly)

Faith and Beverly Sills at the RTR, 1981. (© *Arthur
Schatz*, People Weekly)

Faith, waiters, and Chef Russell Menks for *People* story by Ruth Spear, 1981.
(© *Arthur Schatz*, People Weekly)

Faith, Jerry Stiller, Anne Meara, and Mayor Ed Koch. The mayor's
sixtieth birthday party at the RTR, 1981. *(RTR Archives)*

Sydney Pollack with Dustin
Hoffman (in drag) shooting
Tootsie at the RTR, 1982.
(Archive Photos, Tom Gates)

Uncle Wiggily Reads a Bed Time
Story, *The New Yorker,* 1986.
(© The New Yorker Collection 1986
Henry Martin from cartoonbank.com)

Anne Meara, Faith, and
Jerry Stiller outside
the RTR "Taking Down
the Scaffolding Party," 1990.
(RTR Archives)

Lionel Larner, Anne Hampton Calloway, Faith, and Karen Mason in the Cabaret, 1990.
(© 1999 Jerry Ruotolo)

William Roy and Julie Wilson in the Cabaret, 1990.
(© 1999 Jerry Ruotolo)

Skitch Henderson and Faith, 1990. *(© Jerry Ruotolo)*

Jacques Pépin and Faith, 1990.
(© Jerry Ruotolo)

THE AMERICAN TEA ROOM, MOSCOW

The American Tea Room in
Moscow, *The New Yorker*,
1990. *(© The New Yorker Collection
1990 Peter Steiner from
cartoonbank.com)*

Mary Tyler Moore,
Mayor David Dinkins, and
Faith at the Café Bar in the
RTR, 1992. *(RTR Archives)*

In the RTR Cabaret. Front Row: Michael Kerker (ASCAP), Faith. Back Row:
Andrew Freeman, Steve Lutvak, Ellen Kaye, Craig Carnelia, Anne Hampton
Callaway, Liliane Montevecchi, Joel Silberman, David Friedman, Alix Corey,
1992. *(RTR Archives)*

Sylvia Miles, Faith, and Arlene Dahl at the RTR Academy Awards party, 1993. *(RTR Archives)*

Celeste Holm, Liam Neeson, and Natasha Richardson. Academy Awards nomination breakfast, 1993. *(Photo by Paul Schumach)*

Leonardo DiCaprio and Celeste Holm. RTR Academy Awards nomination breakfast, 1993. *(Photo by Paul Schumach)*

David Brown, Faith, and Liam Neeson. RTR Academy Award nomination breakfast, 1993. *(Photo by Paul Schumach)*

Mel Brooks and Faith, RTR Farewell Party, 1995. *(© Jerry Ruotolo)*

Leslie Caron and Patrick Stewart outside the RTR during filming of the movie *Let It Be Me*, 1997. *(Myles Aronowitz, Rysher Entertainment)*

It was because of Annette that a tiny little woman with dyed black hair dressed in a skating costume and helmet used to roller-skate into the Tea Room once a week and have lunch by herself. She never took off her roller skates, spoke only Polish, and talked only to "Anyet." If Annette was not working that day, she would roller-skate right out again, and was often sighted on Seventh Avenue, skating toward Times Square. We called her Chiquita because of her size, but we had no idea who she really was, and I often asked Annette, the only person who communicated with her, but Annette would just shake her head.

"She only talks to me about what she's going to order for lunch," she would say.

But one day, after Chiquita had finished her lunch and skated out, Annette came up to me and said proudly, "She told me who she is!"

I had visions of Anastasia, returned to us at last, or at least that she would boast the title of Grand Duchess.

"Yes! The mystery is solved!" said Annette. She leaned closer to me and whispered, "She's the wife of a Polish dentist!"

Heartthrob for All Seasons

Peter Duchin, as a young piano player, bandleader, and swain-about-town in the early 1960s, was one of those who considered the RTR home. Peter had startling good looks and a football player's build. Only a strong chin and a facial scar kept him from being downright pretty. Instead he had a young-Hemingway-in-the-North-Woods look that would have landed him in an "old family" series of Ralph Lauren ads today. That winning smile, the shock of brown hair falling over his forehead, the Ivy League accent, the slouch with rumpled clothes to match— I can only say that many young women would gladly have listened to him play "Chopsticks" by the hour. Peter knew this, and enjoyed every heartbreaking minute of it.

Peter lived then in a studio apartment in Carnegie Hall, "the ideal digs for a young bachelor," to quote Peter, where his neighbors were Bobby Short and Don Shirley and a raft of young girls who passed through the halls on their way to dance classes. Peter left his door open just in case. Besides girls, down the hall from his apartment had another perk: Peter knew a way to climb through an air duct that led into the back of the highest balcony of Carnegie Hall's auditorium, where he would go to listen to great jazz concerts and even, once, Lenny Bruce, all for free.

While Peter was playing at the Maisonette at the St. Regis, Don Shirley was appearing at the Embers and Bobby Short at the Blue Angel. When they were in a partying mood, one of the three performers would call the other and arrange to meet at Bobby Short's apartment after work. Peter's entrance was always spectacular, as he had a way of climbing across his roof and going into Bobby Short's apartment through the window, dragging his date, struggling in high heels, behind him.

Peter was making a movie about that time called *The World of Henry Orient,* and part of it was shot, conveniently enough, at Carnegie Hall. He used his apartment as his dressing room and came down when the director called. The best part of *Henry Orient* for me was when Peter brought Angela Lansbury into the Tea Room between takes. She was someone who always made the place light up.

Peter has confessed that when he was entertaining and sometimes burned the dinner, he would call down and ask one of his pals on the RTR staff, "Could you possibly send us up something to eat?" Of course someone always did (and, naturally, RTR management was never advised).

One evening Daniel Selznick brought Brooke Hayward up to meet Peter, carrying Chinese food for dinner as Peter had requested. Peter was at the piano practicing when they arrived and didn't get up to greet them. "Go ahead and eat!" said Peter. Brooke and Daniel had their dinner and Peter still played on. Finally Brooke said, "Let's go, Daniel!" and walked to the door. Peter called after her as she left, "Give me a call sometime!"

Brooke didn't call and didn't see Peter again for many years, at which time they fell in love.

When Peter and Brooke decided to get married, Peter called Averell Harriman, his guardian. He was reluctant to call because when Governor Harriman married Pamela Digby Churchill Hayward, she cut him off from any contact with his family.

Harriman, however, was delighted to hear Peter's voice and his news. "Who's the lucky girl?" he asked.

Peter paused. "Brooke Hayward," he finally said, expecting a negative reaction, as Brooke's father, Leland Hayward, had been married to Pamela, now Mrs. Harriman, and Brooke had accused Pamela in *Haywire,* her autobiography, of stealing pearls her mother, Margaret Sullavan, had given her. There was no love lost between them!

But the connection between Brooke and Pamela was lost on the governor, who was quite deaf. "Wonderful! I'll call her!" he told Peter, and he did, and congratulated Brooke on her felicitous choice in marrying Peter. Then he put Pamela on the phone with the unsuspecting Brooke, and, to Brooke's surprise Pamela cooed, "Oooh, Brooke, this *is* good news!" Brooke must've thought, "That woman will go far!"

Peter was great pals with Nadia, the leader of the Russian waitresses at the Tea Room. (We thought of them as Russian princesses who just *happened* to be working as waitresses.) Peter would come barging through the revolving door after his acting class with Wynn Handman around the corner on 56th Street, a gaggle of young student actresses in tow, and yell, "Nadia!" from the front of the dining room, causing all heads to turn. Nadia would leave her lunch customers flat and come bustling up to "Peotr," as she called him, and, standing on tiptoe, wrap her arms around him in a big hug. Then she would go to fetch Peter's Danish Mary (made with Aquavit) and his special chopped chef's salad in a wooden bowl with the salad dressing ingredients on the side for Peter to mix himself. I was often included in those boisterous lunches, where the Danish Marys were not spared.

Every Russian Easter morning Nadia, on her way to work at the Tea Room, would go up to Peter's apartment, knock on the door, and present Peter with a pascha and a koulich, the traditional Russian Easter cakes. Then Peter would invite Nadia inside and bring out a bottle of vodka from the freezer and pour a little into two glasses, so they could clink them and exchange the Russian Easter toast: *Christos vas Kress!* (Christ is risen!) and the response, *Voisteno vas Kress!* (Verily, he is risen!)

One day in the Tea Room Nadia said to Peter, "I have beautiful boy here I want you to meet. Nureychick. Great dancer, very shy. Needs help with English. You can help him!" So that was how Peter became the English tutor to Rudolf Nureyev!

Peter was in the Tea Room having lunch in a bar booth with Terry

Southern (then considered a writer of obscene material) on November 23, 1963, when he learned from a phone call that President Kennedy had been assassinated. I was there, too, that day, having lunch with Lyn Tornabene. The dining room was noisy and crowded until two o'clock, when the news came. Then dead silence. People, not knowing what to do, started leaving. Lyn and I went upstairs to look for Sidney and found him in his office on the telephone, trying without success to get through to the police. He was convinced there was a worldwide conspiracy connected to the assassination and that we were all going to be blown sky-high. I sat on his lap and wrapped myself around him for comfort, but he was too distracted to deal with the tragedy on a personal level, so I left.

I said good-bye to Lyn and went home. I needed to see Ellen more than anybody. Young as she was, I needed her comforting presence. I went into her room and got her up from her nap and took her in my arms. Then I told her what had happened to the president as gently as I could. I was thinking that it could have been Sidney who was dead, not the president. All the time now, knowing his illness was terminal, I was afraid Sidney was going to die. I wondered when I would have to come into Ellen's room like this and tell her that it had happened. I felt a strange combination of relief and foreboding. It was less than four years before the fears became reality.

Ellen and I went out and roamed through the streets. People were wandering around, like us, not knowing what to do with themselves. We passed storefronts on Fifth Avenue already draped in black with American flags placed in the foreground. The police had been called out in force and were standing around everywhere, not knowing what to do. We went home and watched the unfolding of the tragedy on television all weekend: Jackie's vigil, the funeral, the murder of Lee Harvey Oswald by Jack Ruby, and over and over again the pictures from Dallas, the president's car, Lyndon Johnson's swearing-in on the presidential plane, Jackie's bloody pink suit. I felt it was a presentiment, and watched Jackie's reactions with more pain than I wanted to admit.

Borscht

Many years ago Clementine Paddleford, the food editor of the *Daily News,* was a name to be reckoned with in restaurant circles. She was less than five feet tall but she struck terror in the hearts of many a restaurant owner and chef with her power to make or break a restaurant's reputation. When she called up and announced she was coming to the Russian Tea Room, it was all hands on deck, and everybody scurried around getting the place in tip-top shape. When she came in, she asked, much to our surprise, not to be seated in the dining room, but to be taken to the chef, and headed straight for the kitchen. Gary Siderenko, our chef, who was six feet three, a Georgian known for his hot temper, looked surprised to see the tiny lady in the pink Chanel suit suddenly appear across the steam table, but he put down his carving knife and waited.

"I've come to ask you for your recipe for borscht, Chef," she said, looking up at Gary, who, in his toque, seemed even taller. She took out a pencil and notepad from her pocketbook.

"Sure," said Gary. "Take twenty pounds boneses, twelve pounds beets, fifteen pounds onions—"

Ms. Paddleford put up her hands in protest.

"No, no, no! I don't think you understand. I want a recipe for six people!" she said.

"Can't make borscht for six people!" said Gary, and, turning back to his stoves, he mumbled something undoubtedly obscene in Russian, which was fortunately not reported in the *Daily News*.

Restaurant Etiquette

It took two years of heavy indecision before Sidney and I got married, during which time Sidney tried to teach me the little niceties of the restaurant business, beginning with how to be introduced. Sidney: "I'll take you over to the table and say, 'Faith, *you* know Leonard Bernstein,' and you say, 'Yes, of course I do!' " So the next time Leonard Bernstein came in, Sidney took my hand and led me over to his table, where he introduced me, saying, "Faith, *you* know Leonard Bernstein." And I said, "No, I don't believe I do!"

It was then, in the early 1960s, that we put up the Christmas decorations that stayed up all those years. Starting as a joke during the holidays and as an attempt to cover the stark Art Deco chandeliers, the tinsel and red balls became such a familiar part of the decor that we left them up all year. It was then that Rudolf Nureyev defected from Russia, and came every day in his student's cap, speaking no English, to be taken care of by our team of indomitable, but not so young, Russian waitresses— Nadia, Ada, Vera, and Ducia, who hovered over him and called him Nureychick. They all fought among themselves, except for Ducia, who was married to a former Russian general and felt herself above the strife. One of my early duties at the Tea Room was to prevent Nadia, Ada, and Vera from fighting in the dining room. Vera liked to take a nip from left-over wineglasses, which only made matters worse. Things came to a head one day during lunch when Ada, the fiery redhead, announced that she was no longer to be called Ada, but was changing her name to Vera. This meant that we now had two Veras, and at this revelation the real Vera ran to the basement sobbing, her apron flung over her face. After much negotiation on the floor of the dining room, it was resolved that Ada would henceforward be called not Ada, not Vera, but Ada-Vera, and the real Vera was coaxed back upstairs with wrinkled apron and reddened eyes, so that lunch could be resumed.

It's hard to realize how Russian the Tea Room was in those days. The staff was still mostly Russian and the clientele included Mr. Hurok and Anatole Chujoy, the quirky founder and editor of *Dance News*, who dined alone in the first bar booth twice a day six days a week and once on Sunday. When one day Sidney decided to upgrade the bar service at lunch by putting linen tablecloths on the bar booth tables, Mr. Chujoy, ever the iconoclast, ripped the tablecloth off his table, sending the silverware, china, and glasses crashing to the floor. "I won't let Sidney Kaye raise the prices just for a piece of cloth on my table!" he shouted in his heavy Russian accent, and stalked out. Three days later he was back, having scoured the neighborhood without finding another Russian Tea Room. Besides, all the dancers, including George Balanchine and his wife and ex-wives, Alexandra Danilova, Vera Zorina, Tamara Geva, Maria Tallchief, and Tany LeClercq, and Chujoy's other Russian pals, including the entire staff of the *Novoe Russoye Slovoe*, the Russian daily newspaper, were there at the RTR. But he didn't speak to Sidney for two years and Sidney didn't speak to Mr. Chujoy, either. I was the designated messenger, and would be called over to Mr. Chujoy's table, where he would say to me, sotto voce, "Tell Sidney Kaye the borscht needs more salt," which I would do. And then Sidney would say, "Tell Anatole Chujoy to mind his own damn business!" My life became a lot easier when they began to speak to each other again.

It was at that time that Sidney, in a rare burst of entrepreneurial severity, told Anatole the maître d' to ask the old Russian generals not to sit over a glass of tea all night but to order drinks as well, to earn their keep. Anatole, who was as shy as he was tall, and a great friend of all the old generals besides, went to them with great reluctance, and came back to Sidney in tears. "Mr. Kaye, they told me they would love to drink, but they can't. After all their years of drinking, they no longer have any stomachs!" Sidney relented, of course, and they went on drinking their tea as before, except on the day of the annual reunion of Russian generals, when they would repair to the Boyar Room and drink a bottle of vodka apiece. Afterward the younger and stronger would carry out the older and weaker. Then for the next 364 days they self-righteously drank their tea in a glass with cherry preserves.

Sol Hurok

When Sidney and I went to the Soviet Union in 1959, we ran into Mr. Hurok at the Bolshoi Ballet, marching down the aisle. When he saw us waving he stopped, looked intently at Sidney, and said, "Kaye, who's watching the store?" and then proceeded down the aisle, counting the house, as he always did. But my favorite Hurok story took place one evening when Mr. Hurok wandered into the RTR, as was his custom, while Sidney and I were having dinner. Tears were streaming down his cheeks as he sat down at our table. "What happened?" we both asked in alarm.

"I have just had the most moving experience of my life," he replied, now weeping. "I have just been to see the film of *The Sol Hurok Story.*"

Nureyev's Assessment

Soon after Rudolf Nureyev's defection from the Soviet Union, he established himself in New York and, specifically, at the Russian Tea Room. At that time, he was interviewed by *Time* magazine and asked which were the things he liked most about America.

"The Russian Tea Room!" he exclaimed. His English vocabulary was limited in those days.

"No, no, no!" said the interviewer. "We want to know how you feel about the country in *general*. And what you like *most* about it, of everything you've seen."

"The Russian Tea Room!" was all that Nureyev would say.

"Oh, well, OK, then can you tell us *why* you like the Russian Tea Room best of all in this country?"

"Because there I know I will not be poisoned!" he said, and left the interview.

Nureyev went through several phases in choosing what he liked to eat at the Tea Room. During each phase he would eat the same dish every time he came in. In the beginning phase he couldn't get enough of American steaks. Then he went on to eating shashlik and later a Chicken Kiev phase, which led into Chicken DeVolaille. After that I lost count.

A Retirement Fantasy

I ran into Mike Nichols in another restaurant soon after the RTR closed.

"What are you going to do now?" he asked me.

"I haven't the slightest idea!" I said.

"Well, I'll tell you what you *should* do. . . ." He paused and looked at me with that impish grin of his. "You should buy a white Rolls-Royce convertible and drive across the country between two handsome men!"

I'm still working on it.

Ellen's Early Restaurant Training

Sidney, Ellen, and I almost always had lunch on Sundays together at the RTR. We had the habit of sitting in D40, the first booth on the right. Salvador Dalí and his Russian wife, Gala, who came for Sunday lunch whenever they were in New York, always sat directly across the room from us, in D1. (Mrs. Dalí had previously been married to Igor Stravinsky, who also frequented the Tea Room.) Mr. Dalí would stride around the dining room, draped in a black cape, swinging his silver-handled cane, and muttering to himself in (I suppose) Catalán. He never acknowledged our presence, but I noticed he was eyeing us one Sunday as he strolled by our

136

booth, and sure enough, the next Sunday, as Annette was about to seat the Dalís, he pointed his cane toward the other side of the dining room, at D40, our booth. He must have given it some thought and concluded that if the owner was sitting in that booth it must be the best. So when Sidney, Ellen, and I arrived, Annette, with a perfectly straight face, seated us in D1, as though we had always sat there, and as we ever after did.

Whenever Ellen and I had a meal at the RTR, we would play a game. If I couldn't remember the name of a regular customer when they walked by, I would say to Ellen, "Get ready, Ellen!" and with a signal from me she would leap under the table until I had said hello to the person and he had passed by. Then I would lean down and pull a corner of the tablecloth back and whisper, "OK, Ellen! All clear!" One time I was so anxious to remember the names of two inseparable brothers who came by our table I forgot to give Ellen the signal and said, "Ellen, I want you to meet Mr. and Mrs. Goldberg!" Ellen never let me forget it.

Once Ellen and I were having dinner at the RTR when she was about eight. I noticed she was looking intently around the dining room. Finally she said, "Isn't it wonderful to see a dining room full of people enjoying themselves—especially when it's yours?"

Erroll Garner's Double Take

Erroll Garner was a much-loved patron of the Tea Room. A modest man with great generosity of spirit, his talent shone in everything he did, not only onstage and in his recordings, but in his personal relationships, too. He had a great sense of humor and charmed us with his stories of being on the road and in the concert hall.

Erroll loved to tell this story on himself: One evening in the Tea Room, when he was sitting at the bar, Anatole came over to him and whispered in his ear, "There is a lady standing up front who says she would give anything just to say hello to you. She says she is a great fan and goes to your performances wherever you are playing."

Erroll looked over his shoulder and saw an elderly woman with white hair and a cane waiting near the front door. Climbing down from the bar stool, he went over to her, extended his hand, and said, "Hello, I'm Erroll Garner."

The woman looked Erroll over carefully from head to toe, but didn't take his outstretched hand. "You're not Erroll Garner!" she said.

Erroll, startled, said, "Yes, I am!"

"Oh, no, you're not!" said the woman. "Erroll Garner is much taller than you are!"

Erroll couldn't find the right words, so he stood there in silence. Then it came to him what he must do. He turned around and went to the men's room.

"And when I came out," he said, "I went up to the lady's table and I stood on my tippy-tippy toes, and I said, "How do you do. I'm Erroll Garner."

"Yes!" she said. "Of course you are! *You're* Erroll Garner!"

Czarist Humor

Impatient customer to Anatole: "Do you have a quiet table?"

Anatole: "All of our tables are quiet. We only have problems with our customers!"

A Joke with James Baldwin

Jimmy (James) Baldwin and I were chums, in that way you can be when you spend time together in a restaurant, without knowing or caring that much about each other's private lives. We used to kid around a lot, and one evening Jimmy asked me if anyone had been in asking for him. I paused and said, "Well, there was this person looking for you, all right, but I couldn't see his face because he was wearing a white sheet!"

Jewish Rhythms

Sidney loved to tell about the old Jewish lady who wants to buy a record of *Hello, Dolly!* The clerk asks her, "What speed would you like?" "What speed?" she asks. "*You* know," slowly tapping her foot, "Hel-lo Dol-ly—like that!"

Maître d' Manqué

Zero Mostel, like Julie Munshin, loved to assume the role of waiter at the Tea Room, just to drive Sidney crazy. Zero would throw one of our pink napkins over his arm and go up to a table of diners, his head lowered (the long curl he teased over his bald forehead hanging free) and ask, "Good evening. Will you have the peasant under glass?"

Improving on Arthur Miller

Flora Roberts, a dramatic rights literary agent for many years, represented a kaleidoscope of artists including Stephen Sondheim, Alfred Uhry, Maya Angelou, and Robert B. Parker. She was a stalwart of the Tea Room to the end, and especially enjoyed having lunch with her friend and fellow agent Robby Lantz. The stories about Flora are legion, but I love the one she tells about herself in the early part of her career when she was working for the producer Kermit Bloomgarden, who was producing Arthur Miller's *Death of a Salesman* on Broadway. Flora was in charge of making the deals with the ladies who ran the theater benefits, which brought in very important guaranteed revenue for a play about to open.

The ladies were all invited to a run-through of the play, and Flora talked to them afterward, trying to sell them *Death of a Salesman.*

"Well," said the lady in charge of the largest group, "I would buy the play for my girls, but you'd have to change the title."

"Change the title?" asked Flora, dumbfounded. They had just come out from seeing one of the most powerful modern tragedies in our literature. "How could Mr. Miller change the title? That's what the play's about!"

"My girls want *life.* Can't you change it to *Life of a Salesman*? My girls won't buy death!"

Flora's talent was multifaceted and instinctive. Her knowledge of the theater only made it easier for her to come to her creative decisions as quickly as she did.

When *The Gin Game* came across her desk, Flora happened to look up at a poster on her wall of Jessica Tandy and Hume Cronyn in *The Fourposter,* a play in which she had represented the playwright. That did it. She made one phone call to Hume, messengered him the script, and made the deal with the Cronyns the next day. It was their last great success together.

In the middle of a moving memorial tribute to Flora, Helen Brann, my great friend and literary agent, who was a close friend and colleague of Flora's, told this story about her:

"In 1986 I went into Flora's office and said, 'Flora, we must buy a racehorse!'

"She peered at me over her glasses and said, 'Jews don't buy racehorses.'

"But then, as she did so many other times, she yielded, and found herself entering a new world. She never turned down a challenge or a new experience if it caught her interest. And what caught her interest in this new world were the same things that made her so passionate an advocate about writers in the theater. Thoroughbred racehorses are sometimes very talented, always fragile, always unpredictable. And horse racing, when you own and breed horses and are serious about it, is a pursuit full of beauty, heartbreak, fulfillment of talent and excitement. And sometimes, but rarely, you hit the jackpot."

Flora—the quintessential theater person. There was nobody like her.

Who's the Lady in Pink?

Producers Terry Allen Kramer (female) and Harry Rigby, who were great pals as well as partners, were overheard by director John Hart ordering drinks. One of them said, "I'll have a straight Scotch, no ice," the other said, "I'll have a Pink Lady." The funny part was that it was Terry who ordered the Scotch and Harry who ordered the Pink Lady! You had to know them.

Remembering Yul

After Yul Brynner's wake, several of his friends arrived at the RTR to celebrate his memory. His history at the Tea Room went back to those Casino Russe days in the 1930s, and he was always a great guest over the years. Without a reservation, standing in line, were Robert Mitchum and his son, Sylvester Stallone and Brigit Nielson, Michael Douglas, and Raquel Welch. Fortunately Ona spotted them and got them a table. Tom LoSquadro, our comptroller, had heard the news that Raquel Welch was in the dining room and he came running down from his office. He was crazy about her and avidly followed her career. He stood in the front of the dining room, gazing around.

When Ona came near he whispered, "So where's Raquel Welch?"

"She's standing right next to you, dumbo!" said Ona. "She has on a black veil for the funeral!"

Theatrical Angel

Robby Lantz says Yul Brynner is looking down on us.

"With his tenacity I wouldn't be surprised if Yul came back and took over his role in the new revival of *The King and I*. Once during the run of the original production, Yul called me during the only break he got during the show to tell me he counted ten empty seats in the orchestra. Without skipping a beat I said, 'Don't worry, I have the names and addresses of all of them!"

Chicken Kiev and Cherry Coke

Susie and Warren Buffett have been friends of mine since the early 1950s. Susie and I were sorority sisters at Northwestern, and we have always stayed in close touch since then.

On the night of a party the French Culinary Institute gave in my honor, Susie and Warren were there. On the way to the party Warren asked Susie if she realized that she and I had known each other for over 20 percent of the life of our country? Susie and I were pretty devastated when we learned this. It did not prevent Susie from singing like an angel onstage that night, however. She is a cabaret singer who could make a career of it if only she didn't have half the world to take care of, which she does with grace and modesty.

Susie and Warren were an important part of the Tea Room's life. They gave their daughter Susan's prenuptial dinner there, dined with friends and business associates whenever they were in town. As Susie said to me, "It was home to us in New York. Nothing will ever take its place."

Warren, who always ordered Chicken Kiev and Cherry Coke (which we stocked just for him) remembers that he and Susie usually ran into friends when they were at the RTR, and that they loved the Cabaret. Warren also recalls:

"We made some deals at the Tea Room, too. I remember Murph [Charles Murphy] and I walked over from Sixty-seventh Street to the Tea Room and made the ABC deal there, in nineteen eighty-five."

Warren helped me in innumerable ways. He was always there to look over a potential contract or find me a lawyer—you can't do better than that! The only thing he won't give advice about is the stock market.

"I don't watch the market—I'm looking thirty years ahead," he said. "And don't buy Berkshire Hathaway! It's too expensive!"

Penthouse Serenade

Al Hirschfeld, the theatrical caricaturist, has had one of the longest and most successful careers of any living artist. At ninety-five he is still as charmingly laconic as he ever was, still working every day and keeping up the same routine of first-night theatergoing he always had. He has worked for the *New York Times* for seventy years! Only last year, he says, did they suddenly ask him to sign a contract. But the contract goes on forever, so it doesn't matter.

I first met Al and his wife, Dolly, in the 1950s, with Eddie and Rosemary Chodorov at the RTR. Sidney and I often went out to dinner with them and the amazing thing about Al was that he always drove his Buick convertible around New York, wherever he went. If he decided to go over to the Little Club from the Tea Room, he'd say, "Come on, let's ride over and see what Billy Reed's up to."

"But Al," someone would say, "where are you going to park?"

"Right there," Al would say, and sure enough, he would pull up and there would be a space right in front of the club. And wherever he went the same thing would happen. You'd spot Al driving around New York just as if he were in Henrietta, Oklahoma, always finding a convenient parking place.

Al tells this story: One day in 1932 he was walking in Central Park and he looked up at the Osborne Apartments on West 57th Street, which then had an unobstructed view of the park, and he thought the roof of the Osborne looked like a good place to build a penthouse. So he walked over and talked to Mr. Taylor, the owner, who said "fine," as long it didn't increase the building's insurance costs, so Al had it built. You didn't have to get all those permits and board approvals in those days—it was in the middle of the Great Depression.

Al and Dolly lived there happily in this small apartment with the wonderful terrace and spectacular view until their daughter, Nina, was born in 1945. Al had a weekly poker game with Robert Preston and Yul Brynner and some other men, and when the game was on Dolly had to sleep in the bathtub. Now they had Nina and no place to put her, either, so they started looking for larger quarters and found the brownstone Al still lives in today.

Al remembers the Tea Room, diagonally across from his penthouse in the Osborne, as a cultural hangout for artists and writers who moved up from the Algonquin Round Table, which was by then passé. Moss Hart and his wife, Kitty Carlisle, George S. Kaufman, Clifford Odets, Morris Carnovsky, and the entire Group Theater, and "anyone who could play a musical instrument" came to the RTR. "The culture of the city congregated there," says Al. He remembers that

> The designers Boris Aronson, Ralph Alswang, and Jo Mielziner, and the lighting designer Abe Feder were always there, and the Actors Studio people sat in the bar booths, never inside the dining room—Marlon Brando and his friend Wally Cox, who lived together down the street, were part of that bunch. Also Martin Gable and Arlene Francis. People insisted on sitting in the booth they considered belonged to them, and they would wait at the bar and glare at the people in "their" booth until the people left so they could take their "rightful" place.
>
> Fifty-seventh Street was a marvelous street then. Fashionable stores up and down the street—now it's just honky-tonk. The soul of the city is gone. I have little to do with New York now. I work here in my studio seven days a week—though I love it, it's a lonely life—and there are no more meeting places to go to when I want to go out. The Tea Room has not been replaced.
>
> Of course it changed, too, over the years. You could have dinner there for three or four dollars in 1932, and later it might be a hundred dollars. Reasonableness disappeared everywhere. In Paris in

1924 three of us lived in a bungalow for $100 a year, $33 each. We paid $116 dollars a month at the Osborne and what would our apartment cost now? And the Tea Room became more social. People went there to show off rather than to meet. But everything changes—you can't help that. That's life.

Later, when Sidney and I lived in that same penthouse, Al and Dolly came to visit us, and brought William Saroyan with them, who talked through the afternoon and into the evening, nonstop. He talked in poetry, not prose, and everything he said was lyrical and lush. I felt he was speaking great truths that could change my life, if only I could remember what he said!

The Lady Impresario

Jean Dalrymple was a beloved fixture at the Tea Room from its earliest days. As a producer and director at City Center for more than two decades, her working day spilled over into the Tea Room, where she conducted almost daily lunch meetings in the second bar booth, and then she replaced Mr. Chujoy in the first bar booth after he was gone. She was the quintessence of propriety: small, with pale delicate features, she always wore a suit with an open-collared linen blouse and a hat, usually with a feather (even after women stopped wearing hats), and white gloves. She had a high, squeaky voice, but very soft, like a whisper. And all in all, you would never guess that Miss Jean, as I always called her, was a powerhouse, and, according to rumors I heard, had been a femme fatale. She was married first to the theater critic Ward Morehouse and then to Major General Philip de Witt Ginder.

In 1996 it fell to my friend Isabelle Stevenson, president of the American Theater Wing, to deliver a very difficult message to Miss Jean, a friend and colleague of many years. She had been appearing on the Theater Wing's TV seminars with Isabelle and an august panel since the inception of the program, but, at ninety-three, had started to fall asleep during the tapings. It was now up to Isabelle to break the news to Miss Jean that she would not be welcome any longer to continue the seminars. They had lunch in the first bar booth at the Tea Room.

"Jean," said Isabelle, "I know you will be relieved not to have the burden of continuing the seminars."

"Why don't you let me be the judge of that?" snapped Miss Jean. Isabelle was taken aback. "I don't fall asleep and I have no intention of resigning from the seminars, and you're killing me!" There was nothing else to say. The woman who helped Miss Jean get around came up and started to take her away when Miss Jean slumped forward, and would have hit the floor if Isabelle hadn't caught her in her arms. Two waiters got her into a taxi, and as Isabelle helped push her feet inside, Miss Jean opened her eyes and said, "You were right, Isabelle. You were right."

Jean Dalrymple died at age ninety-six in her apartment across the street from the City Center in December 1998, and was buried next to her husband the general at West Point.

Dame Margot and Danilova

Don Smith tells about the last time Dame Margot Fonteyn, dying of cancer, went out to dinner at the Tea Room with him and Alexandra Danilova. For years Danilova had been jealous of Fonteyn. She used to say to Don, "Why you need Dame when you have me?" But now they had become friends—"Margot, she is so dushka [darling]!" said Danilova—and they wanted a chance to be together and talk.

Don said, "It's madness to sit here in the front booth! Every single person who comes in will stop at the table!" but they paid no attention to him. Sure enough, people streamed by, some bringing their napkins to be signed. Roland Petit, the French choreographer and director, heard in Washington that the two celebrated women would be in the Tea Room that night, and hopped a train to New York to see them. There was much hugging and kissing but Don told Roland he would only be allowed to stay for one glass of champagne.

"Do you ever come to Paris?" Petit asked Dame Fonteyn.

"Offer her job!" said Danilova. "She will come!"

Nureyev paid all of Dame Margot's doctor bills when she was sick. She had no money and her husband continued to live in the grand style anyway. He might decide to go to the New York Athletic Club for a swim, and it would cost $600, because he was confined to a wheelchair, and arrangements had to be made—a fee paid to the club, a car, and chauffeur. Or he might pick out $1,700 worth of books and send them to the hotel. Don Smith said about her, "The tragedy of a woman whose life was movement chained to a man who couldn't move." But another friend replied, "It's harder on us than on her. She loves him."

Nureyev was overwhelmed by her artistry and came to trust her more than anyone else. He was in total denial about her illness and was in Vienna, far from her deathbed in London, when she died. Jane Herman, a friend, flew to Vienna to try to persuade him to come to the funeral at Westminster Abbey, but he just couldn't face it, and didn't go.

The Working Girl and the Producer

Helen Gurley Brown first visited the RTR in 1963 when she and her husband, David, moved from Los Angeles to New York. As she remembers:

Nureyev was sitting in the first booth. That started us off right. It became our neighborhood restaurant. So many memories: taking Yul Brynner there for dinner, hearing about his days as a circus performer, his bouts with cancer. We gobbled and gossiped for two hours, though it was after his performance in *The King and I* and he had two shows the next day. The Tea Room encouraged that in a person. And our dinner the night before I first went to work at *Cosmo* as editor-in-chief. Scary. David said I'd be fine, but during the night I disappeared and he found me under my desk in a fetal position. But David was right: I was fine. I remained editor-in-chief of *Cosmo* for thirty-two years.

I can't remember my last meal at the Tea Room. I never believed it would close. I'm still depressed about it right this minute!

Only once did Faith and I have a falling-out. *Cosmo* was doing an article about the Tea Room as a place *Cosmo* readers might want to know about. The only other four we ever did, as I remember, were the "21" Club, the Four Seasons, the Waldorf-Astoria Hotel, and the Beverly Hills Hotel.

Faith wanted the story but she didn't want us to disturb her celebrities with me running up and down the aisles snapping photos during lunch. She kept telling me that was the Russian Tea Room policy—no photographs in the dining room during lunch. So how were we going to get our story across without pictures of the "famed and famished," as someone called them? There were phone calls back and forth with my editor, Bobbie Ashley, a great friend of mine and Faith's, trying to keep feathers from being ruffled. We finally solved it by bringing a photographer in before lunch began, who took pictures of Tony Randall, Hume Cronyn, Florence Henderson, and Garson Kanin, as prearranged and with their permission. Faith and I have remained buddies in spite of this—of course she *loved* the article! And about the RTR's closing: I didn't quite know how much I missed it until now, when I started reminiscing about it.

David Brown, the debonair producer and writer, is the perfect foil for his wife, Helen Gurley Brown, and vice versa. If Helen weren't so smart they could be Mr. and Mrs. Thin Man. As it is, they each run their own shows with brilliance and style and are still twice as appealing as a couple as they are solo.

David remembers the RTR in the 1920s when, as a boy of ten, he was taken there, and "it was still a hangout for White Russian émigrés, with very little money coming in:

Then it became the watering hole of "doers": its sublime location, the many vodkas, the caviar, the warmth and elegance—many places have one or the other, but only the Russian Tea Room had both—its all-year Christmas, like the song from *Mame*—and its permanent residents! The management always disavowed the "permanent resident" policy, but of course it existed.

Sam Cohn, incidentally, was known for eating napkins for lunch, and sometimes part of his sweater. A Sam Cohn watcher told me he saw Sam devour a whole necktie at a particularly grueling lunch meeting, but this story must be apocryphal because Sam, as far as I know, never wore a necktie.

If you wanted to know who was in town in the entertainment world, you had to cover the RTR for lunch and Elaine's at night.

Elaine herself came to the RTR often for lunch, especially for Pelymeni Siberian on Wednesdays. It was one of my favorites, too, along with the blini, the red caviar omelet, and the duck with red cabbage.

Helen and David liked to spend Thanksgiving and Christmas at the Tea Room, inviting two or three friends to join them. I was sometimes invited and always found those occasions memorable.

A View from the Bridge (Sam's Table)

Robert Benton, a client and friend of Sam Cohn's, often had lunch with him. Bob is a screenwriter and director who won an Academy Award for *Kramer vs. Kramer.*

Bob Benton on the RTR:

It was one of the world's best clubs. A great gathering place. No other place like it in NYC. Movie people, theater people—you had to bring California people there the moment they arrived. It was truly a circus. A director would have a conversation with a writer, a writer with an actor, and an actor with an agent—it went round and round. Once I got a bad review on a movie and I just wanted to duck. But Sam [Cohn] said, "No, don't duck. Let's go to the Tea Room for lunch. You need to be seen." Sam did all the deals; that was not what I did. I came to the Tea Room to talk. Dustin and I often had lunch, but that was because we had become friends. I miss the Tea Room, and miss you, we all do, in ways you will never know.

Animal Crackers

David reminded me of the dog who played a part in RTR history. He mentions a woman who wrote a book about leaving her dog in our checkroom but neither of us can remember who it was.

I do remember, however, Peter Gimbel, the documentary filmmaker, bringing in his adorable Norwich terrier, Billy, who was the mascot in his movie titles, like the MGM lion. Billy was a frequent guest in the hatcheck room. I was so fond of him that when Timmy and Tootsie, my

Yorkies, were no more, I got two Norfolk terriers, not sure at the time the difference between them and the Norwiches. (It was another twenty-five years before I got my first Norwich, but I had many Norfolks, including five home-bred litters, in between.)

Maude Franchot, Franchot Tone's aunt, my friend and neighbor at the Osborne, always brought in her Yorkie and hid him beside her under a napkin, then slipped him into a shopping bag before carrying him out, nobody (but us) the wiser.

Joan Rivers left her Yorkie, Spike, in the checkroom when she came. He attracted a lot of attention because Joan talked about him so much on television, and he had some of Joan's personality, too.

Sandra Hochman, the poet, who goes back a long way in RTR life (I remember a time in the wild 1960s when Sandra came in barefoot with a pink balloon attached to her right big toe), used to bring her Lhasa apso in, and one day, her mind elsewhere, she forgot the dog and he stayed there all afternoon until we were able to track Sandra down. Then, when she brought him out of the checkroom, the dog rushed acoss the aisle to the first bar booth, where Harold Clurman was deep in conversation with Joe Wiseman, and did a big pee on Harold's shoe. Sandra, in shock, got some paper towels from Iris in the checkroom and went down on her knees on the floor to clean it up. Harold didn't notice any of this and kept right on talking to Joe. Sandra, who was blocking the entrance to the restaurant, had to be helped up, handed the dog, which was struggling in Iris's arms, and seen through the revolving door so people could get in.

In Sidney's time the laws forbidding pets (now "animal companions") in restaurants did not exist, and once a customer brought in his pet monkey, who was accustomed to accompanying the man everywhere. They were sitting in a bar booth, the monkey and its owner, when the man in the next booth put his arm up on the divider and the monkey bit him on the elbow. Besides the element of surprise, the monkey's bite was fairly deep and the man yelped in pain. The monkey's owner was horrified and immediately helped the man into a taxi, a pink napkin wrapped around the wound, and took him to the emergency room at Roosevelt Hospital, with the monkey in tow. On the way, the wounded man, a screenwriter, discovered that the monkey's owner was a movie director he had been trying to meet, and the story ended happily when the director offered to read the screenwriter's script that very day.

Unusual Neckwear

In Sidney's bachelor days he was invited to a lot of parties, sometimes by people he didn't know. Late in the evening, after a few drinks, it was not so easy to be discerning about accepting invitations. Anatole the maître d' took a fatherly interest in Sidney, in spite of the fact that he was afraid of him, and one night, as Sidney was setting out for a party in Brooklyn whose host he had only just met, Anatole stopped him at the door of the restaurant.

"Mr. Kaye, I don't think you should go," he said.

"Why not?" asked Sidney, irritated.

Anatole hesitated. "Because, Mr. Kaye, the man who invited you, he had on a tie that had large tears, like sobs, painted down the front of it. That's why."

Sidney, who hadn't noticed this detail, decided not to go and admitted Anatole was right.

Cachet on 57th Street

Geraldine Stutz arrived on West 57th Street in 1965 to take over Henri Bendel's, the old-fashioned, exclusive women's clothing store—once stylish and avant-garde but by then gone to seed—and quickly transformed it into the hottest store in town.

How to describe Geraldine? Picture in your mind Marcel Duchamp's *Nude Descending a Staircase,* and you will have the essence of Geraldine. Not the nude part, but the gliding, constant, animated motion, and the pizzazz. When she makes an entrance—sweeping in in a black cape, a sea green turban, a purple knit sweater, black slacks, and stunning jewelry, her arms moving to express what she is about to say—the room stops, and welcomes her.

Soon after her arrival at Bendel's, Geraldine recalls, Sidney walked into her office one day unannounced and said, "I'm Sidney Kaye. Welcome to Fifty-seventh Street! Come on and let me show you around!" He took Geraldine by the arm and led her up the block to the Tea Room for lunch, introducing her to all the staff and generally making her feel at home. This was the beginning of their friendship and an even longer friendship between Geraldine and the RTR, which lasted until the restaurant closed.

Geraldine remembers that 9 West 57th Street (the big building with the sculpture of the red number 9 out front) had not been built when she came on the scene—Bendel's address was 10 West—and there were still row houses there. Back in 1911, Henri Bendel, who began his career as a milliner, built the first commercial building on the block, an unheard-of nine stories tall. On the corner of 57th Street and Fifth Avenue then was Harry Payne Whitney's house, where the Crown Building is today, and the Vanderbilt mansion was on the other corner where Bergdorf Goodman is. All along the block were custom clothiers, hatmakers (Emmy the hatmaker had a young man in the back room who later became Adolpho), Milgrim's, Jay Thorpe, the Tailored Woman, and the fur shops. Moving toward Sixth Avenue the block changed to music shops, fabric shops, art galleries, and art-book stores. Everything was fashion and culture.

Geraldine met her friend Bobby Short at the RTR, and Leo Lerman, then culture maven about town, who took her under his wing. (Which editor was it that, in the heat of a discussion about the galleys for Leo's book, threw a shot glass of vodka at Leo's beard?)

Most important to Geraldine was meeting Ruth Gordon, who "adopted" her. They bonded right away because Geraldine, who had originally come to New York from Chicago to become an actress, adored the theater, and Ruth Gordon, who had worn haute couture since the 1920s, adored fashion.

One day Ruth came up to Geraldine in the Tea Room, and, in her carefully casual accent, which sounded like Old New York, the way she dropped her *gs*, said:

"Watch the Academy Awards show this weekend. I think you'll find it fascinatin'. I found an old Fortuny dress ol' man Bendel made for me thirty years ago, and it didn't need alterin' at all—I think you'll find it very interestin'."

Geraldine continues, "The Academy Awards were then held in a hotel ballroom with a small stage, a podium, a mike—and that was it." Geraldine watched on TV as Ruth Gordon's name was announced as winner of the Best Supporting Actress Award for *Rosemary's Baby*.

"Ruth flounced down the aisle, her hair pulled back in a bun, her back straight, her hips moving, and the dress—the dress was marvelous! And it covered everything that wasn't hotsy-totsy about her figure. After stopping to talk to people along the way, she climbed the steps to the stage and received her award. Then she pushed the mike away (an actress from the theatah doesn't need a mike!), put the statuette down, and said, 'I've been workin' in the theatah, motion pictures, even television, for the last sixty-five years, and this is the first time I've ever won an award for anythin'!' There was a long pause, the audience fearing the rebuke she was about to deliver. 'I must say I find it very encouragin'!' Then she picked up her Oscar and sashayed off."

Geraldine and I really became friends after Sidney died, when she sensed what I must be going through in taking over the restaurant, and offered her help. I was overjoyed! At first we met for our "training sessions" in her booth at the RTR, the last bar booth, but we needed more privacy, away from prying eyes, so we started lunching at Orsini's, then a popular restaurant around the corner from both of us on West 56th Street.

Geraldine would say things to me like "Don't let them push you into making decisions, kiddo. If you don't know the answer to something, just say, 'I'll think about it and let you know later.' " Or "Ask them what *they* think would be a good solution!"

Words like these were more than comforting: they were lifesavers to the rookie restaurateur.

Through the years, Geraldine achieved much success at Bendel's and among the New York glitterati. Still, she continued to write the copy for her Bendel's ads in the *New York Times* as she had always done, and she stayed hands-on at the store. When we published our *Russian Tea Room Cookbook* in 1981, she threw a book party for us in her Street of Shops on the main floor of Bendel's, which launched us in a big way. Years later, in 1994, when Geraldine had sold her interest in Bendel's and had become a book editor at Clarkson Potter, a division of Random House, we did a book together: *The Russian Tea Room: A Tasting,* and this time we threw the book party at the RTR.

She brought the fashion designers she had discovered—now famous—into the Tea Room: Jean Muir, Sonya Ryckiel, Mary Quant, Steven Burroughs, Zoran, Perry Ellis, and many more. Her talented window dresser, Joel Schumacher, became a big movie producer and remained a nice person. There was a rumor at the Tea Room that some of the saleswomen from Bendel's who came in for lunch were so chic they must have been wearing clothes "borrowed" off the racks from the store. I don't believe it, but it's a funny idea.

One of her treasures, whom Geraldine shared with me, was Gene Moore, the window display artist, who for forty years mesmerized everyone who passed Tiffany's windows with his creations. It was not just as a customer of the Tea Room, which he was, but as an artist that I got to know him, and that was thanks to Geraldine's introduction. Gene was shy and temperamental and Southern, and had a wicked sense of humor, but he needed only to be coddled and then he became a pussycat.

I wanted Gene to come and design our two display windows, which I knew he would make into great showcases. We had begun to decorate the windows in the 1960s and it became an ongoing project, which was my baby, and I had a lot of fun experimenting with it. Almost anything Russian—dolls, samovars, eggs, snow scenes—could be made into a display. I asked Artkraft-Strauss, the sign company, to paint a frame around the two windows, and they designed black, red, yellow, and green stripes as a border. At that time, there was no building to the west of us and we had Inman Cook design a narrow vertical sign along the front edge of our west wall with the letters spelling the *Russian Tea Room* one under the other, in the same colors as the window frames. And to top it all off, we had the front window on the second floor painted in a similar design, with *Russian Tea Room* scrolled across it. It was a lively look, very "with it" at the time.

The main problem for Gene in working on the RTR windows was getting in and out of them through the checkroom. Even as slim as he was, it was almost impossible. Every time he had to push wet coats aside and crawl into the narrow space between the checkroom and the window, he would say with his inimitable drawl, "Faith, I know you're gonna *kill* me!" But I urged him on with the promise of dry martinis when he came back out. And Gene produced miracles in there—hand-blown eggs strung across the space, for instance—always minimal, always smashing, always witty. He could take a simple brass samovar and, by adding a little gauzelike ribbon in a certain way, fashion an eye-catching display. And the lighting Gene effected was a key to his genius. After the windows were done we would go outside to admire them and then sit Gene down in a booth for his dry martinis. When he had finished I would see him through the revolving door and start him on his way back to Tiffany's, to perform more miracles there.

A Femme Nearly Fatale

There were only so many booths in the RTR and sometimes we ran into trouble trying to make everybody happy, even doing the unforgivable—asking an old friend to give up his booth for a celebrity expected at any second.

Lionel Larner was one of the "most-favored agents" at the RTR and has been a friend of mine for many years, and, partly because he's British, he has a special flair. (An example of his Britishness: Lionel sends a Christmas card every year featuring a picture of the "Queen Mum.")

Lionel often brought in his clients, such as Carroll O'Conner, Dame Diana Rigg, and Stacy Keach. Like many of the regulars he prized his booth in the RTR, so when he heard one day that producer Harry Rigby had offered to give up his own booth to Jackie Onassis, Lionel voiced his approval of Harry's gallantry, as only one who adores the Queen Mother would. But when Ona, the maîtresse d', asked Lionel to give up his booth to a certain European film star, Lionel refused. This star—let's call her Madame X—had given Lionel and Harry Rigby endless agony when she was up for the starring role in *The Rose Tattoo* on Broadway, and he felt no obligation to accommodate her now, in the Tea Room.

"Actually," said Lionel, "her talent was not acting but her fluency in translating lire into dollars faster than a computer could!"

Not being familiar with the legitimate stage, Madame X had photos of herself taken in costume for the role, as they do in the movies, but she refused to audition for the part.

"But the producers want to have a look at you in person! They want to see you!" Lionel told her.

"When they buy ticket they see me!" she retorted.

P.S. She didn't get the part.

L'Envoi

All of us at the Tea Room, customers and staff alike, knew that Jessica Tandy was ill. She and her husband, Hume Cronyn, were there so frequently that when he now came in without her we began to worry. Then one day she came back, looking frail, her hair thinner, but as friendly and gracious as ever. Hume was smoking his pipe as usual and I thought that was a good sign. As the Cronyns had their lunch I thought about the time when I hadn't been in New York long, and was hired to be in the "Omnibus Repertory Company" on CBS, with Jessie and Hume as the stars—how in awe of them I was, how kind and unpretentious they were. I was concerned about Jessie's appearance and discussed it with Ona.

"I don't think she has long," Ona said, and I had to agree it looked that way. I got busy talking to some other people and suddenly looked up to find the Cronyns' table empty.

Ona came rushing over to me. "They just left!" she said. "Maybe you can catch them!"

I pushed through the revolving door and looked up and down 57th Street. There they were, walking slowly toward Sixth Avenue, Jessie holding tightly to Hume's arm. I caught up with them and said, "I didn't want you to leave without my saying good-bye!" They both turned and as our eyes met Jessie gave me her wonderful smile, and we clasped hands for a second. Then they were off. I never got to see her again.

Endpapers

Silas Spitzer was one of those writers, like A. J. Liebling and Ludwig Bemelmans, who loved good food and drink and, gourmet that he was, he wrote about both with wit and style.

Silas wrote a piece on the RTR for *Holiday* in 1959 that put us on the map. He captured the flavor of the restaurant in a delightful way. Aside from the story he wrote, I loved knowing Silas for his camaraderie and generous spirit. Rotund and tweedily dressed, his face in a perpetual flush, he came in with his wife, Helen, or with her identical twin sister, Madge, or with both of them together. It was fine when they both came in with Silas, but when only one of them arrived I always wondered which one it was, and I often thought Silas must have wondered, too, even in more intimate circumstances! The three of them animated each other, and you could feel little ripples of excitement emanate from them when they enjoyed beluga caviar with a glass of iced vodka, for instance, or while sampling new dishes, and all the while discussing the different tastes and textures of the food. Something they were eating or drinking would always remind Silas of a story from his long, adventurous life, and he would regale us with it as he moved on to the next course.

Years later, just after Sidney died, I told Silas I wanted to write about Sidney and he said, "Don't wait too long. You'd be surprised how quickly memories fade!" It has taken me this long to do it and though I worried all those years about the diminishing past, I'm happy that most of the memories, including those of Silas, are still fresh in my mind.

Into the Valley

When Sidney found out he had cancer in the summer of 1960, he tried to treat it casually but he didn't hide his fears from me for long.

It didn't affect our lives dramatically right away, but we were always aware it was there, and before long Sidney developed nodes in his lymph system and had to begin radiation treatments.

For the next seven years he was in and out of hospitals, bouncing back so quickly from each bout that many people didn't know he was ill at all. Gradually, though, the cancer took its toll, and I found myself doing more at the restaurant. Mainly I hoped my presence would be reassuring, as I knew the staff were worried about Sidney and wondering what was going to happen to the RTR and to their jobs.

Ellen was in a bad position. The hospitals Sidney was in and out of didn't allow children to visit in those days, and she missed her daddy and felt left out. I knew it was hard being excluded, even from the bad things that were happening. I was spending a lot of time at the hospital and at the restaurant and not much time at home with her.

The summer I worked on Larry's movie Sidney, Ellen, and I were out on Fire Island, thanks to the generosity of Barbara and Reggie Rose, who lent us their house in Fair Harbor for a month. We had been out there for the month of June the year before, renting a little house that belonged to newscaster Charles Collingwood, and we nearly froze to death. The house was on the dunes overlooking the beach, where the wind came whistling through the cracks and the only thing that saved us was that Cruz, our housekeeper and Ellen's nurse, knew from her upbringing in Chile how to make a really good fire and keep it going even when the wind was blowing down the chimney with all its might. Still, the bedrooms were icy at night and we had to keep Ellen covered in layers of clothing. We learned that June was too early to be out there on the ocean, but we did meet the Roses, who had a house next door, and through them we had a magical time the next year.

Betty Friedan and I became friends at Fire Island, just after her tremendous success *The Feminine Mystique* was published. She used to go to our little grocery store in Fair Harbor every day and make sure that the paperback copies of her book were prominently displayed. Betty and her then-husband, Karl, lived in Lonelyville just across the narrow boardwalk from Harold and Ruth Greenwald, who entertained us often around their crowded table. Harold was a psychotherapist and writer who had written a best-seller, *The Call Girl,* in 1958. Bel Kaufman, who wrote *Up the Down Staircase,* would sometimes walk down from Ocean Beach, and there were always psychiatrists, directors, and writers to fill the table. "Doc" (Neil) Simon, Stanley Prager and Georgianne Johnson, Frank Cosaro, Theodore White, Lee and Paula Strasberg, N. Richard Nash, Anne Bancroft and Mel Brooks, and many others were on hand in the community, enjoying the island life.

The Fire Island experience was a kind of paradise for us, away from the city and restaurant responsibilities. There Sidney and I, walking on the beach, could sometimes believe that his illness had disappeared. Then there were other times when fear would seize us as Sidney's awful pain and high fever would come back, and I would worry about getting him off the island to a hospital. It didn't happen, but several times we came close to having to leave.

The Fire Island scene was friendly and casual. You could walk down any lane, on the ocean side or the bay side or in between, and find people you knew or meet people you didn't know. The spirit was carefree, and it was a great place for Ellen to play with her new friends. I loved swimming in the breakers, walking on the beach, especially at night when we would often walk in a group to the lighthouse in Kismet, at the end of the island, to have steaks at a restaurant there. And sometimes we would take a beach taxi or a water taxi to go to another part of the island—Ocean Beach or the Pines—for drinks and dinner. There were parties all weekend, every weekend, at different people's houses, everything casual and spontaneous. In spite of his good spirits, though, Sidney began to have trouble walking and we knew he was in pain. We pretended our life on Fire Island would go on forever but it only lasted that summer.

One of the best days Sidney and I had was with Betty and Karl Friedan and Ruth and Harold Greenwald. We chartered a small steamboat with a captain and went up the bay to the end of Fire Island and then came back along the mainland shore—a brilliant summer day, a picnic with plenty of wine and good conversation—one of those unforgettable times.

During the last two years of Sidney's life, he spent more and more time in the hospital, first at Mount Sinai and then at Sloan-Kettering. I was living in a triangle, from the hospital to the restaurant to the apartment. I took Sidney mail and financial figures every day, and we discussed problems and made decisions, which I tried to carry out. But the day came when Sidney waved aside the questions I needed answered and said, "I don't care. Do what you want to do," and my heart stopped. If Sidney no longer cared about the business he must be giving up, I thought. And I realized I could no longer count on his support. I was really alone.

Meanwhile, Ruth Greenwald helped me get my paper, "The End of Innocence," written, and I managed to complete my two history courses. My plan was to begin my master's in the fall.

Sidney said to me not long before he died, "In my will I've given you three months to decide about keeping the Tea Room. I've been trying to get out of this crazy business since the day I got into it, so you know what I think you should do. Sell it!"

But it was too late. During the seven years Sidney was ill, I had gradually gotten involved with the everyday running of the restaurant and had become committed to its survival. The truth was I had begun to link the life of the RTR with my own, making its continuity vital to mine. These feelings were heightened by the fact that Sidney was dying. He was so inexorably linked to the Tea Room, not only by me but by everybody who knew him and loved him, that it was unthinkable to me that I could let the Tea Room pass to other hands. It would be my memorial to him to continue the life of the restaurant. It was a kind of crusade, which was to last twenty-seven years before I was finally able to take Sidney's advice to get out.

Those intense feelings kept me going as I took on my vigil over the RTR. I simply had to make it work, in spite of the fact that I had no formal restaurant training. Nor had I any interest, originally, in learning the restaurant business. The main thing that intrigued me about it, and specifically about the RTR, was its crossover to the theater, to which I had earlier dedicated myself until I found more disillusion there than reward.

Sidney died on the morning of August 7, 1967, at Sloan-Kettering Memorial Hospital, and the funeral was set for the next day. That afternoon, after I brought Ellen home from camp, I walked across 57th Street from the Osborne, past Carnegie Hall, to the RTR. I pushed through the revolving doors and stepped inside. It was very quiet, as much because it was August, I thought, as because Sidney had died that day. I had decided not to close the restaurant because the policy had always been to stay open every day of the year. I was surprised to see that everything appeared normal. Somehow I had imagined this world that belonged so much to Sidney would disappear when he died, but here it was, every samovar in place. Only the customers were missing. Was it because of the heat (and the treacherous air-conditioning) that they were absent or was it because people had learned about Sidney?

Anne Messavage, the maîtresse d' (still referred to in those days as "hostess"), was sitting at her favorite table in the middle of the dining room. I walked over to Anne and sat down across the table from her. I knew, all of us at the RTR knew, that Anne was in love with Sidney, and that she considered me a young interloper. Young I was, thirty-five that year, but only twenty-three when I first met Sidney in 1955. Anne was already there then, had been there since Sidney, with partners, bought the restaurant in 1947. The age difference between Sidney and me caused a lot of commotion among the staff when I came on the scene. They wanted to get on my good side but they also wanted to show me up in my insecure position as one in a long line of Sidney's girlfriends, so they treated me as a temporary presence.

Now back to 1967. I looked across the table at "Miss Anne," and tried to comfort her. It occurred to me there was something odd about this—that maybe she should be comforting *me*—but I knew this was not what I could expect from Anne. After all, she had worked for Sidney for twenty years, and she felt he belonged to her. It was only right that I honor her position, whether it made sense in the real world or not.

"Anne," I said, "we've got to go on." I wanted to reach out to her but I was afraid she might draw away.

She was crying silently. "Why?" she asked. She sat erect, spreading her hands on the table and staring at them, the way she did when she had something on her mind. I thought of her arranging the gladiolas on the center table every morning. When the flowers were removed from the table to the shelf in back of the front booth, it meant the center table was needed because the dining room was full, so the first question Sidney always asked Anne when he called down to her during lunch was, "Are the flowers off the table yet?"

"*Why* must we go on?" Anne asked me again, still staring at her hands.

"Because we just have to. Because Sidney would want us to. We can't let him down," I said. I think it was at that moment that I felt the resolve I needed—before it had been only in my head. I hoped Anne wouldn't let *me* down, either. How could I go on without her and a few of the other key people? She didn't answer and I finally left her sitting there in tears and I wondered if she would still be there tomorrow.

That evening, I slipped away from family, friends, and lawyers gathered at our apartment and went back to the restaurant in search of Marcel, whom Sidney had recently promoted from waiter to maître d', and who was due back from vacation that night. Marcel was an affable man, but weak. He was a waiter to the bone, but he was the only person in the crew who was willing to step out of the ranks and become, at least in title, a part of management. He was all I had and I needed him now to keep the unruly night waiters from running away with the restaurant.

When I walked in Marcel looked ashen. He seemed overwhelmed at the realization that Sidney was gone. I took him outside onto 57th Street and told him how much I was counting on him to get us through this difficult time. A chain-smoker, he puffed away as we walked up and down the block, beads of sweat breaking out on his forehead. If he could have, he would have ripped off his black bow tie and dinner jacket and bolted, I'm sure, but since he couldn't, he made the best of it and assured me I could count on his support.

My friend Nancy Vale (née Kafesjian) came to help me at the restaurant after Sidney's death. She and I had been good friends and rivals as acting students at Northwestern's School of Speech and had been part of a trio of friends at the speech school, "Faith, Hope, and Kafesjian," the third member being Hope Rissman. Nancy thought I'd go back to acting, and that running the RTR was going to be for me a temporary stopgap.

"Then I walked into the office," Nancy said later, "and there was Faith behind Sidney's big desk, and I thought, 'She's doing it!' "

Hope says she was not surprised.

I could have gone back to acting, it wasn't too late, but the moment had passed. I was now wrapped up emotionally in the RTR and I began to thrive on the challenge. Maybe I was my father's entrepreneurial daughter after all.

Nancy was distressed about a couple of things she noticed: (1) The staff was not friendly to me and seemed to think I wouldn't be there for long, and (2) there was a lot of graft to deal with—payoffs to the laundry and to the garbage collector (neither of which could be changed—there was literally no competition because the Mafia controlled them both), and to the police.

The first Christmas, when the police from the precinct came around with their biggest, fattest detective dressed up as Santa Claus—he was the bag man—I took him aside and told him I was sorry, we just didn't have any money to give to the police that year. Much to my surprise they couldn't have been nicer, and walked away with a smile. I was actually quite fond of "Santa Claus" and the other detectives I had gotten to know and we remained friends. The cops on our beat—who guided traffic at 57th Street and Seventh Avenue—Danny and Joe, have stayed in touch ever since.

It took me a long time to whittle the garbageman down to a decent price, but it happened, and through City Hall of all places, when the city administration finally addressed the problem openly. But that was years later.

The laundry monopoly was the most pressing at the time. After all, we couldn't open the doors for lunch without having tablecloths and napkins on the tables. Our arrangement was to rent laundry from the supplier and they were supposed to be sure we had enough and to maintain the quality by dyeing new batches of pink when the old pink started to fade. I was used to dealing with our laundry representative, Frank Mario, known as "Little Frank," and was fond of him. ("Big Frank" was the nickname for Frank Costello, the Mafia chief.) "Little Frank" or "Frankie" had wavy white hair and wore square glasses, tailored Italian suits, usually in a Prince of Wales pattern, and a large sky-blue ring on his left pinky. He had a friendly disposition and a love of gossip, especially about his Mafia connections. Sidney and I would sit with him in the back booth and listen to his stories about "the Family," which he told in a raspy, high-pitched voice.

The day after Frank Costello was shot (but not killed) in the lobby of the Majestic, the elegant apartment house on Central Park West where he lived, Frankie came in for his weekly check. He was full of indignation about the shooting.

"How would *you* feel, you come home from having dinner out with your wife and some guy comes at you in your own lobby with a forty-five? Bang! Bang! Bang!"

"Not very good," said Sidney. I realized why they called Sidney "the Jewish Rick," as in *Casablanca*. He was a lot like the Humphrey Bogart character sometimes.

"You bet you wouldn't!" said Frankie. "I don't know what the heck this country is coming to!"

Now it was 1967, and I decided to go down to City Hall and talk to Bess Myerson, then commissioner of Consumer Affairs in the Lindsay administration, about the laundry situation. Little Frank, much as I liked him, had not been very helpful about the quality of the laundry we were getting or about the prices, either.

Bess, still glamorous behind her big glasses, greeted me hospitably— we knew each other from the Tea Room—and told me I could certainly change laundries if I wanted to. I waited. She looked in a big book, found the names of three different laundry companies, and called one of them. The answer was no, they wouldn't take the Russian Tea Room account: they had too many accounts already. The second one gave a similar answer. The third one said yes, they would take us on, as Bess was putting some pressure on the guy over the phone. He would make a delivery to the Tea Room tonight. (We needed a laundry delivery every day.) I was amazed, and thanked Bess profusely. I returned to 57th Street feeling jubilant. But no sooner had I got in the door of the restaurant when there was a phone call for me. The new laundry couldn't come after all—they said they hadn't realized it was Friday—it didn't give them time to get ready for the weekend deliveries. Then what would we do for laundry for the weekend? I asked. They didn't know. But I knew. It meant we had to go crawling back to our old laundry, with Little Frank and his torn table linen, "pink" tablecloths that were faded almost to gray, and sky-high prices.

Nancy Vale remembers that I was concerned that 57th Street was already threatened by some "tacky" businesses opening up between us and Bendel's down the street, and that she typed a number of letters I wrote to the 57th Street Association complaining about it and saying, "We can't have that here! The character of 57th Street must be maintained!" And how the street has changed now: Planet Hollywood, the Hard Rock Café, MoTown Café, the Harley-Davidson Café, McDonald's, the Nike Store, the Disney Store, Mangia! Mangia!, Jekyll and Hyde around the corner on Sixth Avenue—it's a different world.

Trying to get a toehold in the business, I was so busy after Sidney's death I didn't seem to have time to grieve. I wondered when I was going to cry. Was it because Sidney was sick for so long and I had had time to prepare myself for his dying? Or was I just running away from my feelings? I later looked back on it and thought of it as a "wild grief" because I never seemed to sit down and collect myself. I was like an animal let off the leash in the forest, kicking up her heels at feeling free and all the time getting deeper and deeper into the woods.

Not only Nancy came to help. Alice Peerce, my sister-in-law, told me she needed something to do and would like to lend a hand. Alice was the kind of person who could tackle anything, but she and I didn't see things the same way, and she didn't know even as much as I did about the business. So, much as I needed help, we had to call it quits.

After the Christmas holidays I took off two weeks in January 1968 and went to Europe, meeting a special friend in Paris. My father offered to come up from the South and keep his eye on things, but after only a week he was wiring me to come back. There were just too many problems that came up that had to be solved right away, and the staff was restless, to say the least. He was a very smart businessman but this was a business so crazy he couldn't understand it! He couldn't get over the way it changed every day: employees left without notice, food deliveries did not arrive, customers complained, liquor disappeared, reservations were lost, coats were missing from the checkroom, fires broke out in the kitchen, meetings were canceled at the last minute, wines were tasted and sent back, recipes changed, unions fought with, lawyers called in, personnel didn't show up—it was a not a business for the faint of heart!

ELEVEN

Fires from Ashes

All my life I had enjoyed a propensity for fantasizing about relationships with men. It must have started with my father's early departure from home. I was always looking for a father, but a romanticized version, beginning with my infatuation with Charles Boyer in my early teens. Boyer became the role model for future fantasies: foreign, preferably French, older, unattainable, mysterious.

Eli fulfilled these qualities. He even looked like Charles Boyer, I thought, and had a delicious accent—was it French? Every afternoon about five in the spring and summer of 1967, Eli, whom I had known only to speak to for years, would come to the Tea Room and sit over a glass of tea, and have a meeting with someone or other to discuss one of his "projects"—I never found out exactly what they were—more likely he was talking Israeli politics, which was his passion.

I came to look forward to stopping off at the restaurant after I had left Sidney in the hospital and dropping into the bar booth beside Eli, if he was alone, and sharing my feelings with him. Sometimes I would greet him by saying, "I think I've lost it," meaning the courage to continue, and he would tease me and ask me to explain. He encouraged me not to "lose it" and would suggest I have something to eat, as, out of anxiety, I had lost my appetite, something very rare for me, and was losing weight.

I began to cling to those chance meetings as a life thread, and I was devastated when Eli didn't appear one day. It was June 6, the beginning of the Yom Kippur War, and everything else in his life stopped. Not mine. I wanted to see him anyway.

After Sidney died our tea rendezvous continued, but the fact that I was now single added a more serious note. The fantasy could not overcome the fact that I knew that he would never divorce his wife and leave his comfortable existence, so I was left with the tea dregs, which weren't enough.

Then one night in the restaurant I spotted Jean-Louis Barrault, who had been an idol of mine since his heartbreaking performance in *Les Enfants du Paradis* in 1947. He was sitting across the room, having dinner alone. His angular face, tousled mop of thick, dark hair, the intensity of his narrow eyes, his gracefulness, and his wonderful crooked smile were all there as I had seen them in the movies. I was with my friend Lyn Tornabene, who could see how excited I was to see Barrault in the flesh.

Lyn said, "If you admire him so much you should just go over and say hello!" Lyn always had a lot of moxie.

"Why?" I asked. "What's the point? He doesn't know me from Adam!"

"Oh, Faith, don't you know—he's alone, he'd be charmed to have you greet him. Just tell him you're the owner of the Russian Tea Room! He'll be enchanted," and pushed me in his direction.

Without the least bit of confidence, I did go over and introduce myself, and to my great surprise Jean-Louis said he had been watching me and wondering who I was. His voice was as deep and rich as I imagined it would be. When I told him that I had recently been widowed and had taken over the restaurant left to me by my husband, which he had advised me to sell and which I knew little about running, he seemed touched. Why did I tell him all that? It was his eyes—so sympathetic, with unseen depths of loneliness and longing. Yes, limpid, too. I think it was because he was attracted to simplicity and directness, and something about my story appealed to these qualities in him. He was not interested in "important" people, he later told me, but in artists and people who were striving to make something of their lives. Naturally I was flattered to be included in that group.

We became friends instantly, and he would sit with me in the late evenings and help me taste wines as I tried to make up my first wine list. "Keep it simple," he advised. "Just wines easy to drink at good prices." Good advice! Jean-Louis had grown up in Burgundy and had, he told me, trampled grapes in those enormous vats with his bare feet as a boy, so he knew a thing or two about wine tasting.

Jean-Louis was in New York to direct a new production of *Carmen* at the Met, and after he finished rehearsing, late in the evenings, he would often call me and we would walk over to P.J. Clark's on East 55th Street in the freezing air and have hamburgers and drinks. We called ourselves "the Two Students," as we felt we had that carefree kind of relationship usually left behind when schooldays are over. He gave me his long navy scarf with the pink stripe as part of the "Students" bond and to keep me warm in the snow.

It seemed all too soon when he left to go back to Paris over the Christmas holidays, leaving me his rehearsal copy of *Carmen* as a keepsake. But we made no plan to see each other again. I mentioned to him I would be coming to Paris in January but he expressed no interest in "the Two Students" meeting in Paris. He was a realist, I concluded, and "the Two Students" belonged to a particular time and place: New York in the fall of 1967.

When I returned late in January from my trip to Paris, Ide, Sidney's cousin and our bookkeeper, told me that Jean-Louis had been calling the RTR trying to find me, and had searched for me all over Paris, calling hotels, airports, and even the police to try to track me down. You never know about men.

Jean-Louis continued to visit the RTR over the years and we always had a glass of wine together when he came, and once he introduced me to his amazing wife, the actress Madeleine Renaud. Even in 1981 I received an affectionate letter from him from Rome, which ended, "Alas, it was impossible for me to come the last day to my dear Russian Tea Room in which for a long time now I have left a part of my heart. Will you accept my sincere and respectful love. Jean-Louis Barrault."

The third of my romantic adventures was with Aron, a visiting Israeli diplomat, here for the UN General Assembly session, which lasted from September to December. We met through mutual friends and Aron decided right away he must win my heart, mainly because I wasn't interested in him. He was not handsome, but his craggy features were attractive, and his youthful appearance and reserved but flirtatious manner were very appealing. I didn't notice all this at the time, because I was emotionally involved with Eli, my "fantasy lover," and busy having tea and sympathy with him every afternoon. Besides, Aron was married, though he told me pointedly on our first date that he and his wife in Israel had an "understanding," whatever that meant. (I have found that it usually means the husband understands what he's doing but the wife does not.)

Still, we finally did become more than friends and developed a relationship that lasted for two intense years. We traveled in Europe, drove in France and Italy in the dead of winter. Then there was the ice storm in Vichy, the time we broke up in Tours, the hotel in Santa Margarita, the lunch near the cathedral at Chartres. . . .

In Israel we traveled all over in Aron's old Peugeot and saw things I would not have seen with anyone else. In Vermont we drove to Bromley for skiing. It was a sport I had never been exposed to, growing up in the South, so Aron said he would teach me. He took me to the top of a small mountain and told me to ski down it. That was the lesson. Fortunately, I was able to do it! Aron took a leave of absence from the Israeli Foreign Office and wrote a book, his first, about his diplomatic adventures in Africa. It was published in this country and during the process, when he was away in Israel, I acted as his "agent," urging the publisher on. I hoped he would dedicate his book to me but he didn't have the courage. He wrote something in his dedication about Africans having "faith" in the future, which didn't quite fulfill my dreams.

By this time he had moved into my apartment and I was beginning to feel somewhat settled in his company. Aron was fond of Ellen and we took her with us on some of our excursions. Ellen liked him, too, and it was a healthier situation for Ellen and me, having Aron there.

And what about the telephone calls to Lusaka and Mombasa and Luandi? And what about the visit from his teenage son, who had an undiagnosed illness? I took the son to Sidney's doctor at Mount Sinai Hospital, which was awkward and painful for me—the doctor and Sidney had had such a personal relationship—but he was able to help him. I paid all the bills, but was left with the feeling I could have done more. I have often wondered where Aron's sense of entitlement came from. Was it from his proud German past or from his adopted country's fierce sense of survival? At any rate it gave me a clue about his character.

Then at Christmastime in 1969 Aron flew to Chicago to visit his brother. Expecting him back for New Year's Eve, I received instead a cable from Israel saying his wife had threatened suicide and he had to return home at once. That was it!

I suppose I knew somewhere down deep that it was a fantasy to think I would leave my life behind and take Ellen to go live in Israel. But at the time I thought we could make it work. Maybe what I really wanted was to escape from the burdens and fears I had to face: real loneliness, real grief, real responsibility. That I wasn't yet able to do.

So again I was abandoned, again I was mourning a loss, less than three years after Sidney's death. I felt tremendous anger, along with grief. And Aron's possessions—his clothes, everything—were at my apartment. As I had with Sidney's things such a short time ago, I packed up his personal effects, symbolically letting go. I dumped them at the apartment house of his wealthy American cousin, to do with them what he wanted. What did Aron think would happen to all of his American belongings? Did he care? Or did he want to leave all the trappings of his American life behind? And what about his wife? Did he stay with her? I never found out.

In that moment of low spirits and vulnerability, after the Christmas holidays of 1969, I met Jim.

I came into the RTR one snowy night in January and said hello to some of the regular bar customers, including Ethel Smith the organist and Gregory D'Alessio the cartoonist, who were sitting at the bar enjoying the free hors d'oeuvres, which they and their gang did every night (until I decided it was a losing proposition and discontinued that expensive tradition).

Gregory introduced me to a stout, short man with thinning white hair, a ruddy, round face and an egg-shaped head. He was nattily dressed in a snug-fitting tweed suit with matching vest and a yellow silk tie. He sounded English and appeared to have a quick wit. Something about him reminded me of Toad of Toad Hall.

"So you're the owner's wife?" he asked, sipping a single malt Scotch.

"No, I'm the owner," I said.

"Ah, the widow! Right!" he exclaimed, as a light went on in what he referred to as "the giant brain."

And thus began a relationship I enjoyed at first but later wished had never happened.

Jim

I suppose the struggle against loneliness is one of the most prevailing things in life, and it can cause us to make decisions we otherwise might not make and that we often live to regret.

The thing that snared me about Jim was that he seemed so familiar. Though he was half British I just felt I had known him before. Was it his sense of humor? After the Russian Jewish family I had been a part of, then the exotic Israelis and the romantic Frenchman I was involved with, Jim felt comfortable. We seemed to speak the same language and I was lulled into thinking I could be happy with him.

One thing has to be said about Jim—his bravado and, on occasion, his sense of humor were over the top.

Once, on a cold winter's night when we were late leaving for the theater and got caught in the rain and couldn't get a taxi, Jim pulled me onto a bus, and then, raising a window as high as he could, stuck his head and arms out and waved wildly as he shouted "*Taxi!*" at the top of his lungs. He found one, of course, and it followed us to the next bus stop, where we got out of the bus and hopped into the waiting cab.

Jim was famous, at least in a small circle, for his ability to pick people up and twirl them around over his head. For that reason, some people would shy away from him at a party after he'd had a few drinks! Growing up in Vermont, he became a professional wrestler as a young man, and was known on the wrestling circuit in nearby Canada as Frank Fagen, the Utica Strong Boy. It was prearranged on the tour that he would always "take the fall," i.e., lose the match to his opponent, Henri Ecraseur, the French Red Devil. But one night he decided he had had enough, and he took Henri to the mat and held him there until Henri gave the surrender sign. The Mafia owners of the wrestling team were watching the match out front and rushed back to the locker room, looking for Jim, but, fearing the worst, he had already skipped town.

Jim and I lived in my penthouse apartment in the Osborne for two years after we were married. Jim bought an apartment underneath us and we planned to break through the roof, which Sidney had secured the rights to when he co-oped the building, and join the two apartments together, as we didn't have enough living space.

Our plan had to be submitted to the Osborne board and the decision was to be announced at the next tenants' meeting. I thought it would be pretty ungrateful of them, after the work Sidney had put in on saving the building from the wrecker's ball, to deny us those rights. Leo Lerman, the president of the board, was a relative newcomer to the Osborne. He was a longtime friend of Sidney's and mine and I thought things would go favorably.

The meeting was held, appropriately, in the Byzantine lobby, which was filled to capacity with the co-op owners. Tensions were high among the tenants—those who wanted things run by the letter against those who had heart. When the attorney who represented the board, a stiff, unyielding man with rimless spectacles, announced that we had been denied access to the roof, I lost my head. It seemed to me an insult to Sidney's memory.

"Pick him up, Jim!" I whispered, and, obligingly, Jim lifted the attorney up off the marble floor and twirled him round and round over his head, to the horror of the assembled board members and tenant owners. The attorney was, understandably, speechless.

No perceptible damage was done, except that the attorney's spectacles fell off and bounced up from the marble floor into a potted fern. But this event and the accompanying bad feelings did speed our decision to leave the Osborne, and we set about looking for another apartment right away.

*   *   *

When I first met Jim in the Tea Room one night in January 1970, I was feeling depressed about my life, having just broken up with Aron. I invited him to my apartment to meet Ellen and, because I couldn't find anything else, served him caviar on some matzohs which happened to be around from the previous Easter, accompanied by the only wine I could find, which happened to be Château Margaux. In spite of that unusual offering, our acquaintanceship blossomed quickly into some sort of friendship. I needed someone to talk to about my broken heart, and when he asked me, a few days after we met, to meet him in Los Angeles, where he was doing a story about witches for the *Reader's Digest*, I accepted. I hadn't been to California since I was there with *New Faces* sixteen years before, and I wanted to get away from New York to clear my head.

When I looked for Jim at the L.A. airport I wasn't sure I'd recognize him, but when someone threw a large bouquet of flowers at me across the baggage carousel I knew it was he.

On our first date—we were saying good night in front of the RTR—I gave Jim one of those lines he never let me forget: "Please don't kiss me in front of the Russian Tea Room!"

Jim's impetuosity could sometimes be winning. One morning when we were still living in the Osborne, we were having breakfast on the terrace and saw the *QE2* steaming up the Hudson.

"What are you doing today?" asked Jim.

"Some appointments at the restaurant, nothing much. Why?"

"Why don't we sail on the *QE2*?"

That did it. In a flash Jim was on the phone to the Cunard Line and booking us for the sailing that day at three. We went down to get the tickets at the Cunard office and then packed what we could find to put in our suitcases, made our quick good-byes all around, and hurried up the gangplank. It was a great feeling just to take off without weeks of planning, to find out it could be done!

Another Challenging Day

A PLAY IN ONE ACT

The Characters: Faith, fortyish owner of the Russian Tea Room restaurant on West 57th Street, and Jim, portly husband in mid-fifties. *Characters offstage:* Greg (general manager) and Tom (assistant general manager).

The Scene: The drawing room of a rundown townhouse on New York's Upper East Side.

Time: Early evening, winter 1976.

Faith walks into drawing room, throws hat, gloves, pocketbook, and *New York Post* on cocktail table, then collapses on sofa. Jim, seated left of table in overstuffed armchair, looks up from his book and reaches over, with difficulty, for newspaper. Faith watches him as he glances at newspaper, tapping his pipe out in ashtray on table without looking at it.

Faith: We had another interesting day today on West 57th Street.

Jim: (Looking up) You look pale. What on earth happened?

Faith: (Stretches legs out in front of her and pushes off snow boots) Nothing much. A manhole cover blew off down the street near Sixth Avenue. It blew about fifty feet into the air.

Jim: (Reluctantly putting newspaper down) What blew up?

Faith: Off. Blew off and up. There was a terrific explosion.

Jim: Was anybody hurt?

Faith: Miraculously, nobody was hurt. A delivery boy on a bicycle was thrown in the air but came down on a car fender and seemed to be all right, though the bike was slightly damaged. He sat on the curb, stunned, for a few minutes and then rode off. (Goes to corner bar and fixes drink) But 57th Street was blocked off between Sixth and Seventh for over two hours.

Jim: Oh my God. (Raises empty glass from table and tries to hand it to Faith without getting up)

Faith: Mmm. It really looked like the lunch hour was wrecked, all right. (Takes Jim's glass and fixes drink) Sort of like the bomb scare. Remember the bomb scare when everybody had to be evacuated for an hour, right in the middle of lunch? (Hands drink to Jim over back of sofa and doubles over with laughter)

Jim: That's not funny. (Lifts drink in Faith's direction to acknowledge her effort)

Faith: (Recovering) Or the months of drilling and blasting? That wasn't funny, either. (Sprawls on sofa) But Greg really used his head today. After he heard the explosion—he was in the basement trying to fix the air-conditioning and didn't hear it at first—you know it's solid granite down there—he rallied right away.

Jim: You mean he went down to the scene of the accident?

Faith: Oh, no. He grabbed some lunch menus and gave them to young Ruth to run up to the corner of Seventh Avenue and 57th Street and give them out, and he sent Tracy with menus down to Sixth Avenue to do the same.

Jim: Did the menus have the extra sheet with today's specials on them?

Faith: Oh, Jim, I don't know. But Greg told the girls to tell the cops at the corners, where they had blocked off traffic—you couldn't get into our block at all—that we were open for business as usual and would they please direct people looking for the Russian Tea Room around the block to 56th Street, and they did!

Jim: Fifty-sixth Street? But we have no entrance on 56th Street!

Faith: Of course we do, my dearest. The delivery entrance.

Jim: (Head in hands) Greg has got to be out of his mind! It's a madhouse back there—men cutting up meat all over the place, all those knives flashing—Good lord! And why give out menus? Why were Ruth and Tracy giving out menus on the corners?

Faith: I didn't quite get that, either. I think it was part of Greg's plan to get people to know we were open and that they could get in in spite of the manhole thing and nobody being allowed to walk on 57th Street between Sixth and Seventh. He brought all the lunch customers in through the kitchen.

Jim: The kitchen! When was all this happening? What time was it?

Faith: Eleven-thirty to one-thirty.

Jim: The kitchen must've looked a mess! All the prep all over the floor—people sliding on shashlik fat—

Faith: Greg said the kitchen looked wonde
whistle. The customers all marveled at it and sa
through the kitchen, that they'd always wanted
would let them come in that way from now on.

Jim: I know I'm a worrier, but please just tell
staff was doing all this time. How could they get any
of Manhattan traipsing through the workplace?

Faith: Don't ask me. Greg arranged it. I think he
and the line cooks something extra to stand aside but l
it was he promised.

Jim: You'd better find out. It was probably a fortun
away. I bet the manhole blowup was one of those Con E
am I right?

Faith: Mmm. Right. Another gas leak. Oh, and Greg p
too, saying we were open, though I don't honestly know
could read the signs if they weren't allowed to pass the R
Room. Do you? Greg said everybody in the whole neighborh
about the explosion. I mean they heard it, of course. The
tremendous noise. The regular customers came right over, as if t
was a gong on an ocean liner, announcing the first seating for
They were even early. I guess nothing frightens them. Greg sai
funny way the explosion was good for business.

Jim: They're inured to fright. Those poor people have been comii
the RTR through blasting, drilling—they've walked under scaffold
for six years—they're ready for anything!

Faith: They certainly seem impassive to untoward events. Gosl
when I think back on it, it was downtown Beirut! But Greg saw i
through. He said one woman came with her car and chauffeur and
told Greg the chauffeur would be looking for her on 56th Street and
could she go back out through the kitchen after her lunch? He was very
gallant about it and personally escorted her out himself. It was that
Russian lady who always comes by herself and has the Cotelettes
Pojarsky.

Jim: I can't believe it. Greg was very cheerful when I spoke to him,
and he didn't even mention the manhole incident.

Faith: Amazing. But it certainly happened, believe me. Greg said tiny

6th Street looked like Times Square on New Year's Eve. And then
e-thirty—whoof!—everything was OK, back to normal.

m: So all the one-thirty reservations got in through the main
nce on 57th Street?

aith: Yep, by then it was all over. Greg was really relieved not to miss
late lunchers. That was just lucky. Well, Greg did a great job!

im: What else happened today?

Faith: Oh, you mean the fire over in the cabinetmaker's shop at 802
nth Avenue? Or haven't you heard about that?

SCENE II

The next day, early evening. Faith enters in full snow regalia—parka,
long scarf, snow pants, after-ski boots, fur gloves. Takes all this off as
she sips tea from a mug, revealing white tennis sweater, white shirt,
white tennis warm-up pants, white socks.

Faith: Great game.

Jim: A real competitor?

Faith: No, she could hardly lift her racket. But I won!

Jim: While you were having fun on the court there was a little trouble
at the restaurant. I tried to call you at the club but they said you were on
the courts and couldn't be disturbed.

Faith: We take our tennis pretty seriously. What happened? (Sits)

Jim: The sprinkler system went off just as we were about to open for
lunch.

Faith: What happened?

Jim: You already asked that. The ceiling above the dining room filled
up with water and started caving in, pouring water on the customers
who were seated in the center of the dining room. Young Ruth and Bartender Paul rushed to the walls and started pulling the paintings down as
the water gushed through the ceiling. It soaked everything in the dining
room eventually, and, of course, a lot of people, too.

Faith: But what about the paintings? Were they damaged?

Jim: Evidently not. Two busboys, Ricky and Francesco, helped carry
the paintings upstairs—and Rosa helped and even some of the kitchen
people came out. George Jenkins was in charge.

Faith: George Jenkins! Oh no! He couldn't fight his way out of a paper bag!

Jim: You're talking about our second in command.

Faith: (Looking at Jim in disbelief) But where was Greg? Wasn't he there? Oh, I forgot, it's his birthday!

Jim: But Greg did come in, anyway. He had to leave his own birthday party. And Tom came in, too. It took Tom two hours to get from his house on Long Island to the Tea Room, because of all the ice on the raiload tracks.

Faith: And after the fire yesterday at 802 Ninth Avenue. Poor Tom. He had just finished dealing with the bus collision over there on Tuesday.

Jim: You mean when the bus ran into the building?

Faith: Yes! Tom said the bus was so far into the building that it was literally holding the building up, and when they pulled the bus out they had to shore up the whole edifice. Tom said the building would never be the same. It sort of caved in, bit by bit.

Anyway, poor Tom. His grandmother died yesterday in the middle of a birthday party for Christie, his six-year-old daughter—he had a magician there and everything—and he was on the phone all during the party, trying to call the insurers about our building and trying to call his family to make the funeral arrangements for his grandmother at the same time. So then the ceiling at the RTR caved in and he had to come back to the city! What else could happen to him? And I thought the Long Island Railroad was on strike.

Jim: I guess it is, but the subway's running. Tom had to walk two miles to the station. And Tom said the train stopped for one whole hour in the tunnel. Can you believe that?

Faith: Tom has done a wonderful job. He got there anyway.

Jim: The same firemen who came when the ceiling collapsed today were at the fire yesterday at 802. They acted like old friends to the staff, and teased them when they left that they'd be back tomorrow in time for lunch. Everybody was in stitches.

Faith: Very funny.

Jim: At least they didn't use their axes this time. Oh, one of the fireman said you'd offered him a free dinner the last time he was there at the Tea Room a few months ago, when the sprinklers went off in the kitchen.

Faith: A what?

Jim: A freebee. He said you'd offered him dinner with his family.

Faith: He must be out of his mind! I never—

Jim: Well, he said maybe it could have been a while ago. Anne Messavage was still there.

Faith: Ten years, then, at least.

Jim: Oh, by the way, your old friend Bill Littler was sitting there in a bar booth waiting for his lunch date to appear when the sprinklers went off.

Faith: Was his date a pretty young girl?

Jim: Of course. She had just arrived when the water started gushing down from the ceiling. Bill rose with great dignity from his seat, turned to his date, and said, "I'm so sorry about the inundation," and walked calmly to the checkroom to get his umbrella. Bill always carries an umbrella. It's really a cane, I think. The girl was already soaking wet and seemed to want to leave, so Bill gallantly took her arm and led her out.

Faith: Bill is really a sensitive guy, don't you think? But what happened to Tom?

Jim: It took Tom over two hours to get home again. He said he'd be a little late tomorrow. He had to go by the funeral parlor first, about his grandmother's funeral, and then to the insurance adjusters for the Tea Room.

Faith: Well, what else can happen?

Jim: The Super Bowl starts at six. So there won't be any business tonight at the RTR.

Faith: Yes, I know. I guess we'll just have to stay home and watch the game. (Phone rings) Hello? (Listens. Then to Jim) It's Greg! He says if we're looking for him he'll be at the precinct. One of the cooks stabbed a waiter in the arm and he has to take him in. Then he's going to take the waiter to the Roosevelt Hospital Emergency Room. (Into phone) OK. Good luck!

Jim: Let's turn the phone off before anything else happens. I feel like an early night!

FINIS

Things soured early in my marriage to Jim, but I needed a partner. I couldn't bear the loneliness of running the restaurant by myself any longer, and Jim was willing to help me. For a while it worked, and we shared a number of interests beside the business, too, but by 1987 I had had more than enough of the downside of our relationship, of trying to make a hopeless situation better, and had to find a way out. I knew this would not be easy to do, knowing Jim's penchant for litigating and going for the jugular. I was certain that when his pride was hurt and he was faced with the potential loss of a standard of living he had become accustomed to, Jim would fight like a tiger, and I was right.

We had been living in a townhouse on East 74th Street since 1976, and I hoped Jim would leave so we could sell it, but he refused. I wanted to settle the divorce without rancor if possible, so I hired a lawyer who would purposefully not antagonize Jim. In fact, she was not even a divorce lawyer (mistake number one). After months of fruitless efforts to deal with one or another of Jim's lawyers—he went through a total of six before we reached a settlement—she recommended that I lock Jim out of the restaurant and the house with a court order, to force him into action (mistake number two). The appointed day arrived and step number one began: the restaurant part went fine, and Jim retreated, never to come back to his office at the RTR. Then I went home for the other lockout to find a bodyguard there to serve Jim with papers when he tried to return to the house, which he did in the early evening. He was sent away, furious, with the papers in his hand.

I breathed a tremendous sigh of relief. All the months of tension fell away. I was alone in the house at last! Elena, our housekeeper, had prepared dinner for me, and I sat in the dining room by candlelight, looking out at the snow in the garden, and enjoyed a glass of wine.

Suddenly there were sounds at the door and then the bodyguard burst into the dining room.

"Your husband is back, and he has signed judge's papers to let him back in the house!" I was dumbfounded. How was this possible? I had been assured that he would be out for the night and that tomorrow he would want to negotiate a settlement. And here he was! And it was all legal. My lawyer didn't have a leg to stand on when she had Jim locked out of the house, and Jim, with his usual bulldog persistence, had located "Turn-'em-loose Bruce," the judge infamous for releasing prisoners at the drop of a hat, and got him to sign papers stating his right to return to his own domicile, all of which took less than an hour. My idyll abruptly ended.

We both stayed on in the house, leading separate lives, for seven months. Then, since Jim refused to leave, I waited until he went away to London during the Christmas holidays, and left myself, on the first of January 1988. I took Teddy and Gypsy, my two Norfolk terriers, and some personal possessions to the Hotel Carlyle, where I planned to live until I could find an apartment.

The day after I moved out, Jim was due back from London. I went to the RTR to work and on my way took the dogs back to our house to stay with Elena, thinking Jim would be glad to have them around when he returned. But Jim was furious when he came back to discover I had left, and called me at the RTR to say he was kidnapping the dogs!

I was in a meeting in the conference room when Elena called in tears to verify the news, and I left the meeting and ran back to my office to call my new divorce lawyer, Bob Cohen.

"Don't worry, I'll get Teddy and Gypsy back," he said, "but I'll have to get a court order and it may take a couple of days."

A couple of days! I was desperate. My animals were my main comfort now and I would be bereft without them, as Jim knew.

I hurried back to the Carlyle to see what I could do to retrieve them. I was supposed to go to a dinner Mayor Koch was giving at Gracie Mansion for a group of friends that evening, and I had invited Robert Osborne, a friend of mine, a columnist for the *Hollywood Reporter,* and presently also the host of Turner Classic Movies. As I came into the apartment at the Carlyle, the phone rang and it was Jim.

"I'll give Teddy and Gypsy back to you if you'll agree to meet with me about the divorce," he said. I couldn't believe it. Was that all I had to do to get them back?

"Of course I will," I said. "But send them back now."

"Ask Elena to come and pick them up. I want to meet with you because it's silly our paying these lawyers all this money when we can perfectly well resolve our differences ourselves."

The voice of reason! I, too, wanted to believe we could outsmart the system and achieve an amicable divorce. The process was painful and costly and the idea of a mean divorce was anathema to me.

Jim and I arranged to meet at our house the next day. I told Bob Cohen about it and he said, "Don't get your hopes up, Faith. You know how tricky Jim is. I'm sure there's a catch in it somewhere."

I arrived at five o'clock, as planned, and came in through the downstairs entrance, as always. Elena, who was already at the stove preparing Jim's dinner, told me "el Señor" was upstairs in the drawing room. I thought that was odd, as we usually sat in the small library/sitting room in the front of the house. The drawing room was enormous and we only used it for entertaining, so it was cold in the winter, and anyhow we never succeeded in making it into a comfortable room. At one point, in desperation, we commissioned a Yugoslav painter named Lali to paint a large mural for the room, which turned out to be strangely reminiscent of Matisse's *The Dance,* and he made a carpet and some decorative screens that he placed around the room as dividers. The carpet was the only thing that worked—the rest of it had to go. The room remained in flux.

As I came into the room I saw that Jim had a blazing fire going in the fireplace, and was sitting, one stout leg tucked under the other, smoking one of his Habana Puros. He greeted me as if I were a supplicant come to throw myself at his feet. I was extremely uncomfortable, but I wanted to keep my word and hear him out. Here I was in my own living room, where a few nights before I had entertained friends on my last evening in the house, and now I was received here like a stranger by someone with whom I had once shared the house and my life.

Not surprisingly, the meeting did not go well. Jim's demands for a settlement were way out of the ballpark, and though he tried to wrap his wolfish demands in sheep's clothing, it was a just a lot of hype and came to nothing. I went back to the Carlyle sadder and wiser.

Elena, Patricia, and Iris had all worked for us in the house, and Elena stayed on to cook for Jim. Patricia stayed to clean house. Iris soon left to work for Leonard Bernstein to take care of Ponchita the parrot, but while they were still in the house they ran a kind of underground railway to me at the Carlyle, bringing me things I had left behind, which Jim wouldn't let me back in to retrieve. They also brought me all the gossip about Jim and his paramours, especially a story about a fur coat he had given one of the girlfriends and then, when she rejected him, went down to Washington and took back! The funniest part was that the woman called Bob Cohen to represent her in getting the coat returned, and he had to tell her he represented me!

The weather was severe that January, with lots of ice and snow, and the day after my meeting with Jim a tremendous explosion rocked the neighborhood. It was the sound of a huge water main bursting on 72nd Street between Madison and Park, flooding the basements of most of the buildings in a two-block radius, causing electrical shortages, blackouts, and the disruption of utilities. Many people had to move out of their apartments or houses and go to friends or to hotels. Many of the residents lost antique furniture and whole wardrobes of clothing stored in their basements—it was a mess. It took Con Ed three days to stop the gushing water and another month to repair the main. When I heard about it at the Carlyle, I ran over to our house on 74th Street to see if the basement wine cellar, where I stored and aged wines for our reserve wine list at the restaurant, was still intact. I still had my house key and I opened the gate and ran through the kitchen and down the stairs to the basement. Inside the cellar the wine cases that had been on the floor were floating around the room. I picked them up and stored them above the water line, took the bottles in the lower bins, now under water, and put them on higher shelves. None of the wines was damaged. (Unlike the time I bought several cases of Romanée Conté, one of the world's most expensive and rarest wines, from one of our wine dealers, only to find it all undrinkable. It turned out to have been shipped from France via the Caribbean, where it sat and baked on the dock in the tropical sun for over a week, waiting to be transferred. Fortunately, the dealer was honorable and took it back.)

Jim meanwhile sat upstairs in the library with his Habana Puro, oblivious to it all.

The divorce proceedings went on for three years, until 1991, at which time we agreed to a courthouse-steps settlement, which stated that I would agree to give Jim half of what I possessed, including the house on 74th Street, the restaurant, and its assets. The year 2000 will finally bring an end to those payments. Yes, freedom is expensive, but it's still worth every penny!

THIRTEEN

Caviar and Vodka and Other Epicurean Delights

Rules for Eating Caviar: It always tastes better when you are in black tie, after dark, by candlelight, after making love, when someone else is paying for it, when you don't know how much it costs.

It also tastes great outside a ski lodge at a winter picnic in the snow, a vodka bottle stuck in a snowbank, to keep it chilled.

It's also not bad in the tropics when you're lounging in the shade beside a pool overlooking a coral beach, the open tin of beluga surrounded with crushed ice and immersed in a silver bowl.

Or, for that matter, on New Year's Day morning, taking a look in the refrigerator, finding some leftover caviar, and spooning it up with a plastic party spoon, along with a glass of bubbly overlooked at the end of the party the night before.

And then, too, it could really be appreciated at a restaurant where the waiter understands the ritual of serving blini: first laying a thin buckwheat pancake on the plate, pouring hot melted butter over it, spreading a spoonful of caviar and a dollop of sour cream on top of that, and rolling it into a fat little package to be cut into with a fork.

And here's where your imagination can go to work, deciding on a vodka to accompany the blini. Maybe a flinty Zubrovka, with the reed of buffalo grass inside the bottle giving it a pungent taste, or a fiery, amber-colored Ohotnik, "the Hunter," with the flavor of honey. Whichever you choose would be served in a special RTR shot glass shaped like a miniature carafe, plunged into crushed ice in a silver container.

Many people thought of the RTR and caviar in the same breath—beluga, osetra, or sevruga, depending on taste and the pocketbook, or red caviar (salmon roe), each of them served in the classic way with toast points, chopped egg, and chopped onion, or in blini or in an omelette.

I'm not sure I should consider it a compliment, but often when I met people I knew in the street, I had the strange sensation they were looking at me as if I were a big, delicious mound of blini, the power of suggestion being so strong. Usually they would turn up at the restaurant the next day, not consciously connecting our encounter the day before with their sudden need for a caviar fix.

Lyn Tornabene used to bring into the Tea Room the handsomest, most celebrated men, week after week—well, it was her job. As entertainment editor for *Cosmopolitan* magazine she wrote a column called "Lunch Date," and I could hardly wait to see which gorgeous hunk she would bring in next. Lyn had crushes on all of them, and probably would have run away with a few of them had she not been already spoken for.

Lyn and Judy Krantz, who was associate fashion editor at *Good Housekeeping*, were two of the Young Turks of the women's magazine world—talented, attractive, and full of beans—and they were friends. The main difference between them, Lyn says, was that Judy had a real crocodile handbag and she had a knockoff from the thrift shop. Judy went on to become one of the most successful novelists around, and Lyn moved to Tucson with her family to get away from it all.

Lyn used to say she and Judy came into the Tea Room because the experience expressed their dreams. It was their idea of being in Paris or *Casablanca* (as in the movie, not the real place). "The RTR gave us the imprimatur of success," Lyn said. "We believed we had made it because we were there."

Lyn said that every man she brought into the Tea Room to be interviewed thought she was on the make just because they were meeting there. One of Lyn's interview lunches was with Richard Burton, whom she introduced to blini and caviar. He was so enthusiastic about it Lyn wasn't sure if Burton would get through the rest of the meal.

"It's an aphrodisiac!" Burton exclaimed. "It's the most erotic thing I've ever tasted!" Lyn had to fight him off through the rest of lunch, a task she didn't appear to mind, and certainly most women would die for.

Postscript about caviar: Obviously what the comedienne Patsy Kelly thought about caviar isn't shared by many. But to her it tasted like "ball bearings immersed in fuel oil."

Postpostscript: The Russian Tea Room served 2,647 pounds of caviar in an average year and 5,884 liter bottles of vodka. Also 8,000 pounds of beets, 15,867 pounds of sour cream, and 43,860 pounds of lamb.

FOURTEEN

Ellen—Heartbreak and After

It seems to me we spend half our lives trying to overcome the injustices done to us by our parents and the other half trying to overcome the injustices we have done to our children.

Writing about my relationship with my daughter is one of the hardest things for me to do, because it forces me to face some hard truths about myself and, even more difficult, to share them. The fact that the story has a happy ending may make it easier but does not remove the sting of telling it.

The night Ellen was born, New Year's Eve 1959, was one of the happiest nights of my life. It had been a difficult birth but now Ellen and I were alone together and I was nursing her in my arms. Outside I could hear the noises of New Year's Eve celebrations, but inside we were quiet and peaceful. I felt an outpouring of love and contentment and wished that Ellen and I could always stay together this way, far from the struggles of the world. It seemed that nothing could ever separate us, but fate had other plans.

* * *

In New Rochelle that New Year's Eve my sister-in-law, Alice, was preparing for her own New Year's Eve party when she learned that Ellen had arrived. She dropped everything and put on her coat.

"I'm going to New York to see Sidney's baby," she told her husband, Jan.

"Alice, you can't go!" said Jan. "Our guests will be arriving any minute!" Jan was used to having his way. "What'll I do?"

"You're a great tenor! Sing something!" said Alice. "I'll be back—but I'm going to see that baby!"

By the time Sidney died I was emotionally drained and physically exhausted, and not in good condition to give Ellen, now seven, the kind of love and attention she needed. She began to withdraw and wouldn't talk about her father's death, and I didn't know how to reach her, so I sought help for her in therapy. But the comfort we might have derived from each other was only sometimes there, and I blame myself for that.

Two and a half years later I was still struggling to continue with the restaurant and trying to find some love and security with Aron when he suddenly deserted me, and Ellen, too. I went into a tailspin, which brought back the abandonment I felt when Sidney died.

Along came James Stewart-Gordon, full of good humor and a happy-go-lucky attitude toward life, or so I thought. I had never been around a man who treated life as a lark the way Jim did. He had a talent for enjoying life, especially in the form of good food and drink, and his hedonism fit right into the vacuum left by losses I hadn't yet dealt with. I didn't want to grieve, I wanted to get away from pain. I had had enough of sickness, death, and abandonment, and wanted to kick up my heels, fly away, and "have fun." That's exactly what I tried to do, and in the process, left Ellen behind. I didn't mean to abandon Ellen emotionally but I put my own needs ahead of hers and paid heavily for it. Ellen suffered the most.

I rushed into marriage with Jim six months after we met, when Jim said "now or never," because, though I had grave reservations, I thought, "What do I have to lose? If it doesn't work out we'll get a divorce! Meanwhile I'll have companionship and Ellen will have a dad." It was an act of desperation, but I talked myself into thinking it would work. I was so tired! But it was not a good solution, as my friends, and even some of Jim's friends at the *Reader's Digest,* tried to warn me in advance. Jim turned out to be a disastrous stepfather, just as he had been a dismal father to his five children, if only I had taken the trouble to investigate.

I was fond of the three children of Jim's whom I knew, and felt especially close to Belle and Christina. Belle worked at the RTR a while and learned to do the same kind of thankless but important work Ellen often did when she was there, like receiving deliveries in the winter in the ice-cold steward's office in the back of our building (the former stable) where the door was constantly being opened and shut. I was happy for Belle when she found happiness for a number of years with the man she lived with. She didn't have an easy life, and it ended much too soon. She died of cancer at age forty-eight.

I never cease to be amazed at and I sometimes despair at women's dependence on men. Some of the most enlightened women subject themselves to the worst treatment from men, all because they are afraid to face life alone. Their self-esteem is so low that they really believe they are nothing without a man. It is sad, to me, that I would get involved with someone like Jim whom I really never loved, though because of my deep need for love I thought I did, and could not extricate myself for so many years. Of course there are always reasons, and they usually have to do with emotional dependence. Economics doesn't always explain it: in my case I was supporting the family but I was also the one afraid to leave!

Jim bullied Ellen and I stood by, not coming to her rescue. He pushed her out of our lives, and I pretended it wasn't happening. I wanted to reach out to her but was too intimidated to do it. And I was too proud and too frightened to admit I had made a terrible mistake.

We continued living in my apartment in the Osborne, and not long after we were married Jim bought the apartment below mine. When the building management refused to let us break through to create a duplex, Jim moved Ellen downstairs with our housekeeper, Eugenia, physically cutting Ellen off from us. I felt terrible about it but didn't know how to stop it. I knew we needed more room but didn't have the guts to say, "Let's move!"

Meanwhile the spirit of the 1960s overflowed into the early '70s, bringing with it the war in Vietnam and continuing upheaval in every area of our lives.

In the restaurant we were grappling with lesser upheavals, like the question of the dress code, which used to be a pretty cut-and-dried situation. If a man didn't wear a jacket, we would supply one, and even a tie. We kept blue blazers in small, medium, and large, in the checkroom, and Nadia, our Russian waitress who formerly worked for Balmain, sewed red RTR letters on the front of the jackets and the bottoms of the ties. We didn't realize this would make them such appealing collectors' items until they all disappeared.

But now, suddenly, grown men were dressing up in blue jeans suits and T-shirts and hanging gold chains around their necks. Classic examples were the Segal brothers, George and Fred. George, the actor, formerly had dressed in jeans, but now as a movie star he dressed more conservatively in jacket and tie. Fred, the older brother, who had formerly dressed in the buttoned-down uniform of Madison Avenue, where he was a big-time ad man, now came into the Tea Room in jeans and chains, exposing the hair on his chest. Women dressed in pantsuits were never a problem at the RTR, but they were at the classic French restaurants, the most famous incident being Jackie O.'s landmark rejection from La Côte Basque. But how were we to maintain any kind of dress standards for men? The social upheaval eventually broke down the dress code and it didn't matter *what* men wore anymore.

Teenagers were following adults in "letting it all hang out," and Ellen, now fourteen, was no exception. Members of her class at Chapin, a private girls' school in Manhattan, "streaked," i.e., ran naked, through Lord & Taylor and other department stores. Drugs were prevalent everywhere, as was the practice of dropping out of school and running away from home, and sometimes violence with guns and bombs became part of the scene, as the Weathermen showed us. Communes flourished, pads where kids lived together in communities like Haight-Ashbury in San Francisco and where they hid out and drugged out. The Patty Hearst saga brought the results home to all of us. The Charles Manson murders were the most violent of all.

Our family situation at that time created the perfect setup for disaster to strike, and it did. The outside rebellious environment and the onset of

Ellen's puberty exacerbated the problems she and I were already having. Jim's attitude toward her made it intolerable and, cut off from us part of the time in the separate apartment, it was inevitable that she would run away.

Ellen was gone for four months, and we had no word from her during that time. It's hard for me to know how I went on, without communication from her, for so long. I came to realize the police can do so little, private detectives even less, if they have no clues. It's a big country, and the trail was cold. Only my anger kept me going, I think. If I had given in to my anxiety and guilt, I would have folded. At the same time I admired Ellen for getting out of a situation that was so destructive, even though she did it out of desperation, and I wished I could find a way to follow in her footsteps.

Ellen did come back; she recovered from her experiences on the road and did a complete turnaround, which is something Ellen seems to do with ease, to the constant amazement of the people around her. This comes, I think, from the time when she was still in the womb, about to be born: she turned upside down and sat on her umbilical cord, cutting off her air supply. Then, just as the doctor was marking a big X on my stomach and preparing to perform a cesarean to bring her out, Ellen flipped right side up and came out headfirst! I have always felt this is a character trait of Ellen's: she may go off the track sometimes but she always comes out right in the end!

Ellen went off to Wykham Rise, a private girls' school in Washington, Connecticut, and then on to Sarah Lawrence College, where she graduated in writing and theater. She spent time in summer stock, and then settled into Manhattan life, where she fell in love with singing and wanted to perform in clubs, so when she turned thirty she took a cabaret workshop and decided to go for a singing career. It was now or never, she said.

Back when Ellen was three years old, her teacher at play school asked the children to tell the class what they wanted to be when they grew up, and Ellen stood up and said, "I wanted to be a ballerina but I think they need me at the restaurant!" Ellen was now, at thirty, going back to the ballerina side of her personality.

At the same time, she took jobs managing restaurants, and worked for a while at the RTR, learning how it operated from the back and front of the house. It was, I think, good experience, but a strain on both Ellen and me, and it was better for us both when Ellen moved on to take a chef's course at the French Culinary Institute as part of her professional education, and then went back to managing restaurants, hoping someday to realize her dream of opening her own place.

Meanwhile she took time out to marry Kim Tsang, a lighting engineer, and produced a son, Ian Sydney, born February 2, 1993. Ian goes to the Little Red Schoolhouse, where Ellen went to school through the sixth grade.

Ellen grew up thinking she would inherit the RTR, and was devastated when I told her I was planning to sell, though I talked to her about the possibility for a long time, trying to prepare her. But I knew the toughest part was the emotional tie, the identification with her dad, and the final realization with the loss of the restaurant that the loss of Sidney was final. This was the toughest part for me, too, but I knew it was the right decision, and I hoped that she would someday see that it was. I think she does understand now, and, oddly enough, as she says, we have become closer since the RTR was sold.

Ellen, I believe, has inherited the best of both Sidney and me. I am proud of her and I think she knows it. Her dream of opening her own restaurant is closer to becoming a reality. I watch her love for her son, Ian, her talent as a mother, her focus on him above all else, and though my heart breaks all over again for the little girl I failed in many ways, I still have another chance to be the best friend to Ellen I know how to be, and a loving grandmother to Ian. I'm lucky, because you don't always get a second chance.

FIFTEEN

The Art Collection

Changing the old ballet murals for paintings we picked out ourselves was an exciting new phase in the life of the RTR. It transformed the dining room, making it dance with color and energy.

The first picture I bought for the restaurant was in keeping with its history and old Russian traditions, but to me it seemed amazingly new because I had the courage to buy it.

A couple brought it into the Tea Room one wintry morning and offered it for sale: *Russian Hamlet in Winter* by Constantin Westchiloff— a scene of a small onion-domed church by a river, with the late winter sun casting a golden light on the snow. I thought it was beautiful, bought it from the couple, and immediately hung it over the cashier's booth up front, where we were standing when the couple showed it to me.

The second painting I bought was at a Sotheby's auction, an exciting but humbling initiation into the auction world. It was a still life, *Les Poires,* by Eva González, the mistress of Manet. I was attracted to it because she was a courageous woman painter (you had to be courageous 150 years ago if you were a woman and wanted to paint, not to mention the competition for attention to her work, living with an artist like Manet) and because the style of the painting reminded me of a still life my grandmother Lilla Bell Burwell had painted in her youth, which hung in our house in Spartanburg and which I had always loved.

In my excitement at bidding at my first auction, I was afraid I wouldn't raise my hand in time. But instead the opposite happened, and I bid twice in a row! In a daze I heard the auctioneer say, "Madam, you're bidding against yourself!" and the whole audience broke up. I was too excited to be embarrassed—I just wanted to know if I had bought the painting, and when the hammer went down and the auctioneer announced with a smile in his voice, "To the lady in the third row, then!" I was thrilled. I quickly left the auction room and went around to the cashier's booth to pay for it, then headed for the packing room to pick it up and take it to the RTR. I couldn't wait to get *Les Poires* up on the wall where we could all look at it.

The third picture I bought from Sotheby's, too. It was what I would now call a space filler, a large canvas with lots of colors but little meaning. After the sale I went around back and picked up the painting but, when I came out of the building, I hit high winds on Madison Avenue and went sailing, all but hoisted aloft, as I held on desperately to the five-foot-square canvas. Sotheby's was then at 76th Street and Madison Avenue, across from the Hotel Carlyle, and I was trying to bring the picture down to our house on 74th Street. It was an impulsive thing to do—I was excited about my purchase and wanted to get it home fast so I could look at it—but I almost didn't make it. The wind tossed the canvas around like a kite, catapulting me with it, and since I couldn't see around the sides, I didn't know that I was threatening the well-being of pedestrians as I zigzagged down the avenue, my quarry out of control, praying I would be able to round the corner on 74th Street and get out of the wind.

When I think about that picture today, I find it hard to understand how I admired it so much. It was an abstract painting, all red with streaks of white and yellow running diagonally across it, and because I knew nothing about abstract art I thought I was doing a daring thing to buy it. And so I was! Did I like it? Well, yes. My reasoning was that I wanted to change the dowdy ballet murals on the walls of the Tea Room to something more contemporary and vital. And I loved the vivid red—very Russian—of the background. And it was big! It would cover a lot of space. Did I think it was good? I don't think it mattered to me.

Actually it was not a painting of much quality, but I didn't see that at the time. Who's to say if my painting was "awful"? I can say only that my taste in paintings has changed. I had a pretty good eye and I was a fairly quick study, but there's no way to learn without having the courage to buy what you like, make mistakes, and then move on. Experience. Buying that picture was the beginning of an ongoing education.

I looked on all our pictures as my children—some more favored than others, some troublesome and disappointing, some that surprised me as they grew in winsomeness with time—but all my very own treasures for as long as they were in my care. Each had its own story and each found its rightful place on the walls of the Tea Room. I hated to part with a single one of them.

In freshening up the RTR I had a number of restaurant models spinning in my head: I wanted it to have the cozy but elegant look of the dining room at the Chambord, the bar at the original La Côte Basque, the downstairs at the "21" Club in New York, the showbiz look of Chasen's in Los Angeles, and the antique charisma of Le Grand Vefour in the Palais Royale in Paris. Ambitious dreams! And where to begin? With those dreary ballet murals, of course.

We decided to have the murals cleaned first and see if they looked any brighter afterward. Jim, a self-proclaimed restorer of paintings, thought we should clean them ourselves. (He once bought a picture called *Lot and His Daughters,* which he was convinced was an undiscovered Rubens, and he worked on it assiduously, thinking his "restoration" would uncover its authenticity.)

Accompanied by Lyro DeFanti, our cabinetmaker, we put masks over our noses and mouths, climbed up on the banquettes, and started to work with cotton balls and turpentine, to clean years of accumulated dirt away. But the fumes from the turpentine soon stopped us dead in our tracks, and we had to abandon our project and turn it over to professional restorers. Even after they were cleaned, however, the murals still looked dreary, so we decided to take them down, one at a time, and try to find paintings to fit into each section of the wall as it was left bare.

While we were busy collecting paintings, Lyro was doing magical woodworking in the restaurant dining room. Lyro came to us through Cruz, our housekeeper, whom he had met in Central Park while she was taking care of Ellen and our Yorkies, Timmy and Tootsie. Cruz came to us through Felicia Bernstein, wife of Leonard, who served as the Osborne's unofficial employment center for domestics hailing from Chile, her native land. Felicia told me she would translate for me if I got into trouble with Cruz, who spoke no English. But I decided to go to Berlitz and study Spanish, in case Felicia was unavailable.

Lyro worked for "Mr. Boris," making furniture at "the factory"— that's all I knew. I always assumed he was happy there, loved "Mr. Boris," and would never leave. But one day I got it into my head to ask him if he would come and work for us, and it seems that that was what he was waiting for all along! He set about trimming all the booths and banquettes, the checkroom, and the cashier's booth in mahogany, and built a beautiful mahogany bar, making it shorter than the old one, so that we could fit in two bar booths in front on that side of the dining room. He built a wine room, too, and always had projects, more than he could keep up with. We lost an artist when he died of a heart attack, still young. He and Cruz had a daughter, Lucy, who became a neurosurgeon and now has a baby of her own.

We had at that time problems with a nightclub called Miss Lacey's, which was located inside the Carnegie Hall building. It had a blue neon sign in front of its entrance. How it got there I never found out, but we did discover that Miss Lacey ran a nightclub in Harlem, and maybe more than a nightclub, in fact—perhaps a "house of ill repute."

The situation was getting out of hand in the restaurant, with flashily dressed young women from Miss Lacey's coming in to sit at the bar for the evening cocktail hour, attracting men who looked as if they would have been happier in a bar on Ninth Avenue.

Then one day help came unexpectedly. I was in Brooklyn for lunch and decided to walk across the Brooklyn Bridge to Manhattan. As I came off the bridge, there was City Hall directly in front of me, and on the steps stood Tom Morgan, an old friend who was Mayor John Lindsay's assistant. I went up to Tom and told him about the Miss Lacey's problem, and before you could say "red light district," the place was gone. It was closed down, it disappeared, finis!

In the same year, 1970, Sherrye Henry invited me to be on her television show to discuss a current innovation—women were being allowed for the first time by some restaurant and bar owners to sit alone or with other women at bars. Members of the women's movement were going around to some of the better-known restaurants in Manhattan, "opening up" bars to women. Sherrye asked me on the air if I allowed women to sit at the RTR bar and I said no. I was thinking of the trouble we had had with the women from Miss Lacey's and wondering what would happen if we changed our policy. But Sherrye shamed me into admitting that I was not very enlightened in my views, and asked me to consider "opening" the bar to women. I agreed to do so. The next thing I knew, a group of women showed up at the Tea Room and asked me to declare the bar "liberated." Of course I did it at once, television cameras rolled for the occasion, and nothing ever happened afterward to make me regret my decision. On the contrary, I regretted it had taken me so long to act. I realize now that I sometimes adopted the old-fashioned, chauvinistic views of many of my male colleagues and mentors, without even realizing it. This consciousness-raising experience made an impact on me, and I started examining my decisions more carefully.

It gave me pleasure that Betty Friedan, the founder of the feminist movement and a friend of mine, was one of the first woman to take advantage of the new bar liberation at the RTR. She often sat at the corner of the bar when she was waiting to join someone for dinner at the RTR. It was great to look over and see her there, as though she were guarding an important stronghold.

One spring morning an elderly man came in carrying a large painting wrapped in a gunnysack and asked to see me. I came down from the office and he introduced himself as Otto Rothenburgh, a Russian artist who lived in New Jersey. He told me he had ridden in on the bus with the picture because he had heard my commercials on the radio and thought I would be interested in seeing his painting, entitled *The Russian Tea Room*. He added that today was his eighty-seventh birthday and that he had gotten married the night before. It was almost too much to take in from this perfect stranger who had arrived on our doorstep with such a wonderful story, carrying this picture in a gunnysack.

The painting was a scene in the Russian Tea Room in 1937 and included portrayals of some well-known New Yorkers of the time— Otto Kahn, the financier, Gertrude Vanderbilt Whitney, the artist, and

Heywood Broun, the theater critic. It was delightful! It was Art Deco in style, and yet whimsical, with a folk art feel to it. I fell in love with it and bought it on the spot. Then we invited Mr. Rothenburgh to celebrate his marriage and my purchase with a champagne lunch—"Vodka for me, please" said Mr. Rothenburgh—and then he got back on the bus and returned to New Jersey and to his new bride, both of us happy with having accomplished our goals.

I never got to meet his bride, but Mr. Rothenburgh lived happily on for a number of years and we later bought another of his paintings.

I became friends with Beryl Cook, the British artist with a naïf's genius, a cartoonist's flair, and a delicious ribald streak, when I saw one of her paintings reproduced on the cover of *The London Times Sunday Magazine* in 1976. I wrote to her and on my next trip to London I took the train down to Plymouth to meet Beryl and her husband, John.

Beryl was having her first big show in Plymouth, which I went to see on its last day, and bought two of her pictures right away. Beryl was still running a boardinghouse but was about to give it up because she needed more time for her painting and more studio space, and her family was growing—their married son and his wife and their little girl lived with Beryl and John—and they needed more room, too.

I was crazy about Beryl and John from the moment we met. They are two pixies with a fey sense of humor, a generous spirit, a droll manner, and a shyness that's endearing. Their love for animals is reflected in Beryl's work. They own a terrier and two turtles, Hercule and Desiree. Hercule is fiftyish and Desiree, who later was discovered to be a male despite her name, is twenty. Both are expected to live another hundred years.

One of my treasures is a painting by Beryl of Teddy and Gypsy, my Norfolk terriers, playing the piano, which Beryl painted for me from a photograph. Beryl's pictures bring joy and surprise to the viewer, expressing a point of view that is both innocent and outrageous, and they enhanced the RTR dining rooms and even my office as our Beryl Cook collection grew.

Once when Beryl and John were in New York I took them to an exhibition of Tamara de Lempika, whose work was a discovery for Beryl.

She was captivated, and as soon as she returned home, copied one of de Lempika's portraits, an amazing replica, and sent it to me. It hung in the Café, and Beryl and I kept the joke alive that it was an original. Well, it was an original Beryl Cook!

Beryl wrote me about their RTR experiences: "On our first visit I was absolutely overwhelmed to see the walls covered with such lovely paintings, and felt that mine were in very good company indeed. I look back with great pleasure to the times we spent there and our friendship with Faith." And I still treasure my friendship with them, too.

SIXTEEN

RTR Advertising

The RTR created two innovations in advertising that were later also imitated with much success.

We were the first restaurant to take out full-page ads in the *New York Times,* which started to appear in 1968. The creative team was led by Danny Stern, who brought in two talented men, Alan Glass, copywriter, and Al Bensusan, artist. It was Danny who came up with the tag line "Where does the Russian Tea Room stand? Slightly to the left of Carnegie Hall." And it was Alan and Al who created the series of full-page ads, featuring drawings of famous dishes of the Tea Room with captions such as "101 Dishes You've Never Had at the Russian Tea Room but Didn't Want Anyone to Know." Each dish was described in handwritten script alongside the drawing. In addition to the full-page ads, we ran small-space follow-up ads, too, selecting one of the dishes like Pelymeni Siberian from the large ad. Alan and Al created special holiday ads, too: for Thanksgiving, for instance, we had "Turkey and Borscht." The *New York Times* published a booklet about these ads and explained how they were created, with photos of Alan and Al and me in the Tea Room kitchen.

The second innovation was our radio ads. June LeBell originally announced the RTR radio ads on WQXR, which were written by the WQXR staff. Then I started playing around with the copy and Judy Fremont at WNCN, where we also advertised, suggested that I not only write the copy but announce it myself, which I began to do. We taped the announcements at WNCN and the station delivered them to all the other stations where we advertised: WOR, WPAT, WNEW, and WQXR AM and FM.

Judy describes the events this way: "We wanted to get the RTR account and never got to first base. The RTR seemed to be wedded to WQXR. Finally, when I found out the restaurant was owned by a woman, I went over there to meet the owner, whom I could never get to come to the phone. I expected to find a little old Russian lady in a wheel-chair, dressed in black, sipping tea from a glass. I saw this youngish blond woman in the dining room and I said, 'Can you tell me how to find the elusive Faith Stewart-Gordon?' And she said, 'That's me!' Then I found out she had been an actress and I told her she should announce her own commercials, as well as write them, and we would tape them at WNCN. The rest is history!"

The wonderful fun of it was that I wrote whatever came into my head, and when I got to the studio I had the invaluable assistance of Vido Colonna, the WNCN engineer, a former priest and an inspiring person to work with. Vido understood my "take" on things, and responded in such a positive way to the stories I wrote that he gave me the courage to share them with an audience. We had wonderful times together.

The ads ran sixty seconds, but my stories could only run fifty seconds, as it took ten seconds to give the opening and closing "billboards"—the advertising parts of the commercial. Many of the stories were about New York City and its history, quite a number had Russian themes, and some were about food. Most of them were meant to be humorous and a few were serious. The response was more than gratifying.

Here are some of the most popular:

New Year's Cure for Low Spirits

Hello! This is Faith Stewart-Gordon from the Russian Tea Room. In the sometimes melancholy aftermath of New Year's Eve we can listen to Sydney Smith, the English wit who wrote in 1820 his list of "cures for low spirits":

1. Live as well as you dare.

2. Take cool shower baths.

3. Read amusing books.

4. Take a short view of life—not further than dinner or tea.

5. See as much as you can of those friends who amuse you.

6. Avoid melancholy people and everything likely to excite dark emotions.

7. Do good—the effort to please others will lead to a happier state of mind.

8. Be as much as you can in the open air without fatigue.

9. Make your sitting room gay and pleasant and keep good blazing fires.

10. Don't be too severe upon yourself.

11. And don't expect too much from life!

Happy New Year from the Russian Tea Room—six minutes and twenty-three seconds from Lincoln Center and slightly to the left of Carnegie Hall. (1/1/85)

The Immortal Miss Stebbins

Hello, this is Faith Stewart-Gordon from the Russian Tea Room. Early one morning in September 1873, we went to Central Park with Miss Emma Stebbins, the sculptress, to see her new creation, the Bethesda Fountain. At the north end of the Mall we descended a stately stone staircase built under the park drive and, emerging through a colonnade of graceful Moorish arches, we saw the startling vision of a sculpted angel rising before us out of the mist, hovering atop a cascade of water which flowed over her outstretched arms onto the figures of four delightful cherubs, into an arabesque basin and finally coming to rest in a magnificent pool on the floor of the esplanade. As we gazed at the bronze incarnation of the biblical angel blessing the waters, a crowd gathered, and recognizing Miss Stebbins as the genius behind this crowning glory of the park, burst into applause. It seemed that before our eyes the new fountain and Miss Emma Stebbins became immortalized together!

The Russian Tea Room—six minutes and twenty-three seconds from Lincoln Center and slightly to the left of Carnegie Hall. (8/3/87)

It's Time

Hi! This is Faith Stewart-Gordon from the Russian Tea Room. It's time—time to retire the beach ball and the white linen suit; time to shutter up the country place, to say farewell to tanned bare feet and hello to green suede shoes. It's time to rediscover New York, time to wine and dine again—relax and feel the warmth and glow of that special place you love to go to. Time to be home again! Opera and theater time, tweed time, red and gold time, 57th Street, Russian Tea Room rendezvous time. Autumn in New York—it's time to live it again!

The Russian Tea Room—six minutes and twenty-three seconds from Lincoln Center and slightly to the left of Carnegie Hall. (9/12/84)

Blini Festival

Hello! This is Faith Stewart-Gordon from the Russian Tea Room. In Old Russia, whenever the winter snow piled up high enough to dig a house inside and the ice on the Moscow River froze thick enough to hold up a carousel with a dozen prancing horses, then it was time for *Myaslanitza*, or Butter Week, a whirling Russian Mardi Gras which preceded Lent. And what a fabulous festival it was! A winter carnival was built on the frozen river with theaters, puppet shows, restaurants, and huge ice hills created for sledding. There were restaurants, too, serving mounds of blini— little buckwheat cakes with melted butter and sour cream, and contests to see who could eat the most. When the celebrating ended, Russian mothers comforted their children: "There'll be more blini at Easter. It's only six weeks away!"

The Russian Tea Room—six minutes and twenty-three seconds from Lincoln Center and slightly to the left of Carnegie Hall. (3/6/84)

The Blini Harvest

Hello! This is Faith Stewart-Gordon from the Russian Tea Room. About this time every year little blini buds begin to sprout in the blini orchards, anticipating a golden harvest of perfect little buckwheat pancakes in the fall. The next few weeks are important, for as the little blini begin to grow, they must be carefully spread on both sides with melted butter every single day in order to achieve that round, firm, fully packed maturity that makes them blend so beautifully with caviar and smoked salmon.

But how many blini harvests have been rained out in the last crucial days of September, when there were only baskets full of soggy blini for the peasants to nibble on! Now, in California, thanks to modern science, blini are harvested all year round and rushed amid the thundering acclamation of hungry blini fans to the Russian Tea Room—six minutes and twenty-three seconds from Lincoln Center and slightly to the left of Carnegie Hall. (6/16/83)

Christmas at the Russian Tea Room

Hello! This is Faith Stewart-Gordon from the Russian Tea Room. People wonder if the Russian Tea Room was created especially for Christmas! It's certainly easy to believe that when you see the deep green walls, red banquettes, pink tablecloths, and red candle lights on the tables. It gives a very Christmasy air. And so do the original paintings and the glow from the brass samovars displayed in lighted niches around the room—and the menu! Of course the special Russian dishes literally speak of holiday dining—and three chandeliers all dressed up in gold tinsel and red Christmas balls— are they put there especially for the season? Many years ago they were, but they became such a part of the Russian Tea Room look that finally one year, 365 days revolved and the Christmas balls and the tinsel were still up there! I guess it's a way of saying that at the Russian Tea Room it's Christmas all year round!

Merry Christmas from the Russian Tea Room—six minutes and twenty-three seconds from Lincoln Center and slightly to the left of Carnegie Hall. (12/3/84)

Chicken à la Electric Light Bulb

Hello! This is Faith Stewart-Gordon from the Russian Tea Room. There's a Russian dish just a little too far out to be in *The Russian Tea Room Cookbook,* and I thought maybe we'd better tackle it head-on. It's Chicken with an Electric Light Bulb, or, if you prefer the French, *Poulet à l'Ampoule.* There are a couple of tricky steps along the way with this dish, and certainly you don't want to be standing in a bathtub, for instance, while preparing it. It starts off with the recipe for Chicken Kiev, a beautiful Russian specialty you can make in great style from *The Russian Tea Room Cookbook*—but when it comes to putting the light bulb inside that lovely boned breast of chicken—well, that's when I leave the kitchen. When the chicken is cooked, the light bulb, with wires attached, is plugged in and the chicken glows from inside as it comes to the table! Don't ask me what happens to the wires—you may have to call in an electrician. But I'm told the Russian court was ecstatic. It's enough to start a revolution! *The Russian Tea Room Cookbook*—all you wanted to know about Russian cuisine but were afraid to pronounce—from the Russian Tea Room, six minutes and twenty-three seconds from Lincoln Center and slightly to the left of Carnegie Hall. (11/9/81)

New York Restaurants of Yesteryear

Hello! This is Faith Stewart-Gordon from the Russian Tea Room. The average life of a New York restaurant is six months, they say. Then the Russian Tea Room has lived 188 lives in fifty-nine years. Fifty-nine years ago the Russian Tea Room was still a tearoom—but there was Peter's on West Tenth Street, the Elysée, the Brevoort on Fifth Avenue, or the Hofbrau—things were happening mostly downtown. In 1939 the Colony was going strong; so was the Stork Club, the Voisin, Billy the Oyster Man's, the Café Chambord, and the Blue Ribbon. Do you remember? The Russian Tea Room was still right here. Blini with caviar was $1.50. Wow! Whyte's, Al and Dick's, Armando's, and the Marguery. You couldn't forget those (if you were around then), and the Little

Club, the Gripsholm, Dinty Moore's, and the Pavillon. What memories! And the Russian Tea Room is still here! The Russian Tea Room—six minutes and twenty-three seconds from Lincoln Center and slightly to the left of Carnegie Hall. (1/15/85)

SEVENTEEN

Making Movies
and
Making Trouble

I thought that movie directors like Woody Allen and Sydney Pollack would be so caught up in the creative process that they would be terribly inefficient with the details of moviemaking, creating a big mess on the set, wouldn't you? And I thought, on the other hand, that an august body like the Academy of Motion Picture Arts and Sciences, known as the Academy, would be very serious and very technical in preparing for their annual East Coast Academy Awards party, wouldn't you? Well, I had many surprises in store.

When Woody Allen shot a scene from his movie *Manhattan* at the RTR, his crew was punctual to the point of punctiliousness. They started work the moment we closed the doors at night and continued working until ten in the morning, when we had to begin setting up for lunch, which began at 11:30. They quit exactly on time every day, and they cleaned up the set, i.e., our dining room, so thoroughly that we didn't have to lift a finger after they left.

The same was true when Sydney Pollack directed and starred with Dustin Hoffman in a hilarious scene from *Tootsie,* shot in the first booth on the left as you entered the dining room (D1), afterward referred to as the Tootsie Booth, as in, "I'd like to reserve the Tootsie Booth for eight o'clock tonight."

Dustin Hoffman was a regular at the Tea Room, and was appreciated by our staff. He once asked Greg Camillucci, our manager, if he could take his young son into the kitchen because he, Dustin, had worked as a dishwasher when he was starting out, and he wanted his boy to see what a dishwasher's work was like.

Dustin played a pivotal role in the celebrity life of the RTR, especially after his amazing success in *Tootsie,* in which, as most of the world knows, he played an actor who masquerades as a woman in order to get a job.

The deal to make *Tootsie* was consummated at the Tea Room with Dustin, Sam Cohn, and the director of the film, Sydney Pollack. *Tootsie* turned out to be one of the most successful movies ever made. We did not charge anything for the shoot, knowing that it would be a gift to us to be a part of it.

Dustin was a fanatic about making the part real. He decided to try out his female disguise on John Springer, the publicist, who was almost always in the Tea Room for lunch, and so he came in in costume and makeup and went over to John's table and said hello. John had no idea who he was, and this boosted Dustin's confidence immensely. The movie shoot took place at night and Greg knew from experience that it was risky to let the crew in later than midnight if we were to open on time the following day—once they got in it would be impossible to force them out until they had finished. It took two nights and nineteen takes to shoot the scene, which was a long dialogue between Dustin, as Tootsie, and Sydney Pollack as "her" agent.

Greg reported that Dustin stayed in character even when he was not performing, and insisted on using the ladies' room during the shoot!

Dustin Hoffman made a number of other deals at the RTR for plays and movies, and the negotiations always set the restaurant buzzing. Greg Camillucci reported that Arthur Miller, an RTR regular, walked in one day unannounced and asked him, "Is Hoffman here yet?" Hoffman? Who was Hoffman? Greg had no idea who he meant until he saw Sam Cohn sitting in his booth with an expectant look on his face and figured there might be a connection with Arthur Miller. Rumors started flying the moment Dustin sat down with them, and it didn't take long before word was out that Dustin Hoffman would be starring in a revival of Arthur Miller's *Death of a Salesman*.

Later Dustin and Sam met again at the Tea Room to plan a revival of Shakespeare's *The Merchant of Venice* for Broadway. Unfortunately the playwright couldn't make the meeting that day.

Sam Cohn is not only an agent but a dealmaker extraordinaire. He had the reputation of being a killer negotiator and deals were not consummated at his expense. Every day he sat in the booth opposite the Tootsie Booth, known as Sam's table (D30). The joke in the movie industry was "Meet me for lunch in the booth next to Sam Cohn." He always wore a rumpled sweater over his unbuttoned shirt collar—dark green was a favorite color of his. Sam had a rumpled look—his hair was tousled and his trousers looked as if he might have slept in them. He was always late for lunch. Many a day Ona and I shook our heads silently in sympathy when some young actor or actress would announce him- or herself brightly and say, "I'm meeting Mr. Cohn for lunch." Good luck! That actor would sit by him- or herself, sometimes for an hour. The self-confident ones drank glass after glass of water; the more vulnerable, with mounting anxiety, ordered cocktail after cocktail. Finally, after frantic calls to his office from Ona, Sam would appear, slipping into the booth with that ubiquitous grin as if he hoped his despairing guest wouldn't notice that he had just arrived. He would immediately lean forward and rest his left elbow on the table, displaying keen interest in what his guest was saying, as if conversation were already at full tilt. By then his baggy sweater sleeves would be pushed up with the shirtsleeves showing underneath. He sat with one leg tucked under him, like a nesting bird, and we were all familiar with his collection of baggy socks, as the one on the tucked leg would be showing. He had the reputation, by the way, of never returning phone calls, and a common remark in movie and theater circles was "I'm having lunch at the Tea Room so I can waylay Sam. I've been trying to get through to him for a week!" Sam, instead of making reservations, was the only person Ona called every day to see if he needed "his booth."

Sam tended to squint behind his glasses, which looped over his ears, and the perpetual grin on his seemingly ageless face was actually not so much a grin as a grimace. You couldn't tell what he was thinking, but the suspicion was that it wouldn't be good news, even if you found out. When the conversation grew intense he scratched himself.

Sometimes Sam would have reason to meet with the agent Robby Lantz for lunch. Robby is European (as in unspoiled Europe before the war) to the core, and one of the most charming men I have ever met. His style is the antithesis of Sam's no-frills presentation. Robby is always gallant and effuses a wonderful joie de vivre. When Robby and Sam had lunch together, it became a matter of high protocol as to who was going to move to whose booth. More often than not, Robby moved up to Sam, but sometimes it was the other way around, and whichever it was, it threw the dining room into a dither, as writers, actors, and directors came in to find one of them in the wrong place! Once they decided to have lunch in a neutral booth on the other side of the room, and that threw the restaurant into chaos. Nobody knew where they were or what was going on!

Sam never drank at lunch, though he was reputed to enjoy a drink or two at night. Like many other RTRnicks, he lunched at the Tea Room and dined at Elaine's. This was especially true of writers, and Elaine was famous for keeping out-of-work authors alive for years at a time.

Sam's diet at lunch consisted of a platter of sliced tomatoes, some dill pickles, and a special tuna salad made by the chef for Sam and Sam alone. If someone else asked for "Sam Cohn's salad" he wouldn't get it, even if he was sitting with Sam.

It was fascinating to see the stars pile up at Sam's table. He represented Meryl Streep for a long time, Whoopi Goldberg (who always went into our checkroom to talk to her old friend Iris, the hatcheck person, with whom she had lived in the settlements years before she became a big star), and many others. John Springer, the much-loved publicist, would often be there, too. John represented Elizabeth Taylor, among others, and it was he who arranged for her to come in to show off the new diamond ring Richard Burton had given her when he and she re-wed in the heart of Africa. And that was when I discovered what they meant about her violet eyes. Yes, they are extraordinary. The diamond was impressive, too.

I felt I had a special relationship with Dustin Hoffman, even though we'd never been introduced, because I used to play tennis with his mother and father in Palm Springs. I once asked Lilly, his mother, how she happened to name her son Dustin, and she told me that when she was in labor she was making up names for the baby and she thought, If it's a boy I'm going to name him Dustin for my idol, Dustin Farnum, the silent movie hero. And so she did.

Four times in the 1980s and once in the 1990s, the RTR was involved in making movies. All but one of the scenes was shot in the Tea Room itself, and they were exciting experiences for us, though sometimes hard on our staff, who were in charge of preserving the RTR from bodily harm. When the crew started hanging heavy strobe lights from our ceiling and plugging their high-voltage cords into our outdated connections, Greg turned pale, but they somehow managed to get out without destroying anything.

Woody Allen's *Manhattan* was our first exposure to the movies. It was a short scene in which Woody brings his young son, carrying a toy sailboat, into the restaurant. As the scene opens they are standing at the front waiting to be seated and Woody is talking to the boy about some pretty young women he sees. Our manager, Greg Camillucci, playing himself, comes up and seats them. Cut. I loved the scene. I loved Woody, the shots of the dining room, Greg's role, everything. I couldn't believe we were in a Woody Allen film!

Woody Allen was a regular at the Tea Room for many years, and was held in high regard by all, indicated by the fact that he was the only man besides Nureyev allowed to wear a hat in the dining room. He often came in with Mia Farrow (and sometimes her children came, too) until their breakup, when they would come in separately. Woody also brought his mother and father in occasionally, and I was fascinated to see that he was physically an odd combination of them both. If you looked at his mother, you saw part of Woody's face, but then when you looked at his father, you saw the other part, and yet the two parts didn't exactly meld.

Among his many gifts, Woody proved to be a meticulous director. He sat in a front booth at the Tea Room during the whole four-hour setup for the *Manhattan* scene, making sure everything was just right.

Another movie shot in the Tea Room was *Unfaithfully Yours,* with Dudley Moore, Nastassja Kinski, and Armand Assante, in which Dudley at one point crawls underneath the Tootsie booth to hide. Or did he slide underneath because he was inebriated?

New York Stories had a scene in the Tootsie booth, too. The movie contained three stories; the RTR story, directed by Francis Ford Coppola, was about an orchestral conductor who is reunited with his wife when their daughter gets them to come to the Tea Room together, and they live happily ever after.

In contrast to the high professionalism of Woody Allen and Sydney Pollack, the East Coast Academy Awards party, held at the Tea Room every year, was the hardest-to-organize event imaginable. A great groan went up from our staff when the first phone call of the season came through to remind us that the time had come to try to plan that year's event, always held on the last Monday in March. TV monitors would be set up in the Café and in the New York Room and everyone would watch the proceedings from the West Coast. The first step was to get the Academy committee together at the Tea Room over coffee and pastries, and let everybody complain about what had happened the year before. I had to make an appearance at the meeting, as did our public events manager and our banquet manager, as well as our chef. The two divas in charge were the beautiful Arlene Dahl and the tenacious and persistent Sylvia Miles, the reigning queen of kitsch. Sylvia, as has been told, had her table at lunch, right across from Robby Lantz (D32), and even on the days she wasn't there, her presence was keenly felt.

Sylvia and Arlene had the difficult task of deciding who should be invited to the Academy party. The problem was that all the members had to be invited, of course, and their wives or husbands. But they were not all movie stars, by any means. Most of the truly famous were in Hollywood that night, attending the gala and the show produced live out there. Sylvia and Arlene needed to glitz up their event with some celebrities, but the trouble was, the West Coast Academy, which gave the big televised gala, didn't want any competition from the East Coast Academy. They wanted all the stars for themselves. Yet if any Academy Award nominees happened to be in New York, as Liam Neeson and Natasha Richardson were in 1993—madly in love with each other, too—when they were nominated, the West Coast Academy didn't want the announcement to be made in New York. But what could they do? Everyone knew the two lovers were starring in a revival of *Anna Christie* on Broadway. The West Coast Academy's effort to rain on the East Coast Academy's parade sometimes backfired, however. Paul Newman, for instance, refused to fly, ever, and he and Joanne Woodward always stayed in New York for the ceremony. The night we had a live TV awards presentation direct from the Tea Room, Paul and Joanne were upstairs at our bar in the Café, having a quiet drink by themselves.

The press was not invited, but Cindy Adams, a good friend of the Tea Room, was always there because she came as my guest and sat with me. What could the Academy do? The worst problem was Radie Harris of the *Hollywood Reporter*, who called me night and day to get an invitation, citing Cindy as an example of the press being included. Things could get a little sticky around Academy Awards time.

Dustin Hoffman brought attention to the RTR again, when he and Anne Bancroft presented an award live from the RTR, thanks to our good friend Gilbert Cates, the director, who was in charge of the television presentation that year. He always said he'd do a live segment from the RTR, and indeed he did—and what excitement we had at the Tea Room! It may never happen again, either, as the West Coast Academy was unhappy that attention was withdrawn from Hollywood for even those five minutes. As quick as you could say "Dustin Hoffman and Anne Bancroft," the magic moment passed, but never, ever would we forget our wonderful moment in the Hollywood limelight.

Anne Bancroft was a longtime friend of the Tea Room. She and her husband, Mel Brooks, came in frequently, and before they were married Mel used to have lunch with Carl Reiner, Mel Tolkin, and the rest of the comedy-writing team who wrote and rehearsed the *Sid Caesar Show* in a studio down on the corner of 57th and Sixth. Anne Bancroft and Shirley MacLaine appeared together in *The Turning Point*, a movie with a scene shot outside the Tea Room. It was directed by Herbert Ross, whose first wife, the ballerina Nora Kaye, had been a great friend of Sidney's.

The story concerned two former dancers who meet after many years. Mikhail Baryshnikov and Leslie Browne, who played Shirley MacLaine's daughter, were the love interests. In addition to a scene shot in front of the Tea Room with Anne and Shirley, another one was shot in a simulated set of the RTR dining room. It seems the movie crew would have had to cut through the wall of the restaurant in order to get the close-ups Herb Ross wanted, so they shot the scene on the set in Hollywood instead.

Greg Camillucci supervised the shooting of the movie for the RTR. He said that two extras rehearsed the scene of Anne and Shirley leaving the restaurant, going through the revolving door countless times. Finally a woman customer in the restaurant came up to Greg and asked, "Why do those two women keep going through the revolving door over and over again?" Greg replied with a solemn face, "Don't you know? We're celebrating the hundreth anniversary of the invention of the revolving door!"

Eleanor Bergstein is a producer and screenwriter whose credits include *Dirty Dancing,* and she recently produced another film called *Let It Be Me,* which has a scene shot in the RTR with Leslie Caron and Patrick Stewart.

Eleanor's memories of the Tea Room go back a long way. She remembers celebrating there when her boyfriend, a poet, sold his first poem to the *Kenyon Review.* She looked deeply into his eyes and asked him, "What do you like best about me?" hoping he would say, "Your eyes!" But he replied, "Your soul," at which she jumped up and ran into the ladies' room, where she wept for a long time in bitter disappointment.

When she got back to the table her boyfriend looked at her reddened eyes and said, "But that's a *good* thing, Eleanor, to love you for your soul!" And sure enough, they ended up getting married.

Eleanor chose for the first scene in *Let It Be Me* the black and white checked sidewalk in front of the RTR. A man in a light coat is standing over the grille that allows steam to escape from the basement of the building, waiting for a lunch appointment to arrive. Eleanor used that image, she says, because she had noticed that people stood on that grille in cold weather, especially if they were poorly dressed for the season, and she took it as a metaphor for New York life: the needy writer or actor wanting to appear more successful than he or she is, in spite of the fact that he or she did not have a warm coat to wear. The heat from the grille helped to sustain the illusion of well-being.

Other movie deals made in the RTR:

Meryl Streep, Dustin Hoffman, and Bob Benton for *Kramer vs. Kramer.*

Joel Schumacher's first movie as producer: *Car Wash.*

Albert Finney for the Daddy Warbucks role in *Annie.*

Larry Peerce's first movie: *One Potato, Two Potato.*

Last Days

Of course we thought the good times would go on forever, and we got terribly spoiled. Even when the stock market crashed in October 1987, business continued as usual. We wondered what all the excitement was about. But then, in 1988, things began gradually to change. The public was pulling in its horns and spending less money. Then the government retracted the 80 percent expense deductions for business meals, which created an enormous hole in our revenue. We began to realize we were in a recession.

Along with the public's new spartan attitude came new tastes in dining. People said they wanted simpler, more basic foods to make them feel less frivolous in a more sober time. But there was a lot of confusion about what was "simpler." Some people were waving the banner of "Lighter! Lighter!" and others were crying, "We want Mom's basic comfort food!" and though they both might be "simpler," Mom's cooking meant the opposite of light—it meant meat and potatoes with gravy. In the midst of the confusion there was one thing we knew: French haute cuisine with all the heavy sauces was out. So Russian cuisine, partly based on the French, partly based on even heavier Russian peasant dishes, was not a good candidate for the public's current tastes. The Russian Tea Room had to go light! We created another side to our menu and gave our customers a choice. The regulars needed more choices, anyway, as they couldn't be expected to eat caviar and blini and Chicken Kiev every day. (Though some might say, "Why not?")

We had to go back to the drawing board in more ways than one. As our sales fell off we had to find out how to operate in a losing economy, something we hadn't experienced in almost ten years. It took us about three years to gear down and it was almost too late when we finally learned how to trim our expenses. For instance, the enormous (to us) flower budget for the dining room, which I had believed was a necessity, had to be minimized. That really hurt at the time—it seemed against the principles I believed made a restaurant work, but I had to learn that lavish flower displays were expendable, like a lot of other things, and that the same effect could be achieved with artistry.

Jacques Pépin, the acclaimed chef, cookbook writer, and teacher, came to us as restaurant consultant and worked on improving and stabilizing recipes. He was wonderful to work with, inspirational, creative and kind, but his time with us was limited and we longed for someone like him as a permanent addition to the staff. ("Dream on!" as they say.)

I hired Clark Wolf, another restaurant consultant, to work with me more in the management area than in the kitchen, though our food and wine tastings were a strong part of his contribution. Even when our direction seemed unclear, the sight of that tall, dapper guy with the small oval glasses and Armani suit swinging his briefcase through the revolving door gave me a tremendous boost. I knew he was on my side and I needed someone to champion me more than anything. Clark stayed with us for three years off and on, and found us a new manager, Wiley Nomura, who brought a feeling of reassurance to a somewhat rocky ship. A stronger team began to emerge.

Clark and I made two trips to Japan on a search to find a franchise for the RTR there. Though we believed till the end that we had made a deal with a Japanese company, we were entirely mistaken. The Japanese are no pushovers to do business with!

Meanwhile, in October of 1990, we started our Cabaret at the Russian Tea Room.

NINETEEN

Cabaret

Hi, this is Faith Stewart-Gordon from the Russian Tea Room. The lights dim slowly in an intimate green and gold room. Spotlights come up on a baby grand piano and a microphone, mirrors reflect silhouettes in a packed room of excited people. Suddenly the buzz of conversation and the tinkle of glasses die and a hush falls over the room as the cabaret artist starts through the crowd. With a burst of applause and a ripple of chords, the magic of Sunday night at the Russian Tea Room begins! The songs of yesterday and the songs of tomorrow—intimate, honest, heartfelt, funny, and sad—it's a love affair between the artist and the audience that creates a special bond. It's what cabaret means. Cabaret at the Russian Tea Room, every Sunday night at 8:00 P.M. and 10:30. It's magic. Right here on West 57th Street. With dinner before or after the show. The Russian Tea Room Cabaret, six minutes and twenty-three seconds from Lincoln Center and slightly to the left of Carnegie Hall. (10/30/90)

This radio announcement introduced the opening of our first cabaret season in October 1990.

Creating the Cabaret at the Russian Tea Room was possibly the most exciting thing we ever did. It came seemingly out of nowhere and blossomed before our eyes. It existed for five and a half years and made a lot of people happy—the public, the performers, and all of us at the Tea Room who worked on it—even the critics were happy. And it was an emotional shot in the arm for the Tea Room at a time when the crash of 1987 was beginning to reap its effect on our bottom line. The Cabaret never made a dime and we stopped it because it was losing too much money, but it brought a new dimension to the RTR and a renewed interest from the public. Our financial people, the number crunchers, finally talked me into closing it, but when they did, I realized it was time to sell the restaurant. If I couldn't enjoy the pleasures the Cabaret had brought to so many of us, then it was time to quit. Andrew Freeman, our Cabaret manager, had left by then, and with him went a lot of the fun of it. Then Don Smith, who had created it with us and booked the performers, had other commitments and had to leave, too. We kept going for a while thanks to Michael Kirker of ASCAP (American Society of Composers and Performers), always a pleasure to work with, but our team had dispersed and the money wasn't there to keep us afloat.

I had been in love with cabaret since I was first exposed to it in the 1940s and early '50s through recordings of cabaret stars like Bea Lillie, Mabel Mercer, Noël Coward, and Gertrude Lawrence. And there was a close connection between cabaret and Leonard Sillman's *New Faces of 1952*. *New Faces* was built around cabaret sketches and cabaret performers.

Cabaret was flourishing when I arrived in New York in April 1954. Some of my Northwestern friends, like Mary Louise Wilson, were already employed in *Upstairs at the Downstairs,* or in Julius Monk's revue at the Plaza, and Brooks Morton was playing piano downtown in the Village at *The Living Room*. Lovey (Lovelady) Powell, my sorority sister at Northwestern with whom I stayed the first week in New York, was singing torch songs to great effect at the Duplex, and Northwestern alums like Charlotte Rae were already well established at the clubs and in the theater.

The Blue Angel, the Embers, the Bon Soir, Billy Reed's Little Club, and the Vanguard were just a few of the spots where rising stars like

Woody Allen, Barbra Streisand, Johnny Mathis, and Mort Sahl were performing. And Mabel Mercer, the queen of them all, was singing at the Byline.

Cabaret remained just a favorite hobby of mine until May 1990, when Dorothy Loudon, the nightclub and musical-comedy star, gave a birthday party in our new New York Room for her agent and good friend Lionel Larner. Dorothy's party was elegant and outrageous, like the hostess herself. It was a black-tie event and the champagne and caviar flowed. Dorothy brought in Billy Barnes, the great cabaret pianist and accompanist, and rented an upright piano for the evening. Of course Dorothy sang and she was never more lyrical or more hilarious. As she walked through the room singing to each guest, I noticed something special about the atmosphere, apart from her performance: the acoustics of the room were terrific and the size and shape of it were perfect for cabaret. I turned to my old friend Donald Smith, the cabaret impresario, who knows more about the genre than anybody, and I could tell by his look that we had the same idea.

"Let's have a cabaret!" we both said at once, just like Judy Garland and Mickey Rooney in *Summer Stock*. To my delight and surprise we did just that, and opened the RTR Cabaret five months later, in October 1990, with Don Smith doing the bookings and the PR, and Andrew Freeman from the Tea Room managing it from our end. We planned a fall, winter, and spring season, later adding short seasons in the summers, with two performances on Sunday nights, at 8:00 and 10:30 P.M.

Andrew took to cabaret as if he had always been involved with it. He had a background in acting and his two areas of expertise were selling and promotion, so we got off to a good start. At first we had only the upright piano. Hildegarde, a great cabaret star since the 1930s, relied on a good sound to enhance her playing (in white full-length kid gloves) and she complained. So we found a way to fit in a baby grand, and we strung up temporary lights before every performance and took them down again afterward when the New York Room once again became a room for à la carte dining. Ed Richardson, who became our sound and lighting man, came with the lighting equipment and stayed to become a crucial member of the Cabaret team. Fortunately he was slim, because he had to slide into what had been a checkroom, now the sound and lighting booth, and remain there throughout the show. Tables full of people were pushed up against the doorway of the booth, so he couldn't have gotten out if he tried!

When we had gained enough confidence in the future of our Cabaret, we bought permanent lighting equipment, which was promptly stolen the first night. Refusing to be daunted, we replaced it and took more precautions for the future.

Isabelle Stevenson, my great friend and longtime head of the American Theater Wing, gave me the idea to call Michael Kirker at ASCAP and see if he would be interested in moving the ASCAP Monday night musical workshop to the RTR. These were informal evenings with composers playing and singing their own songs, often taken from musical works in progress, and accompanied by cabaret singers who wanted to show their support to the composer or were just happy to have a showcase, depending on their status in the cabaret world. They were all chosen by the composer and were performers he or she (in the case of Alan and Marilyn Bergman, he *and* she) enjoyed working with. I discovered on those Monday nights that composers play and sing their own songs better than anybody.

Don Smith says about our Cabaret:

> Every Sunday night I loved to go into the room just before it opened and see it set up. It had such a perfect size and shape. I know Faith must've gone through the agonies of the damned at how crowded it could be. By the time the performer came on everyone at the tables knew everyone else in the room! But we didn't think of it as crowded—we were focused on intimacy. I used to say it gave the word *intimacy* new meaning! The RTR was a throwback in contemporary terms to the "boîte" of the '40's and '50's. You could feel it!
>
> What made it work? The excellent lighting and sound, the good food, and value for your money, too. No other cabaret offered that. And cabaret has got to be so honest. There's no net—it's only

the singer, the material he or she selects, and those people out there—the audience. For cabaret to work for me the audience has to feel at the end of the performance that they know how the singer feels about the lyrics. She doesn't have to tell us—we hear it through the stories she tells us, through the songs. Andrea Marcovicci, who loved the intimacy of the RTR Cabaret, has so many stories to tell the audience, about this composer and that one, and it works for her. On the other hand, Mabel Mercer never spoke a word. It was all in the lyrics.

The performers sang better there because they were presented so well. They were all grateful to be there at the RTR. They became a part of history, being there. The RTR had such high standards, they could float in on that. And it became a hangout. There was as much activity in the audience as there was onstage!

Setting the Stage

You were on your way to the Cabaret, coming up the back stairs from the restaurant's dining room or coming up the front stairs through the side door of the restaurant to the second floor and walking through the Café, the dim light reflecting from green walls, the bar glistening with bottles on the mirrored shelves behind the bartender, dressed in a red tunic. Then you passed by people standing around the bar for a pre-Cabaret drink, walked through swinging doors into the the corridor hung with framed theatrical posters, and there in front of you was a large Bakst painting of Columbine dressed in masquerade costume: a multicolored flounced skirt, a black mask covering her eyes. You climbed a few more steps to the landing where the Cabaret hostess stood, welcoming you and checking off your reservation as you came in.

Then at last you entered the inner sanctum, the room called by one critic "a jewel box," and by another "the inside of a Fabergé egg," and, walking down a narrow aisle, and squeezing past a row of tiny tables where people sat opposite each other, you entered the New York Room itself, filled to the brim with tables crowded with people. The room was decorated like the rest of the RTR, with hunter green walls, mirrors, red banquettes, and tinsel with red Christmas balls hanging from the wall sconces. On the walls were paintings by New York artists, among them *New York Harbor* by Jonas Lie and *Italian Festival on Mott Street* by Howard McLean, and, of course, *The Russian Tea Room,* by Otto Rothenburgh.

At the entrance you would be met by Gary Sullivan, the Cabaret maître d', who also was a familiar personage downstairs in the dining room on other nights. Gary is blond and compact, cherubic in appearance, with a wicked smile dancing over his face, showing his dimples. I always felt like hugging him when I saw him and sometimes I couldn't resist. Straight ahead at one end of the room was a baby grand piano and the tiny stage, which some of the women performers complained about because their narrow high heels slipped through the cracks between the boards. Even Andrew's laying carpeting over the stage platform didn't seem to help. Behind the stage was a black drape hung over the mirror to prevent glare from the stage lights bouncing into people's eyes, a sign on the drape reading RTR CABARET.

Many of the Cabaret regulars came to have dinner about seven o'clock, and the tables started to fill up. People were jammed next to each other and conversations were easy enough to start between tables—in fact, it was hard not to! It was a sophisticated New York crowd, and you might be seated next to Bobby Short and Dame Irene Worth, or Liza Minnelli and Billy Stritch, or Liz Smith and Barbara Walters, or my old friends Lenna and Sidney Fulmer from Spartanburg—you never knew. The short menu worked well and the kitchen turned out the food in record time. How the waiters managed to serve between those tables I will never know, but they did it with great skill. The whole Cabaret experience seemed to be a product of legerdemain— Ed in his lighting booth, Don Smith prowling around the back of the room, his keen eye on every detail, and I, nervously going over my notes before squeezing through the tables and getting onto the stage to say, "Good evening, ladies and gentlemen, and welcome to the Russian Tea Room Cabaret!" I would then thank our sponsor, Broadway Cares/Equity Fights AIDS, talk about upcoming shows, and introduce the celebrities who were in the house that night. Finally I would announce the evening's performer and step down as he or she fought his or her way from the back through the crowded room and onto the stage. The accompanist had meanwhile come in from the other entrance behind the piano, and was playing an introduction, as the room burst into applause. The show was about to begin.

Of all the performers we had at the Cabaret, the sentimental favorite was Julie Wilson. There's something about her New York glamour and sophistication combined with her Omaha earthiness that is irresistible. There is a poignancy in her ability to prevail through more than fifty years of performing without losing her star quality or her humanity, only adding the heartache of experience to her wonderful style and her sense of humor. She is the hometown girl, the waif, the cut-up, and the glamorous woman of the world all wrapped into one.

Two images of Julie stand out: one, the svelte chanteuse in the clinging black gown with the long feather boa draped around her ever-lithe body and the gardenia perched in her hair, and the other, the hardworking showbiz performer walking from job to job on the New York streets in space shoes, without makeup, her head wrapped in a scarf, an enormous duffel bag flung over one shoulder, her costume and makeup and evening shoes tucked inside.

Andrew Freeman remembers asking Julie, when she arrived at the RTR for her first performance and was having a bite to eat, if she needed anything.

"Just give me a glass of water and a doggie bag!" she replied, with that million-dollar smile.

Julie celebrated her fiftieth anniversary in show business with a four-week engagement at the Tea Room. It was the first long run we had attempted, and she and her accompanist, Billy Roy, were a great success. Her indomitable spirit, above all, was what made it work.

The most enduring and, in some ways, most endearing Cabaret star of all was Hildegarde. Her show, entitled "Live at 85," was one of the funniest, and, of course, the most nostalgic of all the shows we presented. Hildegarde is among the most charming people you will ever meet, and her radiant looks and husky voice are still intact, not to mention the famous elbow-length white gloves she wears to play the piano, and she can really punish those keys! I remember seeing Hildegarde when she was at the height of her career—how I worshiped her! And now here she was, forty years later, at our Cabaret. Whenever she sang Ray Noble's "Love Locked Out," I wept. She had not lost that magical ability to move an audience.

It was fun to see her with her old friend and former manager-producer Anna Sosenko, with whom she had shared many successful years both here and in Paris. Anna wrote "Darling, Je Vous Aime Beaucoup" for Hildegarde and it became an enormous hit. Anna and Hildegarde had not been friendly for a long time, but when Hildegarde gave her "Live at 85" show at the RTR Cabaret, I persuaded Anna, an old friend of mine, to come for that important occasion. The lively and slightly barbed exchange between them during the show was unforgettable. And they remained friends ever after.

Hildy is remarkably agile, for her age or any age. Once Tom LoSquadro, our comptroller, was walking by the reception area upstairs on his way home and noticed Hildegarde stretched out on the office sofa, her arms folded on her chest, her feet sticking out under the armrests. She looked very pale and still. Was she alive? He started off to look for help when Hildegarde opened one eye and looked at him.

"Hiya, sailor!" she said, without moving.

Tom stopped dead in his tracks. "I beg your pardon?' he asked.

"Oh, I never miss a good-looking guy!" she replied with a lilt to her voice. "Just catching a little shut-eye," she added, and closed her eyes again.

Marcovicci Sine Voce

Andrea Marcovicci, blessed with wonderful looks and that radiant smile, could entrance an audience just by standing on the stage, with proper lighting. But she can sing, too! And over the years her interpretations have achieved a depth and mellowness that brings us to our feet, and to tears.

My favorite memories of Andrea in the Tea Room are of her having lunch alone, lost in reverie. When anyone would go up to her and say hello, she would make strangulation motions with her hands around her throat to indicate that she was saving her voice and could not speak. This killed two birds with one stone: in addition to saving her voice, she avoided people she didn't want to talk to.

Deborah Winer, a cabaret-watcher who wrote a book about it called *The Night and the Music*, felt the RTR Cabaret belonged to a gentler time, the cozy and sophisticated cocktail party culture of the 1950s. "The RTR Cabaret had a secret," she said, "an insider feeling, yet it was relaxed and homey, too. The audience was talented and glitzy and inspired the singers to raise the level of their performances. And the intense colors of the room gave it just the right tone of warmth and festiveness. There was only one word for the RTR Cabaret experience: luminosity."

A list of our RTR Cabaret performers includes: Karen Akers, Tom Anderson, Judy Argo, Yana Avis, Kay Ballard, Judy Barnett, Laurie Beechman, Richard Rodney Bennett, Alan Bergman and Sandy Stewart, Francesca Blumenthal, Joyce Breach, Betty Buckley, Julie Budd, Liz Callaway, Ann Hampton Callaway, Claiborne Carey, Craig Carnelia, Barbara Carroll, Alix Corey, Daugherty and Field, Mary Bond Davis, Blossom Dearie, Baby Jane Dexter, Cleve Douglas, Peter Duchin, Nancy Dussault, Eileen Farrell, Anne Francine, David Friedman and Friends, Eric Michael Gillett, Natalie Gomsu, Amanda Green, Faye Greenberg, Carol Hall, Julie Halston, Mary Cleere Haran, Jeff Harner, Skitch Henderson, Hildegarde, Dee Hoty, Ellen Kaye, Judy Kuhn, Nancy LaMott, Jay Leonhart, Marcia Lewis, Jo Sullivan Loesser, Emily Loesser, Steve Lutvak, Richard Maltby Jr. and David Shire, Andrea Marcovicci, Karen Mason, Sally Mayes, Marin Mazzie, Amanda McBroom, Audra McDonald, Heather McRae, Liliane Montevecchi, Sheridan Morley, Pamela Myers, Portia Nelson, Phyllis Newman, Melissa Newman, Phillip Officer, Jerry Orbach, Charlotte Rae, Lee Roy Reams, Steve Ross, Spider Saloff and Ricky Ritzel, Helen Schneider, Debbie Shapiro, George Shearing, Joel Silberman, David Staller, Marti Stevens, Stiller and Meara, Billy Stritch, Charles Strouse, K. T. Sullivan, Sylvia Syms, Marlene Van Planck, B. J. Ward, Paula West, Margaret Whiting, Julie Wilson, the Wise Guys, Sara Zahn.

TWENTY

Endings

The Russian Tea Room was open for business for the last time on Sunday, New Year's Eve, 1995. But for me there were three occasions even more memorable than the actual final day: the party we gave for friends of the Tea Room upstairs in the Café on Wednesday, December 27; the events at lunchtime on Thursday, December 28, three days before we closed; and our staff party on Tuesday, January 2, 1996. That really was the end for all of us.

I was reluctant at first to give a farewell party. There were just too many people I knew and had known who were associated with the restaurant for us to limit the guest list to two hundred, the maximum number of people the Café could hold. But as the closing drew nearer many people were calling to ask, "When's the final party?" and I felt more and more strongly that we had to do something, to make some gesture for as many of our friends as we could muster in that busy season. So we set a date and took the plunge, rifling through our Rolodexes to make lists of as many "Russianteanicks" as we could muster.

It turned out to be a wonderful, sad, and emotional parting, and the best way to say good-bye, if there ever can be. The Café had hosted so many fabled events, including Oscar award parties, wedding parties, press parties, election parties, and funeral (memorial) parties, and we had always rolled out the caviar, blini, iced vodka, and champagne, as we did that evening, too.

On Thursday, December 28, at lunchtime there was a tremendous buzz in the restaurant, created in part by the holiday spirit—after all, it was the height of our busiest season—but also by the many fans of the Tea Room who had come to congregate for the last time. Warner LeRoy and I did a live television interview together, discussing the changeover in ownership. In spite of our usual policy not to allow filming in the restaurant when people were dining, there were several TV crews panning the room, the well-known year-round Christmas decorations, and the bustling clientele. That day nobody minded except poor Ona, our maîtresse d', who was going out of her mind because the people waiting for tables were stumbling over cameras and cables as they stood in line. In the middle of all the activity, I got a phone call from my former brother-in-law, Walter Kaye, Sidney's younger brother, saying he was bringing Hillary Rodham Clinton, her mother, and Chelsea in for lunch. Walter said Selma, his wife, would be with them, and there would be two others in the party. Walter had become a great friend of the Clintons and spent a lot of time in Washington with them. He always told me, "I'm going to bring them to the Tea Room!" and sure enough, just in time, he did. Walter, after a very successful business career, was appointed by President Clinton to be the Civilian Aide to the Secretary of the Army. Among his achievements in Washington was introducing the president to Monica Lewinsky, the niece of a friend, when she was looking for a job.

The first thing I thought with all the action swirling about us was "What a way to go!" The second thing was "Ona will have a heart attack! How can I tell her?" The unexpected and very special arrivals would mean, for one thing, putting a large round top on a smaller, square table somewhere up front, which, of course, fell to Ona to execute. The problem was there was no room to enlarge a table: the surrounding tables were already filled with people wining and dining hugger-mugger. And what about the Secret Service agents the Clintons would bring with them, who had to sit somewhere near but separate from the presidential party? There was no table for them, either.

Ona managed it, as always, in great style, and balanced the TV crews with the Clintons' party without merging them into some unholy mess. Before I could get over to say hello to Mrs. Clinton she came over to the table where Warner and I were sitting and shook hands. She was gracious and charming and told me, to my surprise, that she and the president had been to the RTR often over the years, and felt very romantic about it.

Outside the restaurant, word had traveled fast and crowds of passersby and press people were waiting for the Clintons to emerge. We could have pulled our old trick of taking them out through the kitchen, as we did for Princess Pahlevi, the sister of the Shah of Iran. But on that earlier day there was an angry mob of Iranians outside on 57th Street shouting, "Down with the Shah!" and similar epithets. The diminutive princess was sitting with a group of friends over caviar and champagne in one of the back booths, with her security people at the next table, and when we saw that her party had finished lunch, we alerted the security and whisked them all out through the kitchen to our back entrance on 56th Street, much to the surprise of our chef and the kitchen crew, still in the middle of serving lunch. Today, for the Clintons, we didn't need to resort to our escape hatch. There were only well-wishers and the curious and, as always, the man who stood outside every day with his autograph book asking people as they came in, "Are you famous?" I felt we had arrived when he moved his celebrity watch from Sardi's to the RTR.

The restaurant was packed and there was a contagious feeling of exhilaration in the air. It was the RTR at its theatrical best. All the "regulars" had turned up, it seemed, as if called upon to give a last performance. Their allegiance was primarily to lunch, and with the long New Year's holiday weekend coming up, this would be their final appearance before we closed—yet none of us could believe it was really happening. I felt dizzy and euphoric, heady with the feeling that the restaurant was so much loved and appreciated, that all our work and caring had not been in vain.

"This is magical!" I thought. "Why am I letting it all go?" I remembered what my good friend Helen Gurley Brown had drummed into me all those years: "Don't sell, Faith. When you lose your base in New York, nobody will remember you for five minutes." I forgot for a moment how I had arrived at this place in my life, how the problems of running the restaurant had finally gotten to me and tilted my decision, after much agonizing, toward getting out. Right now I could think only of the joy, not the pain. I thought of Lyubov in the final scene of *The Cherry Orchard,* leaving her beloved house for the last time: "Oh, my orchard! My sweet, beautiful orchard! My life, my youth, my happiness, good-bye! good-bye!" And I thought, "This room! All the wonderful people who have come here and all the dear people who have worked here! Where else could there be so much warmth, such camaraderie, as we have given each other over the years?" I was getting carried away.

Then in my mind's eye I saw all the RTR employees from the past slowly swirling through the revolving doors. One by one they came— Nadia, Ada, Vera, Ducia, Anatole, Sidney, of course, Annette, Miss Anne, Rosa, "H," passing before my eyes. Papasha, Ida, Tioshi—as I stood there more and more of them appeared, unmindful of me, unseen by everyone else, some taking up their posts in the dining room, the chefs walking straight through to the kitchen carrying their knives, and still others slipping through the side door at the front of the restaurant to climb the two long flights of stairs leading to our office on the third floor. I wanted to stop them, to ask them about their lives, to find out what had happened to them, to thank them, to beg their forgiveness for closing the restaurant, but suddenly I realized it was only a vision, a waking dream.

I couldn't face going to the restaurant on New Year's Eve, our closing night. Ellen was there—it's her birthday, and she celebrated it with some friends, though I knew she must have been as sad as I was. Most of the "regulars" had left town as predicted. It must have been a difficult night for our staff, but I felt I had already said good-bye so many times, I just couldn't go back again.

The next day, January 1, 1996, the maintenance crew cleaned the restaurant for the last time. We had already cleared out our offices days before, and Tom LoSquadro, our comptroller, and the rest of the financial staff were working out of rented space on Sixth Avenue. There would be enough bookkeeping to keep them busy for months, tying up loose ends.

The last day for all of us who had worked at the RTR was January 2, when we gave our party for the employees. Instead of having it in the Café, as we usually did, we decided to leave the RTR in good shape and go over to Patsy's on West 56th Street, where I had been a friend and customer for many years. We reserved the upstairs room for that cold, snowy Tuesday and had a lunch party so that people who lived outside the city could get home early. Besides, everybody was tired out by the holiday season and the strain of closing and I thought the party would probably not last long. I hoped it wouldn't, in a way, because I was afraid I would break down in front of everybody. I hadn't any idea how many of our people would come, or would want to. After all, it was a sad or, at best, a bittersweet occasion. But almost everybody came. Warner LeRoy had generously presented me with a Methuselah of champagne, the equivalent of six liters, which our bartender Tim carefully transported by taxi, wrapped up like a baby, to Patsy's, and we somehow managed to pour it into glasses after someone got the brilliant idea of decanting it into water pitchers first.

Again there was a sense of unreality about the occasion. We ate and drank, laughed and cried, told war stories and toasted each other, but then it was time to go home. I felt the Tea Room, which had been my present existence for so long, slipping into the past. I didn't break down, but I might have if I had stayed any longer. There were still a lot of people there when I left—I thought they might like some time together without the boss around—and I heard later that the stalwarts closed up the favorite neighborhood bar around the corner on Seventh Avenue before they all finally said good-bye.

I wish for the Russian Tea Room a renaissance, something it has well earned after seventy years of being part of the heart and soul of New York. As for myself, I didn't know how hard the wrench would be, harder than ending a marriage. But of course it *was* a marriage, and the wound will need time to heal.

The wrench of leaving has been made easier knowing that Warner LeRoy has the imagination and theatricality to bring the Tea Room back to life and embellish it with his own vision. Now that he has brought the RTR back to life, my heart is lighter. I look forward to swinging through those revolving doors again to wish him all the joys of the RTR experience.

Epilogue

I wrote this book to satisfy a longing to look back over my life, particularly as it was formed by the Russian Tea Room during a period of forty years; to distill the memories, happy and sad; and to find a closure to that long chapter as I began a new life.

I wanted, too, to share these memories with others for whom the Russian Tea Room meant something special, as well as with those who never got a chance to know its charms.

And last, I wanted to learn from this retrospective what meaning my experiences might have for people of another generation starting out as I did, with big dreams and little experience, learning as they go along. But I have no words of wisdom. I believe we act out of passion and necessity, often impetuously, usually unaware of the consequences. We don't realize at the time something is happening that, as with everything we do, this event becomes part of a larger pattern that shapes our lives. Later, looking back, this pattern becomes what we call Destiny!

The most important thing, I believe, is to have the courage to embrace each new experience, and to live each moment to the fullest. And who could argue with that?

Index

Absinthe House, 53
Academy Awards, 209, 214–15
Actors Studio, 143
Adams, Cindy, 105, 215
Adams, Joey, 105
Adler, Stella, 64, 65
advertising, 202–8
Age of Innocence, The, 69
Akers, Karen, 228
Al and Dick's, 46, 207
Alex (RTR back steward), 36, 120–21
Algonquin Round Table, 143
Allen, Steve, 102
Allen, Woody, 103, 209, 213, 222
Allison, Fran, 102
Alpern, Andrew, 82–83
Alswang, Ralph, 143
Alwyn Court, 69
American Theater Wing, 144, 223
Anatole (RTR maître d'), 27–29, 35
Anderson, Tom, 228
Angelou, Maya, 139
Anna Christie, 215
Annette (RTR maîtresse d'), 108, 128–29, 137, 232
Annie, 217
Argo, Judy, 228
Armando's, 207
Armstrong, Joe, 109
Aronson, Boris, 143
Arron, Judith, 86
Art Deco, 70
Arthur X, 79
Artkraft-Strauss, 153
Art Students League of New York, 69
ASCAP, 221, 223
Ashley, Bobbie, 147
Assante, Armand, 214
Atlanta Constitution, 17
Avery Fisher Hall (Philharmonic Hall), 72, 73, 78, 112
Avis, Yana, 228

Axe, Mrs., 75–77, 79
Axe-Houghton Mutual Funds, 76

Bainter, Fay, 26
Bakst, Léon, 224
Balalaika, 120
Balanchine, George, 104–5, 134
Baldwin, James, 138
Ballard, Kay, 228
ballet dancers, 74, 104, 133–34, 145–46, 216
Bancroft, Anne, 120, 158, 215–16
Barbizon Hotel for Women, 25
Barnes, Billy, 222
Barnes, Clive, 103–4
Barnett, Judy, 228
Barrault, Jean-Louis, 167–68
Barrie, Barbara, 119–20
Barrymore, John, 98
Baryshnikov, Mikhail, 216
Becker, Alan, 26–29
Beechman, Laurie, 228
Beer, David, 87
Belafonte, Harry, 100
Belknap, Norton, 84
Bell, Caroline, 116
Bendel, Henri, 151
    see also Henri Bendel
Bennett, Richard Rodney, 228
Bennett, Tony, 72
Bensusan, Al, 202
Benton, Robert, 148
Bergdorf Goodman, 151
Bergman, Alan, 228
Bergman, Ingmar, 27
Bergstein, Eleanor, 216–17
Bernstein, Felicia Montealegre, 115, 116, 198
Bernstein, Leonard, 71, 114–15, 116, 133, 183
Billy the Oyster Man's, 207
Blackmer, Sidney, 127
Blackwell, Earl, 127

Blatas, Arbit, 124
blini, 186–87, 188, 205, 206
Blond, Susan, 98–99
Bloom, Julius, 85, 89–90
Bloomgarden, Kermit, 139
Blue Angel, 46, 221
Blue Ribbon, 46, 207
Blumenthal, Francesca, 228
Blyden, Ellen, 116
Blyden, Josh, 116
Blyden, Larry, 116
BMI, 26
Bogart, Humphrey, 163
Bolger, Ray, 38
Bolshoi Ballet, 74
Bon Soir, 46, 221
Booth, Shirley, 116, 127
Boyer, Charles, 166
Boy George, 98
Brando, Marlon, 143
Brann, Helen, 140
Breach, Joyce, 228
Breslin, Millard, 81
Brevoort, 207
Brooks, Mel, 158, 215
Broun, Heywood, 200
Brown, David, 146, 147–48
Brown, Eva, 116
Brown, Helen Gurley, 93, 109, 146–48, 232
Browne, Leslie, 216
Bruce, Lenny, 130
Brussels, 46
Brynner, Yul, 71, 140–41, 143, 146
Buckley, Betty, 228
Budd, Julie, 228
Buffett, Susie, 141
Buffett, Warren, 141–42
Burroughs, Steven, 153
Burton, Richard, 188, 212
Burwell, Ernest (father of FSG), 17–18, 19, 21, 41–42
    in naval Intelligence during World War II, 23, 51
    in New York with Faith and Sidney Kaye, 47–48
    at RTR after Sidney Kaye's death, 165

Burwell, Ernest "Buster" (brother of FSG), 21, 22, 42
Burwell, Ethel, 47, 48
Burwell, Faith, *see* Stewart-Gordon, Faith
Burwell, Lilla Bell, 195
Byline, 222

cabaret performers, 71, 141, 220–22, 226–28
Café Society Downtown, 46
Calisher, Hortense, 116
Callaway, Ann Hampton, 228
Callaway, Liz, 228
Call Girl, The, 158
Camillo's, 46
Camillucci, Greg, 210, 213, 216
    management of RTR during crises by, 175–80
Camp Croft, 20
"Campfire Girl, A," 23
Cannata, Anne, 122
Carey, Claiborne, 228
Carlisle, Kitty, 143
Carlyle Hotel, 182, 183, 184
Carmen, 168
Carnegie Hall, 69, 72–73, 74, 75, 78, 83–84, 112, 114–15, 116
    Miss Lacey's location in, 198
    Peter Duchin's apartment in, 129–30
    plans for development of, 80, 82, 84–86, 89–90
Carnegie Hall Tower, 80, 82, 93
Carnelia, Craig, 228
Carnovsky, Morris, 143
Caron, Leslie, 216
Carroll, Barbara, 228
Carroll, June, 23
Car Wash, 217
Casablanca, 163, 187
Casino Russe, 71, 74, 120, 140
Cates, Gilbert, 215
Cat on a Hot Tin Roof, 43
caviar, 186–87, 188
Central Park:
    Bethesda Fountain in, 204
    created, 68

Chalif, Louis, 70–71
Chambord, 47, 197, 207
Channing, Carol, 125–26
Chapin School, 192
Charles restaurant, 54, 91
Charleston, S.C., 15–16
Charlotte Observer, 17
Chasen's, 197
Chauve Souris, Le, 63
Chekhov, Anton, 56, 232
Cherry Orchard, 232
Chertok, Isaac, 56–62
Chicago, Ill., 102
Chickering Hall, 71
Chinese Tea House, 86–87
Chiquita, 128–29
Chodorov, Eddie, 142
Chodorov, Rosemary, 142
Chujoy, Anatole, 134–35, 144
Cirque, Le, 47, 54, 98, 109
City Center, 72–73, 75, 80, 112, 144
City Spire, 80
Civil War, 19–20
Claman, Julian, 101
Clark, Dane, 116
Clarkson Potter, 152
Clary, Robert, 23
Cliburn, Van, 116
Clinton, Chelsea, 230
Clinton, Hillary Rodham, 230–31
Clinton, William Jefferson, 230
Clurman, Harold, 41, 64–65, 95–96,
    149
Coates, Helen, 114–15, 116
Coco, Jimmy, 119
Cohen, Robert, 87, 182, 183, 184
Cohn, Sam, 91, 99–100, 127, 147, 148,
    210–12
Collingwood, Charles, 158
Colonna, Vido, 203
Colony, 47, 207
Columbia Artists (CAMI) Building, 71
Come Back, Little Sheba, 127
Compton, Juleen, 65
Converse College, 22, 83
Cook, Beryl, 200–201
Cook, Inman, 153

Cook, John, 200
Coppola, Francis Ford, 214
Corey, Alix, 228
Cosaro, Frank, 158
Cosmopolitan, 146–47, 187
Costello, Frank, 163
Côte Basque, La, 98, 192, 197
Courtney, Marshall Marcus, 20
Courtney-Burwell, Faith, 16–17, 18,
    20, 21, 22, 25, 37–38, 42
  meeting of Sidney Kaye's mother and,
    48–49
  musical interests of, 27, 83
Coward, Noël, 70, 221
Cox, Wally, 143
Craig, David, 119
Cronyn, Hume, 139, 147, 155
Crown Building, 151

Dahl, Arlene, 214
Dahlrup, Baroness, 45, 116
Dahlrup, Just, 116
Dakota, 69, 115
D'Alessio, Gregory, 170
Dalí, Gala, 136–37
Dalí, Salvador, 108, 136–37
Dalmatov, 63–64
Dalmeida, Louis, 116
Dalrymple, Jean, 55, 144–45
Daniels, Lee A., 80
Danilova, Alexandra, 104, 134, 145
Daugherty and Field, 228
Davis, Mary Bond, 228
Dearie, Blossom, 228
Death of a Salesman, 139, 211
DeFanti, Lyro, 123–24, 197–98
de Lempika, Tamara, 200–201
Depression era, 71
de Sousa, Ona, 92, 93, 94, 99, 102,
    110–11, 124–25, 127, 140–41, 154,
    155, 211, 230
Dexter, Baby Jane, 228
Diners Club, 74
Dinesen, Isak, 45
Dinty Moore's, 46, 208
Dirty Dancing, 216
Disney store on 57th Street, 164

Douglas, Cleve, 228
Douglas, Michael, 99, 140
Downes, Mrs. Olin, 116
Duchamp, Marcel, 150
Duchin, Peter, 46, 129–31, 228
Duplex, 221
Durst, Seymour, 82
Dussault, Nancy, 228

East Coast Academy Awards party,
     209, 214–15
Ecraseur, Henri, 173
Ed Sullivan Show, 103
Eisenhower, Dwight D., 71
Elaine's, 98, 147–48
Ellis, Perry, 153
Elysée, 207
Embers, 46, 221

Fairwell, My Lovely, 113
Fancy Free, 115
Farnum, Dustin, 213
Farrell, Eileen, 228
Farrell, Suzanne, 104
Farrow, Mia, 213
Faulkner, William, 128
Feder, Abe, 143
Feminine Mystique, The, 158
Ferrer, Mel, 24–25, 101
Finney, Albert, 217
Fire Island, 115, 157–59
Firestone, Lee, 24
Fonda del Sol, La, 54
Fonteyn, Margot, 145–46
Fonville, Harold, 116
Forand, Rosa, 99, 109–10, 178, 232
Fornos, 46
Forum of the Twelve Caesars, 54
Fourposter, The, 139
Four Seasons, 54, 98
Foy, Gray, 116
Franchot, Maude, 116, 149
Francine, Anne, 228
Francis, Arlene, 143
Franklin, Freddy, 104
Freeman, Andrew, 221, 222, 225, 226
Fremont, Judy, 202–3

French Culinary Institute, 141, 194
Friedan, Betty, 158, 159, 199
Friedan, Karl, 158, 159
Friedman, David, and Friends, 228
Fulmer, Lenna, 225
Fulmer, Sidney, 225

Gable, Martin, 143
Gallagher's, 46
Garland, Judy, 72, 222
Garner, Erroll, 137–38
Garroway, Dave, 102
Gaslight, 22
Gelb, Jimmy, 41, 64, 65
General Motors Building, 69
Geva, Tamara, 104, 134
Ghostley, Alice, 23, 31
Gill, Brendan, 72, 80
Gillett, Eric Michael, 228
Gimbel, Peter, 148
Ginder, Philip de Witt, 144–45
Gin Game, The, 139
Glackens, William, 69
Glass, Alan, 202
Gloucester House, 46
Gogi's La Rue, 46
Gold and Fitzdale's cookbook, 104
Goldberg, Whoopi, 212
Goldberger, Paul, 82
Goldie's New York, 46
Goldwurm family, 88–89, 90
Gomsu, Natalie, 228
González, Eva, 195–96
Goodbye, Columbus, 120
Good Housekeeping, 187
Gordon, Ruth (actress), 100, 101, 102,
     126, 127, 151–52
Gordon, Ruth (sister of Eliot Janeway),
     117
Graffman, Gary, 116
Graffman, Naomi, 116
Graham, Ronny, 23
Graham, Virginia, 105
Granada, 91
Grand Vefour, Le, 197
Green, Amanda, 228
Greenberg, Faye, 228

Greenwald, Harold, 158, 159
Greenwald, Ruth, 158, 159
Grenouille, La, 98
Gripsholm, 208
Gro, Ida, 45, 116
Gross, Michael, 98–99
Grossinger's, 50
Group Theater, 64, 143
Grubman, Alan, 87

Hagen, Uta, 59, 126
Haight-Ashbury, 192
Hall, Carol, 228
Halpern, Ide, 90, 91
Halpern, Morty, 24
Halston, Julie, 228
Hamilton, Bernie, 119
Hamsun, Knut, 59
Handman, Wynn, 131
Haran, Mary Cleere, 228
Hard Rock Café, 164
Harley-Davidson Café, 164
Harnack, Curtis, 116
Harner, Jeff, 228
Harriman, Averell, 130–31
Harriman, Pamela, 130–31
Harris, Radie, 105, 215
Hart, John, 140
Hart, Moss, 143
Hassam, Childe, 98
Hayes, Helen, 127
Hayward, Brooke, 130–31
Hayward, Leland, 131
Haywire, 131
Hearst, Patricia, 192
Heat, 113
Hector, Bob, 64
Hello, Dolly!, 138
Henderson, Florence, 147
Henderson, Skitch, 228
Henri, Robert, 69
Henri Bendel, 118, 150–53
Henry, O., 70
Henry, Sherrye, 198–99
Hepburn, Audrey, 24–25, 100–101
Herman, Jane, 146
Hesse, Hermann, 59

Hildegarde, 222, 226–27, 228
Hirschfeld, Al, 142–43, 144
Hirschfeld, Dolly, 142–43, 144
Hirschfeld, Nina, 143
Hochman, Sandra, 149
Hofbrau, 207
Hoffman, Dustin, 209–11, 212–13,
    215, 217
    in *Kramer vs. Kramer,* 148
Hoffman, Lilly, 312
Holdouts!, 82–83
Holiday, 155
Hollinger, Gina, 64
Hollinger, Hy, 64
Hollywood Reporter, 105, 182,
    215
Hoty, Dee, 228
Hurok, Sol, 74, 101–2, 115, 134,
    135
Hurwich, Sally, 42
Hyams, Nessa, 101–2

Iglesias, Julio, 98
Italian Festival on Mott Street, 225

Janeway, Eliot, 117
Jay Thorpe, 71, 151
Jekyll and Hyde, 164
Jenkins, George, 178–79
Joe's, 91
Johnson, Georgianne, 158
Johnson, Lyndon, 132
Jones, Carol, 27
Jones, Mary Mason, 69
Josephs, Lawrence, 81
Josephson, Marvin, 87
Julliard School of Music, 72

Kafka, Franz, 54
Kahn, Otto, 199
Kalmanowitz, "Mama," 48–50,
    52–53, 56
Kane, Carol, 113
Kanin, Garson, 100, 101, 103, 127,
    147
Kaufman, Bel, 158
Kaufman, George S., 143

Kaye, Ellen:
  birth of, 43–45, 75, 117, 189–90, 193
  cabaret singing career of, 193, 228
  at Chapin School, 192
  childhood and teenage years of, 117,
    118–19, 127, 132, 136–37, 157–58,
    160, 169, 190–93
  disappearance of, 193
  early restaurant training of, 136–37
  FSG's relationship with, 189–94
  FSG's ring given to, 52
  at Little Red Schoolhouse, 194
  marriage of, 194
  professional training of, 193–94
  restaurant management work of,
    193–94
  restaurant work at RTR by, 191, 194
  at RTR during bomb scare, 95
  RTR hatcheck girls as babysitters for,
    122
  in RTR on closing night, 232
  at Sarah Lawrence College, 193
  son of, 194
  stepfather of, 191, 193
  at Wykham Rise, 193
Kaye, Joel, 37, 40, 41
Kaye, Nora, 216
Kaye, Selma, 230
Kaye, Sidney, 15, 27–39
  army service of, 37
  army uniform worn by, 60, 121
  bachelor apartment of, 40
  Bill Littler and, 30–31, 33–34, 117,
    180
  Bronx childhood of, 36, 37
  daughter of, *see* Kaye, Ellen
  death of, 117, 152, 156, 160–62,
    190
  first marriage of, 37, 40, 77
  FSG's marriage to, 40–45
  generosity of, 58, 60, 63–64
  hungry artist friends of, 63–66
  illness of, 117–19, 132, 157–60
  Jewish background of, 49–53
  as the "Jewish Rick" of *Casablanca*,
    163
  Maria Tallchief and, 104

  Monte's restaurant acquired by,
    76–77
  mother of, *see* Kalmanowitz, "Mama"
  Osborne saved from demolition by,
    116
  preparations for papal visit on 57th
    Street by, 123–24
  psychiatrist housed at RTR by, 79
  as raconteur, 41–42, 138
  restaurant business philosophy of,
    100
  RTR bought by, 160–61
  RTR building bought by, 75–77
  RTR business management by, 77–78
  with RTR customers, 89, 133,
    134–35, 150–51
  RTR employees of, 36, 106–7,
    120–21, 122, 150
  Russian background of, 50, 56, 57
  son of, *see* Kaye, Joel
  visit to Soviet Union by, 73–74, 135
  Zero Mostel and, 95, 138–39
Kaye, Walter, 79, 230
Kazan, Elia, 43
Keach, Stacy, 154
Kelly, Gene, 65
Kelly, Patsy, 188
Kennedy, John F., 132
King, Archer, 110
King and I, The, 141, 146
Kinski, Nastassja, 214
Kirker, Michael, 221, 223
Kissel, Howard, 55
Kitt, Eartha, 23, 31–32
Koch, Edward I., 79, 83, 86, 182
Kramer, Terry Allen, 140
Kramer vs. Kramer, 148, 217
Krantz, Judy, 187
Krause, Alvina, 23
Kravitz, Henry, 114
Krushchev, Nikita, 73
Kuhn, Judy, 228
"Kukla, Fran, and Ollie," 102
Kutcher's, 50

Ladies in Retirement, 22–23
Lali, 183

LaMott, Nancy, 228
Lansbury, Angela, 130
Lantz, Robby, 99–100, 113, 139, 141, 212
Larner, Lionel, 105, 154, 222
Lawrence, Carol, 23
Lawrence, Gertrude, 221
LeBell, June, 202
LeClercq, Tanaquil, 104, 134
Lee, Bobbie, 16–19, 42
Lefkowitz, Sally, 113, 127
Leonhart, Jay, 228
Lerman, Leo, 116, 151, 173
LeRoy, Warner, 54, 81, 230, 231, 233, 234
Les Enfants du Paradis, 167
Let It Be Me, 216
Levin, Ira, 115
Lewinsky, Monica, 230
Lewis, Marcia, 228
Lie, Jonas, 225
Lief, Arthur, 102
Lief, Ruth Hurok, 102
Lillie, Beatrice, 23, 221
Lincoln Center, development of, 71–72, 74–75, 78
Lindbergh, Charles A., 70
Lindsay, John V., 82, 198
Little Carnegie Theater, 88–89
Little Club, 46, 142, 207–8, 221
Littler, Bill, 30–31, 33–34, 117, 180
Littler, Mooie, 30–31, 33–34
Little Red Schoolhouse, 194
Living Room, 221
Loesser, Emily, 228
Loesser, Frank, 112
Loesser, Jo Sullivan, 228
London Calling, 70
Long Christmas Dinner, The, 127
Loos, Anita, 126–27
Lord & Taylor, 192
LoSquadro, Tom, 83, 87, 140–41, 175, 179–80, 227, 233
Loudon, Dorothy, 222
Luks, George, 69
Lunt, Alfred, 101
Lurie, Jerry, 64, 77

Lutvak, Steve, 228
Lynde, Paul, 23, 30, 31–32

McAlister, Ward, 70
McBroom, Amanda, 228
Maccione, Sirio, 47, 54
McDonald, Audra, 228
McDonald's, 164
McDougal, Alice Foot, 70
Macklowe, Harry, 80–83, 89, 92–93
MacLaine, Shirley, 215–16
McLean, Howard, 225
McRae, Heather, 228
Madonna, 121
Maeff, Sasha, 71
Mafia, 77, 162, 163, 173
Maids, The, 113
Maltby, Richard, Jr., 228
Mama Bertollotti, 91
Manet, Edouard, 195
Mangia! Mangia!, 164
Manhattan, 209
Mansfield, Irving, 41
Manson, Charles, 192
Marcel (RTR maître d'), 106, 107, 161–62
Marcovicci, Andrea, 224, 227, 228
Mario, Frank, 163–64
Martin, Jack, 109
Martin, Mary, 23
Mason, Karen, 228
Mathis, Johnny, 222
Maxwell's Plum, 54
Mayes, Sally, 228
Mazzie, Marin, 228
Meara, Anne, 59, 94, 96, 102–3, 114, 228
Meir, Golda, 65
Member of the Wedding, The, 21
Mercer, Mabel, 221, 222, 224
Merman, Ethel, 23
Merrill, Robert, 73
Messavage, Anne "Miss Anne", 35, 88, 105–6, 108, 128, 160–61, 180, 232
Metropolitan Opera, 72, 73, 75
Metropolitan Tower, 80, 82, 92–93
Midnight Cowboy, 112

Mielziner, Jo, 143
Miles, Sylvia, 99, 111–13, 116, 214
Milgrim's, 71, 151
Miller, Arthur, 139, 210–11
Mindlin, Mike, 116
Minnelli, Liza, 225
Mitchum, Robert, 140
Mitzi Newhouse Theater, 72
Moiseyev Dancers, 74
Monk, Julius, 221
Monroe, Marilyn, 126
Monroe, Mrs. Eustiss (school), 68–69
Monte's on the Park, 76–77
Montevecchi, Liliane, 228
Moore, Dudley, 214
Moore, Gene, 153–54
Morehouse, Ward, 144
Morgan, Tom, 198
Moritz, Owen, 79
Morley, Sheridan, 228
Morocco, El, 46
Morrison, Marjorie, 116
Mortimer's, 54, 98
Morton, Brooks, 221
Mostel, Zero, 20, 95–96, 119, 138–39
MoTown Café, 164
Muir, Jean, 153
Mulligan, Richard, 119
Munshin, Jules, 59, 65–66, 138
Murphy, Charles, 142
Murray, Luellen, 22
Myers, Pamela, 228
Myerson, Bess, 163–64

Nash, N. Richard, 158
Nation, 64
Navarro Hotel, 76
Neeson, Liam, 214
Nelson, Portia, 228
Nemy, Enid, 125
New Faces of 1952, 15, 23–24, 25, 31–32, 102, 221
Newman, Melissa, 228
Newman, Paul, 92, 215
Newman, Phyllis, 228
New York, 98, 103

New York, N.Y.:
  Central Park created, 68
  Central Park's Bethesda Fountain, 204
  early apartment buildings, 69
  Fifth Avenue mansions, 69, 151
  Goat Hill area, 68
  Jones Wood area, 67
  Lincoln Center, 71–72
  music world of, 70, 72–73
  northward development of, 67–69
  restaurants in, *see* restaurants
  West 57th Street, 68–71, 79–82, 151, 164
New York City Ballet, 73
New York City Opera, 73
New York *Daily News,* 55, 79, 81, 109
  food editor of, 132–33
New York Harbor, 225
New York Philharmonic, 71, 72, 78, 114
New York Post, 105, 109
New York State Theater, 72
New York Stories, 214
New York Times, 17, 59, 80, 82, 123
  Al Hirschfeld's contract with, 142
  Clive Barnes as critic for, 103–4
  Henri Bendel's ads in, 152
  interview with Carol Channing in, 125
  obituaries in, 100, 128
  RTR advertising in, 202
New York World's Fair, 22, 47
Nichols, Mike, 92, 136
Nielson, Brigit, 140
Night and the Music, The, 228
nightclubs, 46, 71, 74, 198
Nike store on 57th Street, 164
Nixon, Richard M., 73
Noble, Ray, 226–27
Nomura, Wiley, 219
Northwestern University, 23, 51, 141, 162
Novoe Russoye Slovoe, 134
Nude Descending a Staircase, 150
Nureyev, Rudolf, 131, 133–34, 135–36, 145–46, 213

O'Conner, Bill, 84
O'Connor, Carroll, 154
Odets, Clifford, 143
Officer, Phillip, 228
Onassis, Jacqueline Kennedy, 92, 126, 132, 154, 192
Ondine, 24–25, 47, 100–101
One, Two, Three, 120
One Potato, Two Potato, 119–20, 217
On the Town, 65
Orbach, Jerry, 228
Orsini's, 152
Osborne, 69
  Al Hirschfeld's penthouse apartment in, 142–43, 144
  demolition planned for, 116
  FSG's penthouse apartment in, 40, 44–45, 65, 115–17, 144, 173, 174, 191
  James Stewart-Gordon's apartment in, 173, 191
  residents of, 65, 112, 116
Osborne, Robert, 182
Ostertag, Barna, 34, 36
Oswald, Lee Harvey, 132

Paddleford, Clementine, 132–33
Page, Geraldine, 59
Pahlevi, Muhammad Reza (Shah of Iran), 231
Pahlevi, Princess, 231
Palm, 46
Parker, Dorothy, 59
Parker, Robert B., 139
Parrish, Max Field, 37
Parrish-Martin, Woodrow, 40
Parton, Dolly, 124–25
Patsy's, 233
Paul (RTR back manager), 36, 107
Paul VI, Pope, 123–24
Pavillon, 46, 208
Peerce, Alice, 40, 50–52, 57, 62, 117–18, 119, 165, 190
Peerce, Jan, 50–51, 62, 73, 190
Peerce, Larry, 50–51, 119–20, 157, 217
Pen and Pencil, 46
Pépin, Jacques, 219

PepsiCo, 74
Peter's, 207
Peters, Roberta, 73
Petit, Roland, 145
Philadelphia Orchestra, 78
Philharmonic Hall (Avery Fisher Hall), 72, 73, 78, 112
P.J. Clark's, 46, 168
Planet Hollywood, 164
Players Club, 98, 101
Poe, Edgar Allan, 16, 67–68
Poires, Les, 195–96
Poitier, Sidney, 100
Pollack, Sidney, 209, 210, 214
Poston, Tom, 116
Powell, Lovelady, 24, 221
Prager, Stanley, 158
Press Box, 46
Preston, Robert, 143
Price, Jerry, 112
Prohibition (Volstead Act), 70, 71
Proskauer, Joseph, 116
Put Them All Together, 26

Quant, Mary, 153
Quo Vadis, 47

radio advertising, 202–8
Rae, Charlotte, 221, 228
Randall, Tony, 147
Reader's Digest, 191
Reams, Lee Roy, 228
Redgrave, Lynn, 116
Redgrave, Vanessa, 126
Reed, Billy, 142, 221
Rehearsal Club, 121
Reiner, Carl, 215
Rembrandt Building, 71, 74, 80, 84, 124
Renaud, Madeleine, 168
Resnick, Regina, 124*n*
Restaurant Associates, 54
restaurants, 46–47, 53–55, 207–8
  Diners Club introduced in, 74
  downtown, 54, 90–91, 207
  getting "best seats" at, 98
  during Prohibition era, 70
  in Spartanburg, S.C., 17

Richards, Ann, 109
Richardson, Ed, 222–23, 225
Richardson, Natasha, 215
Rigby, Harry, 140, 154
Rigg, Diana, 154
Rissman, Hope, 162
Ritzel, Ricky, 228
Rivers, Joan, 149
Roberts, Flora, 139–40
Rockrose, 84
Romeo Salta, 46
Rooney, Mickey, 222
Roosevelt, Franklin Delano, 69
Rosa's Place, 110
Rose, Barbara, 157–58
Rose, Reggie, 157–58
Rosemary's Baby, 115, 152
Rose Tattoo, The, 154
Rosewood, 87
Ross, Herbert, 215
Ross, Steve, 228
Rothenburgh, Otto, 199–200, 225
Roy, Billy, 226
Ruby, Jack, 132
Russell, Jimmy, 31–32
Russian Hamlet in Winter, 195
Russian Tea Room:
  Academy Awards party at, 209,
    214–15
  advertising of, 202–8
  air-conditioning problems at, 36, 95,
    96
  Alex as back steward at, 36, 120–21
  Anatole Chujoy as maître d' at,
    27–29, 35, 107, 135, 137, 138, 150,
    232
  "animal companions" in, 148–50
  Annette as maîtresse d' at, 108,
    128–29, 137, 232
  Art Deco decor of, 112, 133
  ballet dancers at, 74, 104, 133–34,
    145–46, 216
  ballet murals on wall of, 104, 112,
    195, 196, 197
  blini served at, 186–88, 206
  bomb scares at, 94–95
  borscht recipe of, 133, 134–35

  Boyar Room of, 71, 74, 124, 135
  building purchased, 75–77
  business management of, 77–78, 219
  Cabaret at, 141, 219–28
  Cabaret maître d' of, 225
  Cabaret manager of, 221, 222
  Café atmosphere of, 54–55
  Café on second floor of, 78, 81
  Carnegie Hall's threat to property of,
    84–86, 89–90
  cartoon of Cindy Adams in, 105
  caviar served at, 186–88
  celebrity patrons' recollections of,
    113–14, 115, 143–44, 146–48,
    150–52
  changes in clientele of, 73
  changes in cuisine of, 218–19
  changes in decor of, 197–98
  charge account customers of, 91
  chefs at, 133, 219
  Christmas decorations at, 112, 133,
    206
  closed for kitchen renovation, 96–98
  closing of, 229–34
  "club" members of, 64
  construction of new buildings next to,
    79–83, 92–94
  critiqued by Michael Gross in *New
    York* magazine, 98–99
  customer "regulars" at, 91, 93, 177,
    231, 232
  D1 booth in, 100, 101, 136–37, 210
  daily meal for Sidney Kaye's cousin at,
    58–61
  decorative objects on walls of, 112–13
  demolition of buildings surrounding,
    74, 124
  design for Sidney Kaye's office at, 58,
    60–62
  dining hours at, 90–91
  dress code at, 192
  expansion of, 71, 78, 81
  expansion proposals for, 81, 85, 87
  explosion blocking off entrance to,
    175–78
  fashion designers at, 153
  hatcheck girls at, 121–22, 149, 212

history of building occupied by, 67–71
hotel development plans for, 87
hungry artists' meals at, 63–66
kitchen of, 71, 133, 176–77
laundry supplier to, 162–64
Lincoln Center development and, 72–75
Little Carnegie Theater next door to, 88–89
lunchtime dining at, 90–92
Macklowe's purchase offer for property of, 80–83, 89
mahogany woodwork in, 198
maître d's role at, 107
maîtresse d's role in, 88, 92, 99
Marcel as maître d' at, 106, 107, 161–62
"Miss Anne" Messavage, as maîtresse d' at, 35, 88, 105–6, 108, 128, 160–61, 180, 232
Miss Lacey's nightclub problem in, 198
movie scenes shot at, 209–10, 213–14, 215–16
Mrs. Axe's property ownership of, 75–77, 79
name of, 86–87
new location considered for, 74–77
New York Room of, 78, 222, 224
in 1960s and 1970s, 191–92
Ona de Sousa as maîtresse d' at, 92, 93, 94, 99, 102, 110–11, 124–25, 127, 140–41, 154, 155, 211, 230
owners of, *see* Kaye, Sidney; LeRoy, Warner; Maeff, Sasha; Stewart-Gordon, Faith
paintings on walls of, 104, 112, 124, 195–97, 199–201, 224–25
parties in Café of, 229–30
party for staff of, 233
Paul as back manager at, 36, 107
payoffs for services to, 162–64
payroll of, 120
photographs on walls of, 100–104
police precinct's relations with, 162–63
Rosa Forand as maîtresse d' at, 99, 109–10, 178, 232

Russian character of, 73, 74, 153, 195, 205
Russian clientele of, 63, 73, 109, 134, 135, 147
Russian cuisine of, 206, 207, 218–19
Russian wait staff of, 128, 131, 134, 192
seating arrangements at, 88–89, 98–99, 127, 143, 154
sprinkler system activated at, 97–98, 178–80
"stammtisch" of, 52, 89, 107, 117, 119
summer difficulties of, 95–98
tenant on fourth floor of, 78, 81
Texans' party for governor at, 109
tipping at, 108
upper floors of, 78–79
vodka served at, 74, 187, 188
waiters at, 107–8, 127
waitresses at, 131, 134, 192, 232
window decorations of, 153
women seated at bar in, 198–99
Russian Tea Room, A Tasting, 152
Russian Tea Room, The, 199, 225
Russian Tea Room Cookbook, The, 152, 207
Ruth, Babe, 70
Ryckiel, Sonya, 153

Sachs, Jack, 64
Sahl, Mort, 222
Saint Joan, 23
St. Regis Hotel:
King Cole Bar at, 36–37
Maisonette Russe at, 46, 130
St. Regis Roof, 46
Saloff, Spider, 228
San Marino, 46
Sarah Lawrence College, 193
Sardi's, 46, 109, 231
Saroyan, William, 144
Schneider, Helen, 228
Schumacher, Joel, 153, 217
Segal, Fred, 192
Segal, George, 192
Seldes, Marian, 100, 101

Selznick, Daniel, 130
Sevilla coffeehouse, 70
Shah of Iran, 231
Shapiro, Debbie, 228
Shea, Norrie, 85
Shea, William A., 84–86
Shearing, George, 228
Shea Stadium, 84–85
Shepherd, Bet, 17
Shepherd, Eugenia, 127
Sherry, Louis, 70
Shinn, Everett, 69
Shire, David, 228
Shirley, Don, 129, 130
Short, Bobby, 116, 129, 130, 151, 225
Sid Caesar Show, 215
Siderenko, Gary, 133
Sifton, Eric, 128
Silberman, Joel, 228
Silverstein family, 127
Simon, Neil, 158
Sinatra, Frank, 65, 72
Sloan, John, 69
Smith, Dinnie, 25
Smith, Donald, 145, 146, 221, 222, 223, 225
Smith, Ethel, 170
Smith, Liz, 109, 225
Smith, Sydney, 203–4
Soffer, Sheldon, 22
Sondheim, Stephen, 139
Sosenko, Anna, 227
Sotheby's, 195, 196
Southern, Terry, 131–32
Soviet Union, 73–74, 135
Spartanburg, S.C., 15, 17, 19–20, 83, 195
  friends from, 225
  FSG's wedding to Sidney Kaye in, 41–42
Spewack, Bella, 41
Spewack, Sam, 41
Spitzer, Helen, 156
Spitzer, Silas, 155–56
Springer, John, 210, 212
Stage Door, 121
Staller, David, 228

Stallone, Sylvester, 140
Stebbins, Emma, 204
Stein, Richard, 125–26
Steinberg, Joe, 44
Steinway Hall, 71
Stern, Danny, 64, 202
Stern, Isaac, 78, 116
Stevens, Marti, 228
Stevenson, Isabelle, 144–45, 223
Stewart, Patrick, 216
Stewart, Sandy, 228
Stewart-Gordon, Belle, 191
Stewart-Gordon, Christina, 191
Stewart-Gordon, Faith:
  acting career of, 15, 22–26, 31, 43, 54, 96, 100, 102–3, 119, 155, 162
  acting classes attended by, 59, 119, 126
  advised by Sidney Kaye to sell RTR, 159–60
  Alice Peerce's friendship with, 51–52
  apartment of, 26, 30, 40
  apartment of Sidney Kaye and, *see* Osborne
  artworks bought for RTR by, 195–97
  Betty Friedan's friendship with, 158, 199
  at Carlyle Hotel, 182–84
  Carnegie Hall in legal battle with, 84–86, 89
  childhood of, 16–22
  in children's theater troupe, 22
  cooking classes of, 42–43
  courtship of Sidney Kaye and, 30–40
  daughter of, *see* Kaye, Ellen
  decision not to sell RTR to Macklowe by, 81
  decision to continue operating RTR by, 93, 159–62
  decision to sell RTR by, 194, 221, 232
  divorced parents of, 21–22
  divorce settlement of, 181–85
  dogs belonging to, 42, 148–49, 182, 198, 200
  economizing measures at RTR by, 219
  effect of Sidney Kaye's illness on family life of, 117–19, 132, 157–60

father of, *see* Burwell, Ernest
final RTR parties given by, 229–33
financial hard times of, 51
at Fire Island, 115, 157–59
Geraldine Stutz's friendship with,
  152
Helen Gurley Brown's friendship with,
  93, 146–47, 232
in high-school plays, 22–23
introduced to James Stewart-Gordon
  at RTR, 170
introduced to Sidney Kaye at RTR,
  15, 27–29
Jean-Louis Barrault and, 167–68
job hunting efforts of, 38–39
in Lee Strasberg's acting class, 119,
  126
literary agent of, 140
lost ring of, 54
marriage of James Stewart-Gordon
  and, 172–74, 181–85, 190–91
married life of Sidney Kaye and,
  40–45, 47–48
mother of, *see* Courtney-Burwell,
  Faith
Mr. Goldwurm and, 88–90
in *New Faces of 1952,* 15, 23–24, 25,
  31–32, 102, 221
nickname of, 21
Northwestern alumnae friends of, 24,
  141, 162, 221
at Northwestern University, 23, 51, 162
at NYU, 118, 159
in "Omnibus Repertory Company,"
  on CBS, 155
in *Ondine,* 24–25, 47, 100–101
in *One Potato, Two Potato,* 119–20
as owner of RTR, 159–65, 171,
  175–80
in *Put Them All Together,* 26
radio ads for RTR by, 203–8
real estate decisions made by, 79,
  80–82, 93–94
restaurant business learned by, 44–45,
  88–89, 120, 133, 134, 160
RTR bar opened to women by, 199
RTR business management by, 219

RTR Cabaret created by, 220–28
RTR checkroom managed by, 121
at RTR during Sidney Kaye's illness,
  157, 159–60
RTR management problems of,
  162–65, 198
RTR name protected by, 86–87
separation of James Stewart-Gordon
  and, 86
as Southerner, 21–22
townhouse of James Stewart-Gordon
  and, 181–85
travels of, 73–74, 135, 165, 168, 169,
  174, 219
in *The Trial,* 54
in Uta Hagen's acting class, 59
Stewart-Gordon, James, 81, 82, 84, 86,
  170–71, 172–74, 181–85, 197
Stiller, Amy, 103
Stiller, Ben, 103
Stiller, Jerry, 59, 94, 102–3, 228
Stillman, Leonard, 23, 24, 25, 32, 221
Stolichnaya vodka, 74
Stork Club, 46, 207
Strasberg, Lee, 119, 126, 158
Strasberg, Paula, 126, 158
Stravinsky, Igor, 136
Streep, Meryl, 212, 217
Streisand, Barbra, 222
Stritch, Billy, 225, 228
Strouse, Barbara, 126
Strouse, Charles, 126, 228
Stutz, Geraldine, 150–53
Sullavan, Margaret, 131
Sullivan, Gary, 225
Sullivan, K. T., 228
Summer, Bob, 87
Summer, Susan, 87
Susann, Jackie, 41, 103
Syms, Sylvia, 228

Tailored Woman, 151
Taking of Pelham One, Two, Three,
  The, 120
Tallchief, Maria, 104, 134
Tandy, Jessica, 126, 139, 155
Taylor, Elizabeth, 126, 212–13

Index

Thebom, Blanche, 116
Thomas, Jean, 77
Threepenny Opera, 112
Tiffany's, 153, 154
Tillstrom, Burr, 102
Time, 135
Tobias, Rose, 116
Tolkin, Mel, 215
Tone, Franchot, 149
Tootsie, 209–10
Tornabene, Lyn, 132, 167, 187–88
Torre, Anne, 122
Tower Suite, 54
Town Hall, 27, 112
Trial, The, 54
Tsang, Ian Sydney, 194
Tsang, Kim, 194
Tucker, Richard, 51
Turning Point, The, 215–16
"21" Club, 98, 109, 197
Twice Over Lightly, 127

Uhry, Alfred, 139
Unfaithfully Yours, 214
Upstairs at the Downstairs, 46, 221
Up the Down Staircase, 158

Vale, Nancy, 162, 164
Valois, 47
Vanguard, 221
Van Nostrand, Abbott, 105
Van Planck, Marlene, 228
Vietnam War, 192
Vivian Beaumont Theater, 72
vodka, 74, 187, 188
Voisin, 47, 207

Wagner, Robert F., 85
Walters, Barbara, 126, 225
Ward, B. J., 228

Warhol, Andy, 113
Watts, Andre, 116
Weathermen, 192
Welch, Raquel, 140–41
West, Paula, 228
Westchiloff, Constantin, 195
Weston, Jack, 119
Weston, Sam, 119
Wharton, Edith, 69
White, Theodore, 158
Whiting, Margaret, 228
Whitney, Gertrude Vanderbilt, 199
Whitney, Harry Payne, 151
Whyte's, 207
Wilder, Thornton, 127–28
William Morris agency, 127
Williams, Tennessee, 43
Wilson, Julie, 226, 228
Wilson, Mary Louise, 221
Winer, Deborah, 228
Winters, Jonathan, 119
Wise Guys, 228
Wiseman, Joseph, 65, 149
WNCN, 203
Wolf, Clark, 219
Woodward, Joanne, 215
World of Henry Orient, The, 130
World War II, 20–21
Worth, Irene, 225
WQXR, 202–3
Wykham Rise, 193

Yale Drama School, 23, 24
You Can't Take It with You, 22
Young, Gig, 116

Zahn, Sara, 228
Zoas, Chris, 107–8
Zorina, Vera, 104, 134